GEHRIG & THE BABE

Other Books by Tony Castro

Chicano Power: The Emergence of Mexican America
Mickey Mantle: America's Prodigal Son
The Prince of South Waco: American Dreams and Great Expectations
DiMag & Mick: Sibling Rivals, Yankee Blood Brothers
Looking for Hemingway: Spain, the Bullfights, and a Final Rite of Passage

GEHRIG
& THE BABE

The Friendship and the Feud

Tony Castro

TRIUMPH
B O O K S

Library of Congress Cataloging-in-Publication Data

Names: Castro, Tony.
Title: Gehrig & the Babe : the friendship and the feud / Tony Castro.
Other titles: Gehrig and the Babe
Description: Chicago, Illinois : Triumph Books, 2018.
Identifiers: LCCN 2017049823 | ISBN 9781629372518 (hardback)
Subjects: LCSH: Gehrig, Lou, 1903-1941. | Ruth, Babe, 1895-1948. |
   New York Yankees (Baseball team)--History. | New York Yankees
   (Baseball team)--Biography. | Baseball players--United States--Biography.
   | BISAC:SPORTS & RECREATION / Baseball / History. | TRAVEL /
   United States / Northeast / Middle Atlantic (NJ, NY, PA).
Classification: LCC GV865.G4 C37 2018 | DDC 796.357092/2 [B]
--dc23 LC record available at https://lccn.loc.gov/2017049823

This book is available in quantity at special discounts for your group or organization. For further information, contact:

Triumph Books LLC
814 North Franklin Street
Chicago, Illinois 60610
(312) 337-0747
www.triumphbooks.com

Printed in U.S.A.

ISBN: 978-1-62937-251-8

Design by Amy Carter

Page production by Nord Compo

For Renee

"There has never been anything like it. Even as these lines are batted out on the office typewriter, youths dash out of the AP and UP ticker room every two or three minutes shouting, 'Ruth hit one! Gehrig just hit another one!'"

—Paul Gallico, 1927

Contents

Prologue

*"Pitchers began pitching to me because
if they passed me they still had Lou to contend with."*

—Babe Ruth

Hollywood, California, April 1942

If it hadn't been for baseball, Babe Ruth often said, he would have been in either the penitentiary or the cemetery. But on this day, he felt, there was a third option: If it hadn't been for baseball, he would never have been on a goddamn movie set. A prison or a graveyard might indeed have been better, for he now found himself uncomfortably in the middle of Tinseltown. He hated the idea. He disliked movies as it was, and now the experience of being in film made him despise the industry even more. Babe couldn't see the magic others saw in cinema.

Like most Americans in the first half of the 20th century, most ballplayers often spent their free time in movie houses, enamored by the silver screen and the movie stars projected to the size of pop culture gods. Perhaps if Babe hadn't been screwed over by Hollywood he might have felt the same. But he had been swindled out of thousands of dollars in the 1920s when a producer had jilted him on a movie deal. Babe would have killed him if he could have found him, so baseball fans should be thankful he didn't. He swore then never to appear in another movie. But then that was the Babe. He could swear never to do something one day and go back to doing it the next. So much for the Babe making a stand on principle; here he was on a movie set again. There had been no way of getting out of this film, which was now embarrassing and sad for him and his other New York Yankee teammates who also agreed to be in it.

On the set this day, Ruth's discontent boiled over and became obvious, along with his increasing disgruntlement. Unsurprisingly, Babe's displeasure, like so much else about him, was so "Ruthian" in its visibility that the entire 20th Century Fox set was on edge. Yet no one knew exactly why Ruth was unhappy. It may have been difficult for some to imagine that an American icon who had maintained a fascinating hold on the public's attention for almost three decades could appear as nervous as Babe now seemed to be. Yet here he was, the symbol of boyhood dreams and pure Americana, perspiring so heavily that those who saw it assumed it was a case of nerves. Or perhaps he was truly ill, as some had reported. He had a relatively small role in the film—and it was a role he knew well, having played it his entire life, often with a flair for the dramatic. The movie business, however, could break even the most hardened of men, especially when subjected to the unforgiving heat from stage lights that were often a production nightmare. That was why makeup artists constantly blotted actors' faces to remove the perspiration and oils and then went about setting and resetting the foundation with pressing powder to keep the makeup fresh. The makeup artist who touched up Babe's makeup noticed that he was sweating profusely and asked an assistant nearby for a cup of water.

"Water?" said Babe Ruth, wiping his brow and forcing the makeup artist to reset the foundation anew. "That's all you've got?"

Ruth obviously had something stronger in mind. He was a prolific drinker with an insatiable appetite for booze, food, and women, possibly in a different order. Water? Babe loved to munch on ice, to swig it in his mouth, something he did between innings of games. But water? Water was something Babe rarely drank alone. Cutty Sark and water? Now you were talking. Was there any scotch and water on the set? Ruth made no secret of his behavior, often boasting, "I learned early to drink beer, wine, and whiskey. And I think I was about five when I first chewed tobacco." This was common knowledge within the game and among the sportswriters who wrote about baseball. In another era, one with a 24-hour news cycle and a tabloid newspaper culture, Ruth's off-the-field exploits would have been easy fodder for sensationalism. However, the sportswriting of Ruth's Golden Age of sports was one that turned skilled athletes into legends by "waxing poetic about their accomplishments," as put by the immortal Grantland Rice, the dean of those sportswriters. "When a sportswriter stops making heroes out of athletes," Rice once said, "it's time to get out of the business." So Babe's legendary status as a baseball hero and role model for children remained intact. To the public, he was the incomparable slugger who had hit 60 home runs in 1927 and 714 homers for his career—unheard-of statistics before Ruth.

He was also the New York Yankees teammate and, at least in the eyes of the public, the inseparable partner of Lou Gehrig, the beloved, power-hitting first baseman for whom the nation was still mourning. At the height of his career, three years earlier, Gehrig had been tragically felled by a debilitating, fatal illness whose name few could pronounce or remember but which would become known because of him—ALS, amyotrophic lateral sclerosis,—Lou Gehrig's disease.

If there had been any doubt of Gehrig's heroism as a sports idol, his fight against the illness that struck him down at the height of his career had elevated him to saintlike status. Americans still remembered Gehrig's unselfishness, which had been impressed upon them on July 4, 1939. It had been an extraordinary Fourth of July holiday—still two years before the war that consumed everyone—when people across the nation paused and sat in their living rooms to listen to the Iron Horse, as he was affectionately known, address his teammates and fans at Yankee Stadium. "Fans, for the past two weeks you have been reading about a bad break I got," the gravely ill Gehrig began, following with the words that would be memorialized with him: "Yet today, I consider myself the luckiest man on the face of the earth."

That day, the Gehrig and Ruth friendship was forever immortalized by the emotional photograph of the heroic pair that was published in newspapers all over America—of a gregarious Ruth in a dashing light-colored summer suit consoling his friend in Yankee pinstripes with a loving bear hug, cementing that moment as one of the most memorable in sports. It was this image of Ruth's friendship and compassion that had further endeared him to America in his retirement. And so on the movie set this day, it was this Babe Ruth, a living sports immortal in a town that catered to self-centered stars, who was strangely feeling as if this were the last place he belonged.

Ruth's drinking something far stronger than water to quench his thirst in the middle of a workday might have been unknown to someone unfamiliar with the history of the Babe. But on the set that day happened to be a young radio newscaster from North Carolina who had long followed Babe Ruth—and who wanted desperately to break into Hollywood. His name was Johnny Grant, and this moment presented an unexpected opportunity for an aspiring young man who wanted to work in the movies. Hoping for a role as a movie extra, Grant had enlisted the aid of a friend on the film's crew who helped him sneak onto the set of *The Pride of the Yankees*, a 20th Century Fox biopic of Lou Gehrig starring Gary Cooper. A baseball fan all his young life, the 19-year-old Grant had immediately recognized Babe Ruth, who was in the film playing himself. It was seven years after Ruth's retirement from the game, but he still appeared fit enough to step on the field and play baseball's Great Bambino. Grant also couldn't mistake that distinctive face of the Babe that looked as if had been sculpted from a boulder.

No one questioned Grant's presence there on the set, possibly because he appeared as if he belonged on a studio lot. Grant looked like an actor. He had a slight resemblance to Mickey Rooney, with whom he also shared the curse of being diminutive in size. Grant had always used his size to his advantage. He found that people were drawn to him, unthreatened by his short height, and that usually got them to open up. It didn't hurt that Johnny also had the gift of gab, especially for telling funny stories and sometimes for making himself the butt of his own jokes. It had endeared him to some of the crew on set, and Johnny immediately sensed how he could make an impression on Ruth, whose discomfort was apparent.

"Babe, I think this may be more to your liking," Grant said, handing Ruth a cup half full of bourbon that he'd gotten from a member of the crew. Ruth sniffed the cup, then eyed Grant as he took a sip and said, "*Keed*, ya ever feel like you were in the circus?" But before Grant could answer, he was startled by Babe's next words. "I do. All the time. It's the circus, and I'm one of the freaks."

Babe let out a big roar of a laugh. He took an immediate liking to Johnny Grant, and they would soon form a close friendship that would last until Ruth's death. Years later, after a career in Tinseltown in which he would become friends with many of the industry's movie legends and earn for himself the honorary title "mayor of Hollywood," Grant would consider meeting Ruth to have been one of the most important days of his life.

"I was a nobody—and a short nobody, at that—and Babe, even in 1942, seven years after he'd retired from baseball, was still one of the biggest stars in America. And he wanted to be my friend. Can you imagine that? That's something you expect some Hollywood writer to make up, isn't it? Here I was, just trying to get my foot in the door in this town, and on the set where I'm not suppose to be, I become friends with Babe Ruth, a man who knew presidents and kings and could open the gates to the White House and royal palaces. Only in Hollywood!"

That night, bonding over drinks at the Roosevelt Hotel on Hollywood Boulevard, Ruth regaled Grant with story after story about his outrageous exploits. Babe regularly made no great effort to keep from being caught breaking team rules and curfews, and he confessed that he used to fear that his incorrigible ways would cause Yankees manager Miller Huggins to suffer a heart attack. Huggins, who managed the Yankees from 1918 until his death in 1929, once fined Ruth $5,000 for staying out three consecutive nights, a figure that was 10 times more than any previous fine in major league history. Ruth boasted to Grant, as he had to writers in New York, that no amount of money—either in fines or threat of losing his contract—would change his ways. "I told Huggins, 'I'll promise I'll go easier on the drinking and I'll get to bed earlier,'" Grant later recalled Ruth telling him. "'But not for you, not for your fines, or for 50,000 or 250,000 will I give up women. They're too much fun!'"

Grant learned that even in retirement Ruth remained in need of constant company from women, as if their sheer numbers were, in addition to pleasure, a validation of his Ruthian self-image. On this trip, Ruth was nightly entertaining a string of women in his rooms, Cabana Suite 229, which overlooked the pool and offered him more privacy than in the main building of the hotel. Grant later recalled, with his encyclopedic knowledge of Hollywood, that this was the same suite where Marilyn Monroe stayed for almost two years in the early 1950s as her career began to take off. Her first magazine shoot, in fact, had taken place on a diving board within view of the suite.

"Heaven knows why he was telling me so much about himself," Grant said years later in an interview in the same Roosevelt Hotel, where he resided until his death in 2008. "I was flattered. Me being Babe Ruth's confidant. What a dream come true. As that night wore on, and as I got to know him over time, I sensed a deep sadness in Babe. I wondered if he had many friends, or any at all. I mean, I'm sure he had a lot of people around him—and did have for years. But I don't know how much he truly let them into that private part of him. They knew the public Babe Ruth but not the private one, the real one. And I got the impression that this was where his relationship with Lou Gehrig came in. 'Lou was different than all the others,' Babe told me. He meant the teammates. He said he tried to get to know Lou and that for a while there was a friendship, but that it bothered him that he felt Lou disapproved of the way he lived his life. 'I could never have been Lou,' he said, 'and Lou could never have been me.'"

In the 1930s, they had been estranged for several years, Babe confided, before Ruth learned that Gehrig was sick and dying. Ruth had been grief-stricken and almost to the point of despair, blaming himself for allowing their friendship to erode. All that, Babe said, had come back to haunt him during the making of *The Pride of the Yankees,* and Grant finally understood what Ruth had meant about feeling that he was in a circus. Although Ruth was no stranger to filmmaking, having starred in a few in the 1920s when Hollywood first tried to exploit his name, he had only a common man's understanding of how films were really made. This now troubled him because he witnessed some strange tricks in the production trade that were being employed in the making *The Pride of the Yankees.*

"[Babe's agent and manager] Christy Walsh told me the producer knew absolutely nothing about baseball," Ruth said to Grant, referring to Samuel Goldwyn. That was true. By the early 1940s, Samuel Goldwyn's name had become synonymous with Hollywood; some might even have called him the

Babe Ruth of Tinseltown. He was famous for his relentless ambition, bad temper, and genius for publicity—and became Hollywood's leading independent producer mainly because none of the other movie-making big shots, not even his partners, could stand him.

Goldwyn had not been interested in making *The Pride of the Yankees* until a screenwriter pleaded with him to watch the newsreels from Gehrig's Appreciation Day ceremonies—and his "luckiest man on the face of the earth" speech. When the lights came back on in Goldwyn's screening room, the producer was wiping away tears. "Run them again," he cried. Goldwyn was so touched by the Lou Gehrig story that he promised Gehrig's wife, Eleanor, final editorial control. The final cut of the film, he assured her, "would be changed just the way I wanted it if I found anything to criticize in the uncut version," she recalled in her memoir. "I felt I wanted to know if it was Lou's real life story and not colored and overdramatized." She received a special screening at the studio and left remarkably impressed. "I saw Goldwyn, who was waiting for me... I told him of my gratitude for the fine treatment and the careful attention to every detail. I didn't ask for one solitary deletion or addition. I accepted the picture exactly as it was made. That's how good I think it is."

The making of the film, however, was a challenge—something that Ruth and others could easily see. "Christy was right," Babe told Grant. "This fella Goldwyn knows nothing about baseball and very little about Lou. They've got a guy playing Lou who can't hit left-handed [Gehrig was a left-handed hitter] and hits only slightly better from the right side. Then, when he hits, they got him running from home to third base and not first base, and they've got the numbers on the backs of the jerseys on backwards!"

Ruth was right about what he had observed, but there was more to the story. Gary Cooper, who had begun making a name for himself in westerns, could ride horses as well as any cowboy. Baseball, though, was another matter. But he was an actor Samuel Goldwyn took credit for discovering, and Goldwyn had been adamant from the start that Cooper would play Gehrig. All the instruction and coaching in the world, however, weren't enough to turn the actor into looking like even a journeyman player. Most of his shortcomings could be covered up in the way he was filmed, and a lookalike double who could perform the more difficult baseball action would be used in other wider shots, with no one able to tell the difference. But on the movie's playing field, where the shooting was done, Ruth and other Yankees players in the film had seen what no amount of movie magic could hide: Cooper's ineptness in mimicking Gehrig's powerful left-handed swing. But this was Hollywood, where the Red Sea could be parted along with the re-creation of biblical miracles. How tough could baseball be by comparison? In getting ready to portray Gehrig, Gary Cooper had managed to become a passable hitter as a right-hander, but there was no hope of teaching him to hit as a lefty. An innovative film editor, though, quickly came up with a clever solution. Filmmakers would shoot Cooper hitting as a righty, then make him appear to be hitting as a left-hander by reversing the film. The idea was utter genius, something only movie magic could accomplish. But that created a new set of problems. Gehrig had worn No. 4 on the back of his uniform shirt, so reversing the film required flipping the numbers as well as the lettering on the front side of the shirts—not only for Cooper but also for all the players in those shots. That meant that in real-life the movie-set players were often wearing shirts with numbers and team names that looked backwards.

"It's crazy the way everyone looks!" bellowed Ruth.

"Don't you think they know what they're doing?" asked Grant, hoping his new best friend would understand that moviegoers would never see the bizarre sight that had so upset him.

"On top of that," Ruth continued, "they have Coop, when he hits the ball, running to third base as if it were first base, and the first baseman playing third base, and if I'm on first base [as a runner], I'm actually on third base, taking a lead from third base toward second base and then running the bases the wrong way! Good lord, it's good that Lou didn't have to see this."

Ruth's cherubic face turned sullen, Grant noticed, and sweat beads appeared to run down his cheeks. But it wasn't perspiration. They were tears.

"I let my friend down," cried Babe.

Grant tried to assure Ruth that what filmmakers did was completely out of his control. Moviegoers also would never see how the film was made. All they would see on the silver screen was Gary Cooper hitting left-handed, running to first base, and every players' uniform lettering and numerals correctly in their place. It was something Hollywood did all the time, Grant said.

The Babe shook his head and waved his hand.

"Not that, keed!" Ruth called almost everyone "keed," Babespeak for "kid." "I'm talking about my friend. Our friendship. Most people don't know this, but we had a falling out, and, you know, we didn't talk for years."

Grant sat stunned. Like most fans, he had never heard about a feud between Gehrig and Ruth. His image of the two men was that shared by much of America: Gehrig and Ruth were the country's greatest sports heroes—heroes who played on the same New York Yankees teams and who were joined at the hip. They even batted back-to-back. Ruth, who wore No. 3 on his shirt, batted third in the lineup that came to be known as Murderers' Row. Gehrig batted right behind him in what is known in baseball as the cleanup spot. The image of their glory had come to be known to American moviegoers through the Universal Newsreels shown before every feature film and released twice a week. In an era when motion pictures defined the nation's culture, those newsreels were a primary source of visual news reporting to many. The newsreels regularly showed Ruth—known as the Great Bambino, among his nicknames—slugging a home run, running the bases in his distinctive pigeon-toed fashion, and crossing home plate, where he received a congratulatory handshake from the waiting Gehrig on deck. Sometimes the newsreels would show Gehrig hitting a home run with Ruth on base and the two rounding the bases. Ruth would cross home plate, then wait for Gehrig as the camera followed the pair all the way to the Yankees dugout, where they would be greeted by teammates and cheering fans. But now Ruth was presenting Grant an entirely new scenario.

"I didn't know," said Grant.

He waited for Ruth, now in a pensive mood, to say something. But Babe continued brooding, lost in drink and thought. "What was behind the falling out?" Grant asked at last.

Ruth shook his head, as if disgusted. "Women," Ruth finally said. "It's always broads, keed."

Grant was again surprised. The thought of a woman coming between the two men came totally unexpected. Gehrig's reputation had been one of a loving son and faithful husband, almost to a fault. Had the great Gehrig been a womanizer like Ruth? "What specifically?" Grant was intrigued.

"Keed, I'll tell you the full story another time," said Ruth. "It's too petty. Friends shouldn't part over broads, but they do, all the time."

All Ruth would tell Grant for now was that, as a result of the feud, they stopped speaking. They didn't speak during Ruth's last years with the Yankees. Ruth retired in 1935, and Gehrig played three more full seasons until early in the 1939 season, when he benched himself after a record–setting 2,130 games over 15 years. Grant was astounded that Ruth had his friend's records and statistics committed to memory and how it had all started. "In baseball, we count everything," Babe said. "Baseball's a math teacher's dream for teaching kids arithmetic. It's numbers and statistics. It's long division and decimals. I never knew a hitter who couldn't do long division in his head and figure out his batting average minutes after every game."

Ruth then recounted how in 1925 Gehrig had replaced Yankees first baseman Wally Pipp, who had complained of a headache and been told by Miller Huggins to take the day off. Pipp never returned to the lineup.

"I remember the day," Ruth said. "June second. And you know, keed, when Lou died last year, it was 16 years to the day that he replaced Wally."

Babe then broke down and cried like a child. Grant first tried to console him, then realized that maybe this was something the big man simply needed to let out of his system. And he did.

"I didn't really cry for Lou when he died," Babe said as he began to collect himself. "Not this way. I—I just never thought I would miss him this much."

That night, Ruth offered the first of several toasts that he and Grant would make to Gehrig's memory. Babe then said that perhaps it might have been a good idea that Gary Cooper couldn't replicate Gehrig physical prowess, other than a vague facial resemblance that some people on the set marveled about but which he didn't see.

"Lou was one of a kind," Ruth said wistfully. "He was the best friend a fella could have. I wish I had told him that. I wish I had told him a lot of things. I loved him. I wish I had told him that, too. Oh, how I loved that man."

1   The Black Sox Scandal

"I may be a pitcher, but first off I'm a hitter.
I copied my swing after Joe Jackson.
His is the most perfectest...."
—Babe Ruth to Grantland Rice, 1919

IN 1921, THE NEWLY APPOINTED COMMISSIONER OF BASEBALL, federal judge Kenesaw Mountain Landis, imposed a lifetime ban on all eight players of the Chicago White Sox baseball team who had been accused of conspiring with gamblers to intentionally lose the 1919 World Series to the Cincinnati Reds in what is the biggest scandal in major league history. Landis, who had been appointed to investigate the fix, banned the players despite their acquittal of wrongdoing by a Chicago jury. "Regardless of the verdict of juries," Landis declared, "no player that throws a ballgame; no player that undertakes or promises to throw a ballgame; no player that sits in a conference with a bunch of crooked players and gamblers where the ways and means of throwing games are planned and discussed and does not promptly tell his club about it, will ever play professional baseball."

The most high-profile player accused of throwing the World Series was star outfielder "Shoeless" Joe Jackson, who in his

13-year career compiled the third-highest lifetime batting average in major league history. More than a century after his rookie season, Jackson's .408 season average remains the sixth highest since 1901, widely regarded as the beginning of the modern era for the sport. His average that year also established the record for batting average in a single season by a rookie. However, the Black Sox Scandal, as it came to be known, destroyed his reputation. After the heavily favored White Sox lost the 1919 World Series to Cincinnati, Jackson and seven other White Sox players were accused of accepting $5,000 each to throw the Series. It didn't seem to matter to authorities that Shoeless Joe had played a nearly impeccable World Series. He led both teams with a .375 batting average, including a dozen base hits that set a Series record that was not broken until 1964. He committed no errors, and threw out a runner at the plate. Allegations that Cincinnati batters hit an unusually high number of triples to Jackson's position in left field are not supported by newspaper accounts, which recorded no Reds triples at all to left field.

In September 1920, however, a grand jury was convened to investigate the allegations. On September 28, Shoeless Joe appeared before the grand jury and in sworn testimony confessed to his role. His testimony:

> Q. Did anybody pay you any money to help throw that series in favor of Cincinnati?
> A. They did.
> Q. How much did they pay?
> A. They promised me $20,000 and paid me five.
> Q. Who promised you $20,000?

A. Chick Gandil.

Q. Who is Chick Gandil?

A. He was their first baseman on the White Sox club.

Q. Who paid you the $5,000?

A. Lefty Williams brought it in my room and threw it down.

Q. Who is Lefty Williams?

A. The pitcher on the White Sox club...

Q. Does she [Mrs. Jackson] know that you got $5,000 for helping throw these games?

A. She did that night, yes.

Q. You say you told Mrs. Jackson that night?

A. Did. Yes.

Q. What did she say about it?

A. She said she thought it was an awful thing to do.... She felt awful bad about it, she cried about it a while.

Jackson testified that he tried to back out. "I did tell them once, 'I am not going to be into it. I will just get out of it altogether.'" According to the 1921 trial testimonies of two of the men who organized throwing the World Series, Jackson did not attend any of the pre-Series meetings when the fix was discussed. But it was too late. Sensing a serious threat to the game as America's national pastime, baseball officials took sweeping steps whose impact is still felt. The position of baseball commissioner was created with the extraordinary power of permanently banning players from the era of Shoeless Joe Jackson to Pete Rose three-quarters of a century later. To this day, every major league clubhouse prominently displays a large sign reminding players of the strict rules prohibiting gambling.

Shoeless Joe's fall from grace was complete, the jury acquittal notwithstanding. Jackson later sued the White Sox for lost wages, and a jury found in his favor. The presiding judge, however, set aside the verdict ruling that Shoeless Joe's grand jury testimony in 1920 contradicted what he had sworn to in trial and constituted a prima facie case of perjury. That judge had found Jackson to be a liar and perjurer on top of someone who had accepted a bribe to throw the World Series.

"Jackson's fall from grace is one of the real tragedies of baseball," said a disheartened Philadelphia Athletics owner and manager Connie Mack when he looked back at Shoeless Joe's ban from the game. "I always thought he was more sinned against than sinning."

Shoeless Joe, though, would have an inordinate impact on baseball. Nostalgic sentimentalists years later erected remembrances to the player—from statues and museums to a Congressional resolution lauding his career and induction into the Southern California–based Baseball Reliquary's Shrine of the Eternals, a fans' alternative to the Hall of Fame in Cooperstown, New York, from which Jackson is also banned. But it is perhaps the biggest irony known to baseball that Shoeless Joe Jackson's biggest legacy may have been his influence on the one individual credited for saving the game after the tarnish of the Black Sox Scandal—the baseball player who would become the game's greatest star.

George Herman "Babe" Ruth loved Shoeless Joe. As his granddaughter Linda Ruth Tosetti said in a 2013 interview: "Babe Ruth's idol was Shoeless Joe Jackson. He kind of fashioned his swing at the beginning like Jackson's. In his earlier days he had his bats whittled by the same man who whittled Joe's."

In 1911, when Jackson captured fans' imagination with his sensational rookie season, Ruth was 16 and living at St. Mary's Industrial School for Boys, a reformatory in Baltimore where he was honing his own baseball skills and still not yet the player who would become the immortal Babe. It would be another three years before Ruth was signed to play minor-league baseball for the Baltimore Orioles, then of the International League, and subsequently sold to the Boston Red Sox of the American League in midseason. Over the next two seasons, Ruth built a reputation as an outstanding left-handed pitcher who sometimes hit long home runs, which was unusual in the pre-1920 dead-ball era.

All the while, Ruth wanted simply to be the next Shoeless Joe Jackson. As a kid, young Babe had seen Shoeless Joe at his best—slugging baseballs as no other player ever had before, using a swing that was just as unique. Ruth was only one of many aspiring ballplayers who admired Shoeless Joe's swing, which was so unusual for that time that no one seriously tried to copy it. No one, that is, except young Babe. "I decided to pick out the greatest hitter to watch and study," he later said, "and Joe Jackson was good enough for me."

Babe, did more than just imitate Shoeless Joe's swing. Each day, while taking batting practice with the Red Sox, Ruth worked on the swing as best as he could remember it. Then, on one of the White Sox's trips to Boston, young Ruth decided to get a lesson on how to swing like Shoeless Joe from Shoeless Joe Jackson himself. "What'd I have to lose except Joe laughing at me?" Ruth would ask Johnny Grant decades later. "'Joe, show me, how you hit, step by step,' I said. I don't think he quite believed I could hit swinging the way he did 'cause nobody else ever had. But he saw that I'd already gotten a hang of it."

Jackson personally showed Ruth how to stand properly at the plate to hit the way he did, according to an interview Shoeless Joe gave in 1932 to the *Greenville News-Piedmont* in Georgia. Jackson even went so far as to loan Babe on several occasions his prized personal bat, nicknamed Black Betsy, while borrowing Ruth's own bats in return. Fortunately for Babe, Mother Nature had given him a head start. Like Shoeless Joe, Babe was pigeon toed, and they were both distinctive pigeon-toed batters. "In the history of the game, they would be the only two great hitters who hit identically alike," Jimmie Reese, who played in that era and roomed with Ruth one season, recalled in an interview years later. "They stood close to the plate with their left toes facing in and their right toes turned in and pointing to the far right hand corner. Their hands were down on the end of the bat. They gave it all they had in the only way they knew."

And did the Babe ever. In 1920, the year after the Black Sox scandal, Babe Ruth, in his first season with the New York Yankees, slugged 54 home runs, breaking the record of 29 that he had set himself the previous year. Two years earlier, when he was still a part-time outfielder with the Red Sox, his league-leading mark had been a modest 11 home runs. Suddenly, though, Ruth's power hitting had made a quantum leap, taking baseball with him to an unimagined new level of excitement. This was how baseball survived the Black Sox scandal, as gambling's influence declined but, more importantly, as Babe Ruth transformed the game.

"Every big leaguer and his wife should teach their children to pray, 'God bless Mommy, God bless Daddy, and God bless Babe Ruth,'" his Yankee teammate Waite Hoyt later said about Ruth's importance to the game. "I've seen them: kids, men, women, worshippers all, hoping to get his name on a torn, dirty piece of paper, or hoping for a grunt of recognition when they said, 'Hi-ya, Babe.' He never let them down. Not once. He was the greatest crowd pleaser of them all."

The unique relationship between America and baseball must be understood to fully appreciate Babe Ruth's place in the equation. This was the age when baseball players were the princes of American sports, along with heavyweight boxers and race horses and the odd galloping ghost of a running back from the Midwest or the occasional lanky basketball player in short-shorts. Baseball players were the souls of their cities.

By the turn of the 20th century, every major American city had a major league baseball team—New York, St. Louis, Chicago, and Boston each fielded two—and towns throughout the country were studded with minor league franchises. Baseball had undergone a transformation from its origins in the 19th century as an aristocratic club sport to the game of all Americans. As historian Steven A. Riess observed, although the game had become an urban experience, fans nevertheless "saw baseball as an extension of rural America into the cities," where ballparks were "green oases in a largely concrete world... where spectators could readily slip back into an idyllic, rural past." Never having had a national pastime before in its history, America suddenly had one.

Long before Babe Ruth, his hero Shoeless Joe Jackson, and Lou Gehrig, long before baseball became an industry of multinational owners and millionaire players, Walt Whitman wrote, "Well, it's our game. That's the chief fact in connection with it: America's game. It has the snap, go, fling of the American atmosphere. It belongs as much to our institutions, fits into them as significantly as our Constitution's laws, is just as important in the sum total of our historic life." Baseball is, to be sure, an American cultural declaration of independence. It has come to express the nation's character—perhaps never more so than during the years immediately after a scandal threatened to ruin the integrity of the game. That time ushered in a preoccupation with defining the national conscience, and particularly defining the national identity, which Babe Ruth came to symbolize.

"Sometimes I still can't believe what I saw," Ruth's teammate Harry Hooper recalled. "This 19-year-old kid, crude, poorly educated, only lightly brushed by the social veneer we call civilization, gradually transformed into the idol of American youth and the symbol of baseball the world over—a man loved by more people and with an intensity of feeling that perhaps has never been equaled before or since."

It was the Jazz Age, the decade of the flapper and Prohibition. It was the age of Babe Ruth, the most photographed man of the time. Newspapers had become the media giants of America, and New York City at the time had 11 dailies for which Ruth's melodramatic life on and off the field was the ideal subject for their increasing emphasis on pop cultural sensationalism. The Babe's exploits on the diamond and his garrulous charisma off of it helped revolutionize baseball from a game to a major force in the modern entertainment industry. Radio broadcast baseball games throughout the season, and fans flocked to see Yankees games in record numbers.

"When he came over to the Yankees from the Red Sox in 1920, the Yankees were sharing the Polo Grounds with the Giants," Eric Jentsch, a curator of culture and the arts at New York's American History Museum said in appraising Ruth's legacy. "After Ruth came and made such a dramatic change in the game with all his home runs, Yankees attendance doubled and totally surpassed the Giants', so the Giants kicked them out. The Yankees built this beautiful, huge stadium because they got so popular from Ruth, and then were able to create this dynasty that they've had. The Yankees ended up running both the Giants and Dodgers out of town because they were so popular."

The rise of the New York Yankees, of course, only mirrored Babe Ruth's own remarkable ascendance. He went from being one of the best pitchers at the end of the dead-ball era over the last half of the 1910s to ushering in the live ball era in the 1920s by becoming baseball's greatest player.

In March 1921, Babe was in Shreveport, Louisiana, for a month of spring training, and as biographer Robert W. Creamer wrote, having "roared into that Louisiana city like cowboys coming to town on Saturday night." Shreveport citizens treated baseball's home run king like royalty, showering him with gifts, and jam-packing games and even practices by the thousands. A local Essex automobile dealer gave him a car to use during that month with a license plate read simply BABE RUTH'S ESSEX. Unsurprisingly, the car was found one morning abandoned in the middle of the street where Babe had apparently left it and rode off with someone else during a night of carousing.

On March 12, Ruth went hitless in five at-bats in the team's exhibition game, though the Yankees still beat the local Gassers 7–3. Preparing himself for a big year, the Babe boldly began predicting he would hit 60 home runs in the coming season. Meanwhile, at baseball's headquarters in New York, Kenesaw Mountain Landis, just two months on the job as commissioner, suspended Shoeless Joe Jackson and seven of his teammates following a report that their conspiracy bribery trial in Chicago would be delayed. "I deeply regret the postponement of these cases," Landis said in his announcement. "However, baseball is not powerless to protect itself. All of the indicted players have today been placed on the ineligible list."

Almost five months later, a Chicago jury acquitted Jackson, seven other White Sox players, and two gamblers on charges that they conspired to defraud the public by throwing the 1919 World Series. Several hundred spectators in a Chicago courtroom celebrated and cheered "Hooray for the *clean* Sox!" But the celebration wouldn't last 24 hours. The following day, the baseball commissioner banned the eight Black Sox players for life. The Yankees were well on their way to capturing their first American League pennant in franchise history by winning a team-record 98 games and the White Sox fell to seventh place by the end of the season, 36½ games behind the new champions.

Babe Ruth and the New York Yankees would never look back. They, like baseball, owed a king's ransom in gratitude to Shoeless Joe Jackson and the Black Sox Scandal.

"God knows I gave my best in baseball at all times," Shoeless Joe would say near the end of his life, "and no man on earth can truthfully judge me otherwise."

2 Babe's Resurrection

"I've never heard a crowd boo a homer,
but I've heard plenty of boos after a strikeout."

—Babe Ruth

"ARE YOU GOING TO KEEP LETTING DOWN THOSE DIRTY-FACED little kids?" New York state senator James J. Walker, an up-and-coming politico—and no saint himself—admonished Babe Ruth for his cavorting, late-night escapades and behemoth appetite that kept him constantly out of shape. It was Babe's ways, he claimed, that led to an embarrassing 1922 World Series loss to the Giants. Ruth, once one of those dirty-faced little kids himself, broke down in tears at a dinner in the New York Elks Club, and Walker continued unloading on him in the men's room: "You're a dead man, Babe. Hell, even Jesus Christ couldn't get resurrected in this town."

That's how low Babe Ruth's image had sunk after his third season with the New York Yankees. He had been sold by the Boston Red Sox to the Yankees before the 1920 season and had arrived amid great expectations, having been part of two World Series–winning teams. He had then raised New Yorkers' hopes by slugging a record number of home runs in his first two seasons, only to disappoint with a second straight World Series loss in 1922. So one could see how his scandalous personal life could be used by a politician to paint him as a failure—a dead man without a second chance in New York, even as the Yankees were opening their new stadium. Possibly not, but New York in the 1920s, while not Sodom nor Gomorrah, was hardly first-century Jerusalem either.

Ruth would show that he had it in him to resurrect himself. Not overnight, but in a season that began with Babe christening the new Yankee Stadium with a game-winning three-run home run on April 18 that would lead beat writer Fred Lieb of the *New York Post* to appropriately call Yankee Stadium "the House that Ruth Built."

Two months into the 1923 season, though, it was hardly promising. On a cloudless June day, the Babe seemed to be brooding as he stared out through the misty morning air into the vast expanse of the freshly cut outfield of the new Yankee cathedral. Babe Ruth, one hand on a bar supporting the batting cage and the other on his hip, stood a few feet behind home plate between two protective but aloof teammates who, along with him, were watching first baseman Wally Pipp take batting practice several hours before a game. A few feet behind them, a New York writer milled about, waiting with bated breath for the Babe to speak. But the Babe said nothing.

The outfield on which Ruth set his eyes was unique. In the coming years, Yankee Stadium would gain a reputation for being a left-handed hitter's park, its right-field foul pole a mere 295 feet from home plate. But for the moment, the Babe's eyes trained themselves on the vast acreage of right center field, where the distance suddenly deepened to 429 feet and then to dead center, where the fence in the stadium's original design measured an incredible 490 feet. The dimensions dwarfed the Polo Grounds, the home of the New York Giants and the Yankees' previous ballpark. It was in the Polo Grounds that the Babe, as the Yankees' $120,000 acquisition from the Boston Red Sox, had dramatically transformed the game: 54 home runs in 1920, 59 in 1921, and then the drop to 35 in 1922 when he had missed almost a third of the season because of suspensions.

The Polo Grounds held a special place in the hearts of New Yorkers, including Ruth. In the first decades of the 20th century, the original stadium was the signature of Coogan's Hollow, a scenic meadow in north Harlem enclosed by the Harlem River to the east and a large bluff to the west. Admission to the stadium was 25 cents, though free seats were there for the taking at the top of Coogan's Bluff. When the original Polo Grounds burned down before the start of the 1911 baseball season, it was replaced later the same year by the stadium that would become symbolic of those future ballparks known as the game's cathedrals. Italian marble boxes surrounded the front of the upper deck grandstands. American eagle sculptures adorned the cantilevered roof, from which blue and gold banners blew in the breeze. Each of the National League's eight teams who competed with the hometown New York Giants were honored in the grandstand with their team logos emblazoned on shields.

Already in this 1923 season, Ruth had slugged prodigious drives that would have been home runs in the Polo Grounds, whose modest dimensions included a 258-foot distance from home to the foul pole in right field. In Yankee Stadium, however, Ruth's wallops had been contained for doubles and occasional triples—or, worse, they had died as desolate long outs in the gloves of outfielders who sometimes even gave chase up the slope of grass that ran from foul pole to foul pole.

"All the parks are good for hitting home runs except [Yankee] Stadium," Ruth would lament. "There is no background there at all... I cried when they took me out of the Polo Grounds." If this indeed had been the house that Ruth's fan-drawing power had financed, the Babe, in his first months of residency, was perplexed by his own new home. His batting average was a career high, and he would finish the season only seven points under .400. But Babe, concerned about his power numbers—especially after what for him had been a mediocre year in 1922— felt he was not the same hitter he had been in past years. And though not mired in a slump, Ruth nevertheless now faced doing what every struggling ballplayer ultimately winds up having to do: the Babe was taking extra batting practice.

On this particular June morning, the Yankee hitters shared the Stadium infield with several pitchers there to get in their throwing between starts. Ruth had already taken his first round of swings in the cage and given way to Pipp when their attention turned toward the Yankees dugout. The Yankees' scrawny, diminutive manager, Miller Huggins, was walking toward the cage in his inimitable toes-turned-outward fashion, trailed by a clean-shaven player of imposing build who towered over the New York skipper but who looked uncomfortable in his new pinstriped uniform. "Hey, Wally," Huggins said to the man who from 1915 to that moment had played in more games than any other Yankee, "let the kid hit a few, will ya?"

Just half an hour earlier, Ruth had been introduced to the kid in the Yankee clubhouse when trainer Doc Woods had brought him over to his corner where the Babe was signing baseballs. "Babe," Woods had said, "I want you to meet Lou Gehrig from Columbia." Ruth looked over the newest Yankee, the Columbia University baseball star who had signed a minor league contract with a $1,500 bonus a day earlier, and gave him a friendly smile. "Hiya, keed!"

Gehrig had frozen at the sight of Ruth. Suddenly he was face-to-face with perhaps the single person, other than his mother, who had influenced him. "I wanted to be Babe Ruth," Gehrig would later admit, though he was quick to clarify that "I wanted to be Babe Ruth, the baseball player."

That day, Gehrig had arrived to his first practice nervous and without a bat. Now, with all eyes on him, he picked out a bat resting against the back of the batting cage, unaware that it was Ruth's personal bat and at 48 ounces the heaviest bat in the stadium. The Babe noticed but graciously said nothing. "Ordinarily, a batter prizes his bat more than he does his watch," Yankee right-hander Waite Hoyt would later recall. "In this instance, Ruth could have said, 'Oh, no, kid, that's my good one. Grab yourself another stick.' But somehow the Babe didn't protest. It choked in his throat. He said nothing."

Perhaps it was the unusually heavy weight of the bat, or possibly it was just nerves, that caused Gehrig to miss the first two pitches and then dribble a few harmless ground balls to the infield. Fortunately for Gehrig, among the early arrivals at the Stadium were some friends from Columbia, where in only one season he had established himself as a slugger whose power begged the most obvious of comparisons.

"I think I've just seen another Babe Ruth," Yankees scout Paul Krichell, himself a former major league catcher with the St. Louis Browns, had told Yankees general manager Ed Barrow. Suspicious, Barrow sent Krichell back to take another look. Krichell became even more impressed, urging the GM to take on the kid.

The Columbia fans who that morning watched pregame batting practice from box seats behind the Yankees dugout shouted encouragement. "Show that big guy, Lou," yelled one of the Columbia men, obviously referring to Ruth. "He's not the only one that can hit it out of the park." Gehrig put the next pitch in the right field seats—or bleachers, to be exact.

At the time, the historic greenish seats that came to be associated with the short right field porch in Yankee Stadium were still years away. When the Stadium opened, the triple deck grandstand and signature roof with the copper facade above the third deck had stopped short of both the left and right field foul poles. In the Stadium's early years, wooden bleachers surrounded the outfield. Atop the bleachers was a manually operated, wooden scoreboard in right-center field, surrounded by advertisements. It was not until 1928, with the Stadium's first major facelift, that the triple-deck grandstand in left field was extended beyond the foul pole. The right field grandstand was extended in 1937, allowing "upper deck" home runs in both directions. But for now, two months after its opening in 1923, this new Yankee Stadium had proven to be an humbling experience for even the player for whose enormous left-handed power it had been designed.

In his new home, Ruth was having to acclimate himself to a different range. It would take several seasons. He would go on to hit only 41 homers in his first year in the new ballpark and not hit the magical 60 until his fifth season in Yankee Stadium.

In this maiden season at the Stadium, Ruth was coming to work early for extra batting practice and now found himself watching a hulking left-handed hitter effortlessly impress with his power. After Gehrig parked another ball in the bleachers, the Babe turned to one of the other hitters standing at the cage.

"That kid sure can bust 'em," Babe said in a gravelly baritone. The writer standing nearby thought he had heard Ruth call Gehrig "Buster," and shortly thereafter began calling him "Buster" Gehrig. Ruth would laugh for the rest of his life at how writers could get it so wrong so easily. Gehrig, as it happened, did not appreciate the nickname, which the Babe later often used in addressing his teammate, according to Ruth biographer Robert W. Creamer. But for the Babe, it was a term of friendly affection. He also rarely remembered people's names and called most everyone by the same term he had used to greet Gehrig the first time they met: kid.

"Hey, keed!" Babe called out to Gehrig as he walloped another pitch. "I got a $35,000 check in my wallet. It's all yours if you put the next three pitches in them bleachers." The players chortled and chuckled, and Gehrig stared at Ruth in disbelief. Then, as if on cue, Gehrig turned each of the next three pitches into majestic rainbows, the balls clanking as they landed and ricocheted in the right field bleachers.

Clang. Clang. Clang.

"Aw! I'm broke!" Ruth feigned disgust. Gehrig did not take the bet seriously and would learn in years to come it had been best that he not, for he would have been the butt of one of Ruth's jokes. The $35,000 check was from the Kessel-Baumann Picture Corporation of Hollywood, California, which had capitalized on the Babe's popularity by signing him to costar in a 1920 exploitation motion picture *Headin' Home.* The producers, who included director Raoul Walsh, paid Ruth only $15,000 of the $50,000 they had promised him. For years afterward, the Babe carried around a worthless $35,000 check as a souvenir of his first experience with Hollywood, often bringing it out in conversation. It was the first—but far from the last—time Gehrig would fail to be amused by the Babe's sense of humor.

But on this day, with the season still young and the long shadows of September a distant summer away, the Babe was consumed with his own game and his own insecurities, hidden as they were to the world by the veneer of the outsized, loud, and sometimes profane image that had come to be associated with Ruth. The nation talked more of Ruth than any single individual in its athletic history. Boys, young men, old men, girls, and elderly ladies alike besieged him for his autograph. He greeted them all the same way with the same kindly "Hello, keed," or "Glad to oblige you, keed." He made a movie. He gave his name to caps, suspenders, candy bars, soft drinks. His endorsements brought in even more income than his big Yankee salary, the highest in baseball.

The Babe was in the second year of a five-year contract, calling for over a quarter of a million dollars. Colonel Tillinghast L'Hommedieu Huston, one of the Yankees owners, signed the document while with Ruth as the Babe was melting off some of his fat in a tub at Hot Springs, Arkansas. The contract called for $52,000 for each of the seasons of 1922, 1923, and 1924, and gave the club the right to extend it at the same terms for 1925 and 1926. The first year of the new contract was one of the Babe's poorest in his major league career. A long suspension in the spring got him off on the wrong foot when he finally became eligible to play in late May. The Babe got into an argument with umpire Tommy Connolly and used such strong language that the late Ban Johnson, then American League president, fined him heavily and took his newly acquired captain's commission away from him. Babe's batting average fell from .378 to .315, and his homer crop from 59 to 35, but the Yankees—strengthened by the acquisition of Joe Bush, Sam Jones, Everett Scott, and Joe Dugan from the Red Sox—again won the American League pennant after a tough struggle with the Browns.

In the World Series with the Giants, both the Yankees and Ruth hit their low in blue ribbon competition. The best the American Leaguers got out of five games was one 10-inning tie, while two hits in 17 at-bats gave Babe the slim batting average of .118. Giants fans in New York laughed shrilly at the fate of the American Leaguers and changed Ruth's name from the Big Bam to the Big Bum. Ruth was further humbled when New York City mayor Jimmy Walker said that he had let down the "dirty-faced kids."

The Babe cried at the notion. Perhaps because of his own tough childhood, Babe always had time for children. He frequently returned to the orphanage where he spent much of his youth to play ball, even the tuba, and raise money. Teammate Jimmie Reese, one of his many roommates on the road, recalled how Ruth would often stop his car near Central Park and tell him to wait while he got out and signed autographs. Two hours passed on one occasion as game-time neared: Ruth had to make sure that each and every youngster got an autograph. The Babe vowed to overcome his humiliation of 1922. He worked out all winter, trimming 15 pounds of fat and reporting to spring training weighing 215 pounds, his lowest weight as a Yankee. Ruth's rededication to the game had given the 1923 season special meaning beyond the christening of Yankee Stadium.

On that June day, as Ruth and the other Yankees watched Gehrig take batting practice, no one would suspect how their lives would intersect with one another. Ruth's name would become synonymous with baseball and home runs, just as his incorrigible, bawdy lifestyle made him a symbol of excess. Lou Gehrig's accomplishments on the field would make him an authentic American hero, and his tragic early death made him a legend. They were polar opposites who were magnetized as one. They would become inseparable in baseball's lexicon, as much as the legendary double-play combination of Tinkers to Evers to Chance. "Nobody would've mistaken them for brothers—they had nothing in common except the Yankees and baseball, and for what mattered to them, that was enough," said Jimmie Reese, who played with them in 1930 and 1931. "Lou tended to the sublime, Babe sometimes to the ridiculous."

But then the legend of Babe Ruth operated at the intersection of reality and absurdity, beginning with his birth. The Babe who watched Lou take batting practice that day was 29—or so he thought. Babe offered up his birth date as February 7, 1894, and would do so until 1934, his last season with the Yankees. It was not until Ruth applied for a passport for an extended barnstorming tour to the Far East and on to Europe that Babe learned differently. According to his official birth certificate filed with the State of Maryland, Ruth's birthday was a day shy of being a full year later than what he had always believed: February 6, 1895. Whether 29 or 28, Ruth in 1923 was in the prime of his career. However, it was a Yankees career as yet without full glory. In the three seasons since being sold to New York, Ruth had yet to win a World Series with the team with whom his name would forever be linked in baseball lore. With the Boston Red Sox, the Babe had won World Series championships in 1915, 1916, and 1918, at one point pitching a World Series record of 29 consecutive scoreless innings. "Babe Ruth probably gave me more trouble than any other left-hand pitcher," said the premier hitter of the era, Ty Cobb. "He would have been the greatest left-hander of the generation if he hadn't moved to the outfield." Ruth had been moved to the outfield because of his hitting, of course. The Babe hit .325 in 1917, .300 in 1918, and .322 in 1919 while slugging 42 home runs in that three-year span. In 1919 he led the league with 113 RBIs, 103 runs scored, and 29 home runs, more than double his total from the previous year.

At the age of 24, Babe Ruth was the best player in the game. He had given the Red Sox three world championships in the span of four years and, unbeknownst at that time, Boston's last World Series title of the century. But in 1919, the Red Sox and Ruth could not agree on a contract. Although they were the best team in baseball, the Red Sox were having money troubles. Or, more accurately, the new owner of the Red Sox was having money troubles. In 1917, Broadway producer Harry Frazee bought the team and initiated its slow demise. When Ruth asked for $10,000 for the season, Frazee replied, "I wouldn't pay one of my best actors that much," not realizing that Ruth would be greater than all the actors and actresses he ever engaged put together. Ruth agreed to $9,000 for the year, modest compared to the $15,000 per year that baseball's other top players were earning.

Despite Ruth's emergence as a home run hitter, the Red Sox fell to sixth place in 1919, and Frazee saw his solution to the money crisis. His show, *No, No, Nanette* needed funding; his Longacre Theater was in dire straits; and he faced a $300,000 mortgage on Fenway Park. So on January 3, 1920, Frazee sold Ruth to Yankees owners Col. Jacob Ruppert and Col. Tillinghast L'Hommedieu Huston for $125,000 cash and the guaranty of a $300,000 loan collateralized by Fenway Park. But it wasn't just Ruth; Harry Frazee had loaded up the Yankees to get money to cover his theatrical investments. Watching Gehrig with Ruth that June morning were three other former Red Sox players who Frazee had sold to the budding Yankees dynasty: pitchers Carl Mays and Herb Pennock and infielder Everett Scott. Only a month later, on July 11, 1923, Frazee sold the entire Boston Red Sox franchise for $1.15 million, making a hefty profit on the $400,000 he had paid for the team six years earlier. To the chagrin of Boston fans everywhere, Frazee's time with the Red Sox would be Boston's loss and New York's gain.

Neither Ruth nor baseball looked back. Ruth single-handedly moved baseball from the "dead-ball era," a time when runs usually were scored with a walk, a stolen base, a single, and little muscle. The Babe injected both his personality, his strength, and the long ball. "Some folks say I was responsible for the development of 'swing hitting,'" he later observed. "Maybe they're right. Other fellows, particularly the big, burly, powerful chaps, began taking their bat at the end and 'swinging from the heels,' as the boys say. And 'swing hitting' came into prominence."

The period of Ruth's ascendancy and his impact on the game corresponded with the conclusion of Ty Cobb's great career with the Detroit Tigers. A maniacal, give-no-quarter competitor, Cobb despised Ruth. The rivalry was understandable. Cobb was the game's greatest player of the early 1900s. But Cobb saw in Ruth a man who put an end to his spikes-first, 90-feet-at-a-time brand of baseball. Cobb took every opportunity to disparage the Babe, even calling him "nigger" because of his broad nose. When teams would gather around the cage before a game, Cobb would ask, "What smells?" The Babe, however, took it in stride. "Things like that didn't seem to bother Ruth," said biographer Robert W. Creamer. "He just didn't worry; he was much more adjusted to life than Cobb was. Ruth had a lot more fun playing ball than Cobb."

Cobb and Ruth finally met head-to-head for four games on June 11–14, 1921, a series billed as a grudge match. When the Yankees ran into trouble with their pitching in the June 13 game, Miller Huggins called a clubhouse meeting and asked, "Who can pitch today? There isn't anyone left." "I'll pitch, Hug," Ruth volunteered. Huggins gave Babe the ball, even though he hadn't pitched a single inning in more than a year. Ruth went five innings and won the game against the Tigers. He struck out only one batter in the game, but it was significant for Ruth—he struck out Ty Cobb. In the four-game series, Ruth slugged six home runs and got the better of Cobb as the Yankees swept all four games.

It was important to Ruth that he also got the better of Cobb off the field as well. The Babe's other reason for taking extra batting practice in hopes of finding his home run swing was to impress the newest conquest of his life. Earlier that spring, not long after Yankee Stadium opened, the Babe was introduced in a casino to Claire Hodgson, a pretty and brainy young widow from Georgia who had come to New York in 1920 with her three-year-old daughter, Julia. Shortly after he began seeing her, Ruth learned that Claire had previously dated Cobb. Her standing in Ruth's life was suddenly elevated, even though he was then still married to his first wife, Helen, who lived in Sudbury, Massachusetts, with their adopted daughter, Dorothy.

Claire Merritt Hodgson alone may have the only person who knew the depths of Ruth's despair with his game. The night after they met in Washington, DC, that spring, Hodgson had dined with Ruth in his hotel suite along with a girlfriend and a room filled with hangers-on. To her surprise, Ruth poured his heart out to her. "He was afraid, in fact, that he was washed up before he was 30," Hodgson would later recall. "All the world adored him. He thought all the world hated him. And he knew he hated himself."

Clang. Clang.

When Gehrig put two more balls in the bleachers, his Columbia cheering section resumed heckling Ruth. He turned, smiled, and bowed in mock genuflection. "Keeds," Babe sneered playfully in Huggins' direction. The Yankees manager stood on the other side of the batting cage studying Gehrig. "But this one here's as big as me, Hug."

"Yeah, Jidge," said Pipp, calling Ruth by a corruption of George, a nickname that had been given him by Yankees teammate Joe Dugan. "And he plays right field."

Ruth, the Yankees' regular right fielder since joining the team, roared back, "He also plays first base, Pipp."

Babe roared again, though he could not have known the significance of the dig. Pipp was a good hitter with three .300 seasons and six 90-plus-RBI years. However, two years later, in his 11th season with the Yankees, he would ask for a day off because of a headache. Gehrig, who had pinch-hit the previous day for another player, would come in to play first base and never give up the position. Pipp would be shunted off to the Cincinnati Reds and obscurity.

Nearby, Huggins sneezed. He had a bad cold and sneezed again. The players paid no attention except Gehrig. "*Gesundheit*," said Gehrig, momentarily stepping out of the batter's box.

Ruth walked a few steps over and, reaching into the hip pocket of his uniform, pulled out a big onion that he offered to Huggins.

"Here, Hug, gnaw on this," he said. "Raw onions are cold killers."

Huggins looked at Ruth dismissively. "I'm fine."

Ruth stuck the onion back in his pocket and winked at Pipp, who could barely contain himself. No one could predict what vegetable Ruth might pull out of his uniform. Stories abound of how during heat waves Ruth would place heads of cabbage in the dugout water coolers. Or how each inning, before going back to his position in right field, Babe would take a fresh cabbage leaf and put it under his cap to keep himself cool.

Only Ruth could get away with such absurd behavior, but then he was a showman. He drew the crowds. He was the only Yankee immediately recognizable, not only for his familiar physique but also for the face that was ever-present in the newspapers. One had to be more discerning in recognizing other Yankees players. And a program would have been of little help. In 1923, the Yankee uniforms were blank on the back. The team did not introduce uniform numbers until 1929;

Ruth was given No. 3 because he batted third in the lineup and Gehrig was given No. 4 because he batted fourth. In 1923, the Yankees did not even have their famous interlocking *N* and *Y* on the left breast of their uniforms. The only similarity of those Yankees home uniforms with those of later years were the pinstripes. Owner Colonel Ruppert had them specially designed for the team, believing that the vertical pinstripes would make the Babe look trimmer.

For Ruth, the Yankee pinstripes were an extension of his own fashion consciousness. Later in his life, much was made of his sartorial choices, swaddled in an elegant wraparound camel hair topcoat with a flat camel hair cap on his round head perhaps. Fashion was a major part of the atmosphere of the Roaring '20s. And Ruth was ever the fashion plate then, a time when the trendiness of clothes reflected the superficiality and rebellion of the era. Outward appearance was celebrated over personality, fashion helped create that feeling. Ruth, of course, had both: the personality that encapsulated the decade and the appearance that made him as instantly recognizable on Broadway as the Ginza in Tokyo. *"Baby Roos! Baby Roos!"* cried excited crowds following him through the streets during a barnstorming trip to Japan with an all-star team after the 1934 season.

The Columbia students who accompanied Gehrig to batting practice were making fashion statements of their own. They wore summer suits and straw hats. They stayed after Ruth, who occasionally would turn and smile at them—Columbia kids would be the last to get to him. He had been to Columbia himself, though not for school. Ruth had been invited there two years earlier, after his 59–home run season, when two scientists asked him to participate in a battery of tests. The doctors Albert Johanson and Joseph Holmes were illuminating. They discovered that the pitch Ruth could hit hardest was just above the knees, on the outside corner of the plate. And when he hit perfectly, in still air, with the bat moving at 110 feet per second, the ball would carry 450 to 500 feet. In a clinical test of steadiness, made by inserting a charged rod successively into small holes of different sizes, Ruth was proved to be the best of 500 volunteers. Ruth's eyes responded to flashing electric bulbs in a darkened chamber 2/100 of a second quicker than did the average person's—a skill critically valuable for picking up a moving ball as it left a pitcher's hand. In short, medical science corroborated what the fans already knew: Babe Ruth possessed preternatural eyesight and equally impressive hand-eye coordination. Perhaps his teammate Jumping Joe Dugan was right: "Born? Hell, Babe Ruth wasn't born! The son of a bitch fell from a tree!"

Gehrig's experience with Columbia had been more traditional. He would later credit his Columbia education for helping him learn to appreciate reading, good books, and classical music. To sportswriters, he came to be known as "Columbia Lou," although he had actually left the school after his sophomore year to pursue baseball full-time, becoming Columbia's most eminent dropout since Alexander Hamilton. However, Gehrig also felt that he never gained full acceptance from his fellow students at Columbia. With two parents who struggled with English, along with his shyness, he was often picked on. He ran up a small debt to his fraternity, which he was hesitant to repay even after his success with the Yankees. The treatment he received from his fellow classmates at Columbia gnawed at him; it made him feel unworthy and only drove him further into his shyness. He was never able to forget the snobbery he confronted.

Years later he appeared as guest lecturer at Columbia's Teachers College in the 1930s, an indication that he held no grudge against the school itself. Indeed, Columbia effectively had given Lou the opportunity to display his talents to the Yankees. In addition to the $1,500 bonus for which he signed, the Yankees had also agreed to a $2,000 minor league salary for the remainder of the season—exorbitant by the standards of the day. By comparison, 26 years later, the Yankees would sign Mickey Mantle for $1,500 that included a $1,100 bonus and $400 in minor league salary for the remainder of his first professional season.

But then, the perception of Gehrig, both when he signed and throughout his career, was that of a college man: studious, deliberate, and thoughtful to the point of almost romantic brooding. "Mom and Pop have made enough sacrifices for me. Mom's been slaving to put a young ox like me through college," Gehrig said when he signed. "It's about time that I carry the load and take care of them."

His mother had wept. To many foreign-born parents, a career in professional athletics seemed a poor substitute for a real profession. Even after her son became famous, she would proudly remind reporters that he had once been a college man.

Gehrig was much more humble. "The only B.A. I have," he always cheerfully insisted, "is a batting average."

And power, too, as he first showed his future teammates while taking his introductory batting practice as a Yankee.

When he had finished, he put the bat—Babe's bat—back where he had found it. "Not too heavy, was it, keed?" Ruth asked.

Gehrig stopped, looked at the bat and then at Ruth and realized whose bat he had been using. He grinned and nodded in Ruth's direction. "To be honest," Gehrig said, "it felt a little light."

Ruth looked at the rookie. Then, unable to contain himself, the Babe let out a roar of laughter that echoed far into the man-made caverns of the new stadium.

3   Beginnings

*"I'm not a headline guy. I know that as long as
I was following Ruth to the plate I could have stood
on my head and no one would have known the difference."*

—Lou Gehrig

THE NAMES OF BABE RUTH AND LOU GEHRIG ARE INTERTWINED IN Americana and baseball lore like that of historic brothers or rivals. In truth, they were both and they were neither. They were teammates, a designation often as misleading as it is all-encompassing. Their lives and their careers happened to overlap during a troubling period in the nation, where at one point the excess of the 1920s belied the outlawing of alcohol and where at another the country's obsessive inwardness blinded it to the external forces that would forever change the world.

Some might suggest that Babe Ruth symbolized the America of the Roaring '20s, Prohibition, and the Jazz Age—and Gehrig the sobering wake-up call of the Great Depression and the New Deal. That, however, might be as romantic as the notion that they were true contemporaries. Which, arguably they were not—at least not in the world of professional sports, where the designation of teammates can include a worldly veteran nearing the end of his career and a naive rookie barely beginning his own. Though the names Ruth and Gehrig will forever be inseparable in baseball legend, the men's differences offer testament to the incredible bonding forces of the game, both for players and for fans.

The day in June 1923 when Ruth and Gehrig crossed paths during batting practice at Yankee Stadium was the beginning of their story, though they had come to that point by dramatically different routes. Gehrig's pedigree was from a New York City that had once been known as a haven for German immigrants in the Bowery. Ruth, on the other hand, was born to rough beginnings in Baltimore, an American street urchin before his "reformation" as a youth at St. Mary's.

Babe Ruth was born on February 6, 1895, to Kate Schamberger Ruth and George Herman Ruth Sr., in the upstairs rented apartment of his maternal grandfather, Pius Schamberger, at 216 Emory Street in Baltimore, Maryland. He was the first of eight children born to Kate and George Herman Ruth, who were 19 and 23 years old, respectively, when George Jr. was born. Unfortunately, six of Kate and George Ruth's children died in infancy. Only George Jr. and his sister Mary Margaret, who was born in 1900 and who came to be known as Mamie, survived past childhood.

According to his official birth certificate filed with the State of Maryland, Ruth's birthday was a day and a year later than what he had always believed it to be, but Babe chose to dismiss the corrected date. He made no apologies for his life, least of all his age. The Babe also wondered, and at least one of his biographers concurred, whether the birth certificate with the later date had not belonged to one of his six non-surviving siblings.

The Babe's father was a bartender in the family-owned grocery store/saloon near the Baltimore waterfront. The Babe's mother was the daughter of a lower-middle-class German immigrant who made his living as an upholsterer. Kate also worked at the tavern with her husband and, according to one account, she made the two-and-a-half-block walk to her father's home to give birth to Babe, with a neighborhood midwife named Minnie Graf assisting. The Babe's maternal grandfather, Pius Schamberger, had been born in Germany in 1833. He worked as a grocer just after the Civil War and later as a saloonkeeper on Pratt Street in Baltimore. As an upholsterer, he became an active trade unionist and at one point served as vice president of the Woodworkers Local 6.

Both Babe and Mamie believed their mother to have been Irish, although there is no firm record as to her background. More is known about the Ruth side of the family. According to family tradition, Ruth's paternal line was originally Pennsylvania Dutch, and his grandparents relocated to Baltimore, which is only 60 miles south of Pennsylvania Dutch country. The Babe's paternal great-grandfather, Peter, was believed to have been born in Bucks County, Pennsylvania, in 1801, and his paternal great-grandmother, Kaziah Reager, was born in Lancaster, Pennsylvania, in 1805. German was spoken in the house as fluently as English. Their son, John Ruth, was raised in Baltimore, where in 1873 he was in the business of making lightning rods for people's houses. Later he opened the combination grocery store and saloon on Frederick Avenue, where his son George Ruth and his wife, Kate, were working at the time Babe was born.

George and Kate Ruth were both poor, uneducated people who had moved from one apartment to another in their run-down Baltimore neighborhood. In addition to his work as a saloonkeeper, George Ruth had worked as a lightning-rod salesman, a wagon driver in the days before automobiles, a laborer, and a harness salesman—with none of the jobs ever lasting very long. Soon after Mamie's birth, when George was five years old, his parents bought a saloon at 426 West Camden Street, which was underneath an apartment into which the family moved.

Young George experienced little, if any, real love from his parents, who made no time for their son. His parents said nothing when he didn't bother to go to school, so day after day he roamed the streets with other aimless boys. He spent the first seven years of his life running around the dirty, crowded streets of the Baltimore waterfront watching street fights and stealing from shopkeepers. Among some of his reputed early exploits were throwing apples and eggs at truck drivers, stealing food, and running into his parents' saloon, where he would drink the last drops of whiskey from the almost empty glasses on the tables. The rough street boys he ran around with taught him to swear, chew tobacco, steal apples from fruit stands, and fight.

"I was a bum when I was a kid,' Ruth said sadly, recalling those early years. "Looking back on my boyhood, I honestly don't remember being aware of the difference between right and wrong."

It was unavoidable for young George to spend an inordinate amount of time around his parents' saloon, even though it was a terrible influence on a young boy. In the spring of 1902, a big fight broke out in the saloon. Shots were fired, and the police were called. One of the officers learned that a small child was there when the shooting took place. Not only that, a neighbor told the officer, but the boy was there at all hours of the day and never went to school. It was, of course, young George. When the police reported this, the local school and truancy authorities intervened.

It didn't take long before young George became well known by local police. When their son was seven, Kate and her husband finally decided they could no longer tend to the mischievous boy and took him to St. Mary's Industrial School for Boys. On June 13, 1902, George Herman Ruth turned over his seven-year-old to St. Mary's. Not only did he place young George in the school, but he also signed over custody of the boy to the Xaverian Brothers, a Catholic order of Jesuit missionaries who ran St. Mary's. This was both a reformatory and orphanage, surrounded by a wall similar to a prison with guards on duty. There were approximately 800 children at St. Mary's. The reformatory had four dormitories that housed about 200 kids each. George Jr., who by the age of seven had already proven mischievous, was classified as "incorrigible" upon his admission. For a few brief periods he was returned to live with his family, but he was always sent back to St. Mary's, and no one ever came to visit him while he was there.

This part of the narrative of Ruth's early years has existed since his rise to fame in the 1920s and became an accepted part of the Babe's history through the 20th century. But it appears to have been as much of the myth and legend as anything else in the Babe Ruth story. It would not be until more than a century after Ruth roamed the halls of St. Mary's that a fuller understanding of the forces that put him in what was effectively a group foster home would come into view.

In 2011, Julia Ruth Stevens, Babe's adopted daughter, pulled back the curtain on what was largely an unknown fact of George Herman Ruth's biography—that his parents had separated when he was a child. Ruth's home life had been chaotic and turbulent, that much had long been known. But that his parents had actually separated? That news came as a shock to even the most knowledgeable of Ruth's biographers, the most recent being Jane Leavy.

"In the course of speaking with [Stevens], she suddenly blurted out, 'You know his parents were separated,'" Leavy said in an interview during the Cooperstown Symposium on Baseball and American Culture at the Baseball Hall of Fame in 2016. "That was a reportorial shock. And I remember saying to her, 'I never heard that.' And she said, 'I just thought everybody knew.'

"His mother and father separated," Leavy recalled Stevens telling her. "He stayed with his father until he couldn't control him anymore and sent him off to St. Mary's. It was never mentioned. It must have been a blow to [Babe] to have his mother and sister go off and leave him, and his daddy put him in St. Mary's and hardly ever came to visit him."

According to Stevens, she never heard Ruth speak about his mother. Perhaps it helps explain why he would tell biographer Bob Considine, "I think my mother hated me." In *The Big Fella*, Leavy adopts parental abandonment as a defining biographical fact of Babe's childhood, as it would be of any childhood.

"It was like looking through a lens that suddenly has been clarified: 'Now he makes sense.' This big overgrown boy who never grew up had to invent himself completely because his parents left him in the care of the brothers who ran St. Mary's Industrial School. He wasn't, I don't believe, such a hooligan, such a reprobate at age seven that he had to be incarcerated. It was clear to me that the catalyst for his incarceration, and that is the word that was used, was his parents' divorce. They just didn't have any use for him, basically. How, at age seven, do you explain to yourself that six of their eight kids died and they still sent me away? How bad do I have to be? Do you start trying to live up to that reputation? I started doing all the reporting and as a person he started making sense. And the more I followed that down the more I was able to put together a profile of a person that I find believable. So here's this guy who first, as a boy and as a young man, has to create a life for himself. And then here's this guy who creates a persona that in some ways assuages the pain of the boy that he was and buffers him from it."

In Babe's institutionalization at St. Mary's, here again reality was to meet absurdity. Ruth mythology has long maintained that young Babe was carted off to an orphanage, abandoned by his parents, and ostensibly adopted by a member of the Xaverian Brothers. The facts, though, do not fully support the myth. St. Mary's indeed was a reform school that also housed orphans, but in some instances it also served the same disciplinary role that military schools did for the sons of well-to-do families. In Ruth's case, there may have been several reasons for his enrollment, not the least of which was his truancy. Also, the Babe could neither read nor write when he entered St. Mary's.

According to most accounts, he stayed at St. Mary's for only a month before returning home. He was back at St. Mary's for another month in November, but was back with his family by Christmas and remained at home all of 1903 and until sometime in 1904. "His mother missed him when he was in the home and she would cry and ask her husband to get him out," recalled an older cousin, John Ruth, who was one of the Babe's boyhood companions. "Then when he came home, she'd have trouble with him and hit him, and his father would put him back in again."

When biographer Considine years later asked Ruth why he kept returning to St. Mary's, the Babe shrugged and said, "You know, I'd do things... Drinkin'."

Ruth's sister, Mamie, would later recall, "He just wouldn't go to school... We used to visit him once a month. We used to ride out on the trolley. We had to change cars there at the convent."

Though he didn't realize it at the time, St. Mary's would be home throughout his adolescence. George was released to live with his family on a few occasions, but one way or another he would return to St. Mary's. He didn't adjust well. Living on the streets was the life he was accustomed to; suddenly confronted with rules to follow he began to feel miserable and regretful. Added to that pain was the sense of abandonment. One of Ruth's fellow students at St. Mary's, Lou Leisman, would later recall feeling sorry for himself because he had no visitors in two years. Ruth consoled him, saying, "You're lucky, Fats. I haven't seen my father in 10 years... I guess I'm too big and ugly to have visitors. Maybe next time." According to Leisman, Ruth never had visitors again.

While at St. Mary's, George was taught to be a tailor. He was paid six cents for every collar he sewed onto a shirt. But as fate would have it, tailoring was not all he was suited for. Ruth was often teased by his peers, who called him "Nigger Lips," and he was just as often in trouble himself.

Back home, the Babe's family life had become more dysfunctional than ever. George Ruth was still working as a saloon-keeper, but his wife's health had deteriorated. The family had also moved several times and had wound up at the corner of Conway and Charles, just a block from the city's inner harbor. In 1908, when he was 14, the Babe was released from St. Mary's to live once more with his family. He was at home for two years until the death of his mother on August 12, 1912.

The head of reform at St. Mary's was a Jesuit called Brother Matthias—an imposing man who became like a second father to George. It was Matthias who first inspired Ruth to play baseball. At age eight, Ruth was playing ball on the 12-year-old team; at 12, he was one of the best players on varsity. In 1913, at the age of 18, Ruth was the star of St. Mary's team and the best young player in Baltimore. He was a left-handed pitcher and also a tremendous hitter—and he could play every position. During the final game of the team's 1913 season, Ruth was scouted by the Baltimore Orioles, at the time a minor league team in the International League. On February 21, 1914, George signed with the Orioles, but there was one problem. When George's parents gave over custody to the Jesuits, he was to remain at the school until the age of 21. George was 19 when the Orioles offered their contract. To get around this problem, the manager of the Orioles, Jack Dunn, adopted George and became his legal guardian. Young George's relationship with

Dunn led to him being given his famous name. One day Dunn brought George to the ballpark to show him the ropes. When the other players saw the new player, one remarked, "Well, here's Jack's newest babe." Soon, all his teammates were calling him Babe.

Of course, as was often true with Ruth, there were always other explanations. One is a story in Babe's autobiography about crying himself to sleep his first night at St. Mary's.

> I could see the family gathered about the table for supper and my chair empty, and I was wondering whether they missed me as much as I missed them. I looked up from my pillow in the darkness there, to see a great six foot six man standing over me. He said it in a whisper because he knew that one kid would be sensitive about having the others know him to be homesick....
>
> "What's the matter, Babe?" Brother Matthias whispered.
>
> I don't remember having been called Babe before that. Perhaps that's where the name originated.

Lou Gehrig shared two things with Babe Ruth at birth. Like Babe on his mother's side, Gehrig was the son of German immigrants. Lou was born Heinrich Ludwig Gehrig II on June 19, 1903, to Heinrich Gehrig and Christina Fack, inside the family's cramped apartment at 94th Street and Second Avenue in the lower-middle-class section of Manhattan's Yorkville. The Gehrigs were part of the large wave of German immigrants who had come to America at the turn of the 20th

century. Christina, who had emigrated as a teenager in 1899, was born in 1881 in Wilster in Schleswig-Holstein, a province of pre–World War I Germany near the Germany-Denmark border. Heinrich Ludwig Gehrig Sr., the seventh of nine children, was born in 1867 in Adelsheim, Baden, and came to America in October 1888. His father, Johann Philipp Gehrich, was a carpenter who had married Sophia Johanna Pfeiffer in November 1856 out of necessity in that time. Sophia was nine months pregnant and gave birth to their first child three weeks after the wedding. For reasons unknown, by 1870 the family had changed its surname from Gehrich to Gehrig.

As a youth, Heinrich Sr. trained as an iron metal worker who made ornamental grilles for doors and railings. He was 20 when he left Germany, settling first in Chicago before moving to New York. There he appears to have bounced around to various odd-jobs, living as a boarder with few prospects for any future—until 1901 when, at the age of 32, he met Christina Fack, 14 years his junior.

Christina was literally just off the boat—the *Pennsylvania*, on which she traveled from Hamburg to New York in third-class steerage. She knew no one in New York and didn't know where she would be staying, she told the recording clerk at Ellis Island. Christina also told him that she was arriving with 25 dollars. It was money she had saved while working as a servant. She presented herself as a healthy-looking, stout, tall young woman who had recently turned 18. Imagine teenage Lou as a young woman, and that was Christina Fack: powerfully built, with strong hands and forearms, no waist, and without much of a personality. She had had a hard life, after all. When she was one year old, her mother had died giving birth to a stillborn son. Her father, a carpenter, soon remarried, and Christina was shuffled off to live with her grandparents.

Heinrich and Christina were an odd marriage of two people who seemingly had little in common beyond being German and Lutheran. However, they connected in perhaps the most important way for each of them. Christina was almost four months pregnant with their first child, Anna Christina, who was born May 26, 1902, six months after the Gehrigs' marriage. Unfortunately for the Gehrigs, their firstborn child died barely three and a half months later. Christina was already pregnant with her second child, and he was born the following June.

At birth, Lou weighed almost 14 pounds. His birth certificate accounts for the curious way in which his name was Americanized. The midwife, Phillipine Jandas, appears to have been prepared to write Lou's first name as Heinrich, after his father, as was often customary with first sons. But as she began to write the name—Hein...—it appears she stopped, struck a line through the letter *I* and wrote the name as Henry. The Gehrigs' newborn son would be called Henry Louis, and he would be known as "Lou," the lone and prized child of Heinrich and Christina Gehrig, the latter of whom would dote on him his entire life.

"I don't pretend Lou was born with a silver spoon in his mouth," Christina told one interviewer. "But he never left the table hungry, and I can say he had a terrible appetite from the first time he saw daylight. Maybe his cloths were torn, dirty, and rumpled after playing baseball and football, but he was always clean and neatly dressed when I sent him off to school." The feelings in the Gehrig mother-son bond were mutual. "I'm like one of those Al Smith cigars, up from the street," Gehrig later said. "And if it had not been for my mother, well, I'd be a good-natured, strong-armed, and strong-backed boy, pushing a truck around New York, loading and unloading boxes that less powerful truck drivers could not handle."

There were few similarities in the childhoods of Gehrig and Ruth, beyond the fact that, like the Babe, Lou lost several siblings at childbirth or in their childhood. Lou was the only one of four Gehrig children to survive. His father worked as a janitor in a fraternity house. His mother was a cleaning woman. Young Lou was a good son and never got into much trouble. As a young boy, he was often left out of the neighborhood baseball games. As a matter of fact, he was never very good at baseball as a child, but he enjoyed collecting the baseball cards that came with his father's cigars. On one birthday, his parents gave him his first baseball glove, a catcher's mitt. Little did they know that they had bought a glove for a right-handed thrower (their son was left-handed). The other kids in the neighborhood began to let him play baseball with them, but he still struggled. He fumbled with the ball and was a terrible hitter. However, by Lou's teenage years, the tables had turned dramatically.

As a Yorkville youngster and later, after his family moved to Washington Heights, Lou played in the streets and school-yards and swam in its rivers. His father was often ill, and sometimes drank too much. By all accounts, Heinrich was an alcoholic, drawn to the neighborhood saloons. He had some skills as a metal worker, but often found it hard to gain employment. Like a lot of people in New York after the turn of the century, Heinrich faced growing discrimination aimed at the city's growing Irish, Italian, and German immigrants. That anti-German sentiment increased when World War I broke out in the summer of 1914. Among those stirring up anti-German prejudice was Teddy Roosevelt, the former president who had lost his 1912 election comeback attempt to Woodrow Wilson. Roosevelt had declared that "hyphenated Americans" who considered themselves "both German and American" were "not Americans at all but traitors to America and tools and servants of Germany against America." In the anti-German hysteria, some German immigrants suffered unprovoked beatings and job terminations. The Gehrigs maintained an emotional attachment to Germany during the war years that brought them anguish.

When Gehrig enrolled at Commerce High School in 1917, he was so shy that it took his bookkeeping teacher forcing him for him to show up for a school baseball game. "I went up to the stadium on a streetcar," he later recalled. "When I got there and saw so many people going into the field and heard all the cheering noise, I was so scared I couldn't see straight. I turned right around and got back on the streetcar and went home. The next day the teacher threatened to flunk me if I didn't show up for the next game. So I went."

At Commerce High School, Gehrig became a star in both football and baseball. As a baseball player, he received attention in the school and local papers and from scouts for his exploits as a pitcher and outfielder. In 1920, the Commerce team was invited to play Chicago's best high school team, Lane Tech, in a special "national championship" game at Chicago's Wrigley Field—a game that elevated him to a schoolboy legend. Former president Howard Taft was among dignitaries at the game at which Gehrig slugged a ninth-inning home run with the bases loaded, a feat that earned him his first New York newspaper attention. Only 18 home runs had been hit at Wrigley in the previous season, the *Chicago Tribune* reported, and "Gehrig's blow would have made any big leaguer proud, yet it was walloped by a boy who hasn't yet started to shave." Lou was hailed as "the Babe Ruth of the schoolyards" by the New York papers, and he and his teammates were greeted at Grand Central Station on their return home by 5,000 people and a band.

That early fame, though, did not encourage Gehrig's parents. "This baseball is a waste of time," Christina told Lou. "It will never get you anywhere." Heinrich had long been convinced that baseball was a "peculiar game" without any future.

The next fall, Gehrig moved on to Columbia with his mother still convinced that the only good that would come of college was a degree. She hoped Gehrig would become an architect like his uncle Otto in Germany or some other white-collar professional. Lou, though was on an athletic scholarship, recruited because of his formidable size for the time—six feet tall and 200 pounds—to play football. Gehrig spent two years there, which later won him the nickname of "Columbia Lou" in the nation's press. That was far preferable to "Biscuit Pants," which he was also called on occasion, or "Little Heinie," the name bestowed on him by Sigma Nu fraternity members when he was still a boy.

Gehrig left after his sophomore year to sign with the Yankees. On one hand, Gehrig's time at Columbia was quite productive. It was on the Lions' campus that he apprenticed for stardom in Major League Baseball, and it was where he gained the friendship and advice of baseball coach Andy Coakley, a former big league pitcher who recognized and nursed Lou's large talents.

But Columbia also presented Gehrig with another side, demonstrating that despite how far he had risen, there was still a long gap between his world and that of the Ivy League. As biographer Ray Robinson, who witnessed Gehrig's "luckiest man on the face of the earth" speech at Yankee Stadium, later recalled, "Gehrig felt that he never gained full acceptance from his fellow students at Columbia. At Phi Delta Theta fraternity, where he was pledged, he waited on tables and often performed other tasks. In an era when many fraternities emphasized the social backgrounds and bank accounts of its members, Gehrig lacked such credentials. He had to rely on his athletic prowess to win the condescending approval of his fellows."

Even after several seasons with the Yankees, writer Niven Busch of *The New Yorker* portrayed him in an article titled "The Little Heinie" as an unsophisticate and a mama's boy. Asked if he would ever marry, Gehrig said, "My mother makes a home comfortable enough for me." Gehrig's mother, Christina, who often went to spring training with her son, was described in the article as "continually cooking for him, making apple cake, and cookies with raisins and pieces of bright red suet in them, making roasts, and frying the fish and eels he catches in the Sound."

According to the article, Busch wrote that Gehrig surprisingly failed to be "stimulated or discouraged by the reactions of the crowds that watch his ponderous antics at first base for the Yankees, or cheer the hits he knocks out with startling regularity and almost legendary power." Gehrig's main amusement, Busch concluded, was fishing, and the primary influences on his life were "his mother and Babe Ruth."

Ruth's influence at this stage of Gehrig's life was understandable. In 1929, Ruth's dominance as a sports figure was unquestioned. In 1923, the Yankees' maiden season in their new stadium, Ruth carried the team to its third straight appearance in the World Series, in which the Yanks at long last won their first championship. It was a triumph of enormous ramifications. The Yankees defeated their historic New York rivals, the Giants, who had long been the city's dominant team. That World Series marked a change in baseball's hierarchy. The Yankees would again win world championships in 1927 and 1928, and the 1927 team would go down as one for the ages. This was the team on which Ruth hit his record 60 home runs that would stand for 34 years, leading a lineup featuring six future Hall of Fame players: Ruth, Gehrig, Tony Lazzeri, Earle Combs, Waite Hoyt, and Herb Pennock. That Yankees team won a then–American League–record 110 games with only 44 losses, and swept the Pittsburgh Pirates in the World Series.

The 1927 season is best remembered for Ruth's landmark 60 home runs. As great as that accomplishment was, however, Gehrig's year was even better. After signing with the Yankees in 1923, Gehrig played parts of that season and the next at Hartford, where in 193 games he slugged 61 home runs while batting .344. He saw limited time with the Yankees, mostly as a pinch hitter, but the team didn't put him on its 1923 championship World Series roster. By 1927, however, Gehrig was as feared in the lineup as Ruth. He put up one of the greatest hitting seasons of all time. Ruth's home run record may have upstaged Gehrig's 47 round-trippers, but Gehrig batted .373 with a then-record 173 RBIs and a .765 slugging percentage.

Sportswriters took note. Despite Ruth's home run record, those writers named Gehrig the league's Most Valuable Player.

By 1929, Gehrig was 27 years old and a confirmed bachelor, largely because of his mother. A devoted son, Gehrig had grown up unusually close to his mother; and he had spent his adolescent years conforming to her domineering and possessive ways. Christina Gehrig lived with the disappointment of having married a man who, though loving and faithful, had a serious drinking problem and was frequently unemployed because of his alcoholism. Like the son of many alcoholics, young Lou ended up trying to make up for his father's shortcomings and attempting to be the man for his mother that his father had failed to be. His mother had also struggled with depression, and her loving son learned at an early age that he should put aside his own needs and wants to tend to those of his mother. Gehrig sensed his mother's suffering, including the loss of three children. He had seen her work herself to exhaustion to take care of her family, and he sought desperately to make it up to her. Well into Gehrig's adulthood, his mother remained the most influential female in his life, setting the stage for all future relationships.

"He was just hopeless [around women]," Gehrig biographer Jonathan Eig quotes Yankee infielder Mike Gazella. "When a woman would ask him for an autograph, he would be absolutely paralyzed with embarrassment."

Longtime baseball writer Fred Lieb, who knew Gehrig as well as anyone, remembered how Christina Gehrig always seemed to come between her son and any woman to whom he was attracted. "Even though he was shy, he had known lots of girls, but whenever he started to get serious with one, Mom Gehrig filed her objections," Lieb recalled in his book *Baseball*

As I Have Known It. "He loved his mother dearly and could not think of marrying a girl unless he obtained his mother's okay. At least twice he brought prospective wives over to our house, asking us what we thought of them. Lou's girls were always attractive, with both brains and humor. Then one time, he had been smitten with a girl and was thinking of proposing. On learning this, Mom journeyed to the young lady's hometown, looked around, made some investigations, and filed an adverse report, which Lou accepted."

What made it easy for Gehrig's strong-willed mother to act as the gatekeeper of his personal life was that Lou continued to live at home with his parents until he was 30, away from baseball's raucous scene in the 1920s and '30s. This had been Lou's decision; he used his signing bonus in 1923 to pay off the family's mountain of medical bills. Heinrich's medical problems by this time included epilepsy, and Christina had been slowed by double pneumonia. Gehrig also sent his parents on their first-ever vacation and bought them a house in suburban New Rochelle, New York. He splurged little on himself and lived the social life of a virtual recluse.

It was as un-Ruthian an existence as could be imagined.

4   The Tale of the Most
Costly Headache

"I am a slave to baseball, and only because I really love the game, hate to think of taking even one day away when we are playing."

—Lou Gehrig

LOU GEHRIG'S RISE TO BECOMING ONE OF THE MOST FABLED HEROES of baseball could have sprung from Greek mythology—the one who gets everything he wants but who ultimately has a curse put on him by the gods. Certainly, at least, there was a sense of myth building that came to be attached to the start of the young Gehrig's historic playing streak that would eventually distinguish him as a legend of the game. For decades, the source was said to have been a headache that opened the way for the promising 22-year-old Yankees prospect. That headache had forced Wally Pipp, New York's longtime first baseman, to beg Yankee manager Miller Huggins for a day off on June 2, 1925. Gehrig, who had pinch-hit the previous day for another player, joined the Yankees lineup at first base, and didn't relinquish it for another 14 years.

In baseball history, poor Pipp has been relegated to a historical footnote at best and, at worst, the answer to a trivia question.

And had it really been a headache—a headache, for crying out loud!—that had changed the fortunes of two Yankees players at the height of one of the team's greatest decades? Pipp had been the regular first baseman since the 1915 season, playing 136 or more games nine of 10 seasons until that fateful 1925 campaign. And before Babe Ruth revolutionized baseball with his extraordinary long-ball numbers, Pipp had led the American League with a dozen home runs in 1916 and nine round-trippers in 1917—becoming the first Yankee to win a home run crown. Then came the Babe, ending baseball's dead-ball era and ushering successive Yankee pennants in the early 1920s.

The 1923 World Series championship changed the game's pecking order and placed greater pressure on the new Bronx Bombers—pressure that immediately caused cracks in the lineup. In 1924, the Yankees lost the pennant to the Washington Senators, and in 1925, New York's poor start ushered another disappointing year. Ruth would miss the first two months of that season. His weight, normally 215 pounds, skyrocketed to a massive 260 pounds during spring training. The Yankees' great star collapsed on a train and spent several weeks hospitalized with a mysterious ailment that gave rise to rumors about his excessive lifestyle. Ruth's numbers plummeted to 25 home runs, 67 RBIs, and a .290 batting average—his worst season until his final year with the Yankees almost a decade later.

Many writers that spring had Babe Ruth finished. Ruth had gone broke because of his drinking, gorging, and carousing ways, one reported. He had arrived at spring training weighing 270 pounds, 50 pounds overweight. "Day and night, broads and booze," teammate Joe Dugan told reporters.

Early in spring training, Babe began suffering from horrible stomach cramps and high fevers, a condition complicated by his excessive drinking and eating. During an April 7 stop in Asheville, North Carolina, Ruth collapsed at the train depot as the team readied to depart. He collapsed a second time trying to board a train for New York, slamming his head and causing a sensation that led to London newspapers reporting his death. When his illness was blamed on his diet, the episode became known as "the bellyache heard 'round the world." Diagnosed with an intestinal abscess, Babe underwent surgery in mid-April. He was 30 pounds lighter when he rejoined the team, gaunt and in no condition to play at a high level. Babe Ruth was 30 years of age, and many felt over the hill.

It was no wonder, then, that the Yankees began June that season near the bottom of the standings and 11 games below .500. The mood in the clubhouse was miserable, leading Miller Huggins to shake up the lineup in hopes of revitalizing the veterans and finding fresh talent among the younger players. On June 1, the day before Pipp was benched in favor of Gehrig, Lou had actually pinch-hit in Yankee Stadium against the Washington Senators and began his games-played streak, a fact that is virtually lost in the more dramatic story. Gehrig stepped in for Paul "Pee Wee" Wanninger, made an out, and returned to the bench. Coincidentally, earlier that season, Wanninger had replaced Everett Scott at shortstop, ending Scott's much-remarked-upon string of 1,307 straight games, then the longest consecutive game streak in major league history. On June 1, the Yankees lost their fifth straight game and fell to 11 games under .500 for the season and 13½ games behind the first-place Philadelphia Athletics. The next day,

Yankees manager Miller Huggins benched three of his regulars: catcher Wally Schang, second baseman Aaron Ward, and Pipp, who was batting .244. According to some accounts, Pipp was also beaned in batting practice on June 2, the truth about which Pipp has taken to his grave.

"Charlie [Caldwell, better known in later years as Princeton's football coach] whistled one in and, somehow or other, I just couldn't duck," Pipp maintained in an interview almost three decades later. "The ball hit me right here on the temple. They carted me right off to the hospital. I was in that hospital for two solid weeks. By the time I returned to the Yankees, Gehrig was hitting the ball like crazy and Huggins would have been a complete dope to give me my job back."

Pipp was also later quoted as famously saying, "I took the two most expensive aspirin in history." Another time he told the story of arriving at Yankee Stadium with a terrible headache and being told by manager Miller Huggins, "Wally, take the day off. We'll try that kid Gehrig at first today and get you back in there tomorrow."

The Yankees had originally picked up Pipp on waivers from Detroit in 1915. For nearly the next decade, he was a fixture in the Yankee lineup. He anchored Yankee pennant winners in 1921, 1922, and the championship 1923 team, which was the Yanks' first. He was also coming off a career year in 1924, when he hit .295 with nine home runs, 110 RBIs, and an American League–leading 19 triples. When Pipp sprained an ankle in 1923, Gehrig was called up from the minors for a few games— in which Lou batted .423, including his first homer, and drove in nine runs in limited duty. In 1924 Gehrig had hit .500 in a dozen at-bats with five RBIs.

With Pipp out of the lineup, Gehrig did indeed start at first base on June 2, 1925, and never gave up the position or his place in the batting order until he voluntarily ended his legendary career. "Miller Huggins took his favorite lineup and shook it to pieces," the *New York Times* reported the next day. "Wally Pipp, after more than 10 years as a regular first baseman, was benched in favor of Lou Gehrig, the former Columbia University fence-wrecker." Gehrig responded by getting three hits in five at-bats, scoring once, and raising his batting average from .167 to .241. Until then, the highlight of Gehrig's season had been in the first week, when he got a hit off an overpowering Walter Johnson, the Senators' great pitcher who, at age 37, would rack up his final 20-win season.

As for Pipp, game logs for 1925 show that he did appear in games on the June 3, 4, and 10, along with five other games in June. Pipp also worked with Gehrig before each game after June 2, helping him improve his technique around first base. He apparently was holding out hope that he would eventually win back his job. As for the account of Pipp's beaning in batting practice, it appears that actually may have happened a month later, on July 2. According to various accounts, he suffered a fractured skull or a concussion—certainly more serious than a headache. Pipp, nearly 32, played sparingly the rest of the season and was ultimately traded to the Cincinnati Reds before the 1926 season. After baseball, Pipp toyed with a writing career, moonlighting as Babe Ruth's ghost writer, and later broadcasting a pregame baseball show for the Detroit Tigers.

It was a cruel fall from grace for Wally Pipp, made worse by the fact that his replacement had hardly made a Ruthian impression. There had even been talk early on of the Yankees

trading Gehrig to Boston for Phil Todt, a veteran first baseman. Gehrig had not yet lived up to his Columbia baseball reputation. When he took over for Pipp, Gehrig was batting just
.167 with no homers and zero RBIs. He was having trouble hitting left-handed pitchers, and the New York Times reported in
its June 11 edition, "Huggins is not completely satisfied with
the daily exhibitions of Lou Gehrig. The mite one went so far
the other day as to send Fred Merkle, the ancient ex-Giant, to
first base against a left-handed pitcher." Lou was subbed by
pinch-hitters three times that first month and didn't start on
July 5, although he came into the game later.

Then he caught fire. He hit .344 (31-for-90) with six homers
and 14 RBIs for the month of June, and his 1925 stats included
20 homers, 68 RBIs, and a .295 batting average. One of those
round-trippers, against the Senators on July 23, was the first of
Gehrig's league-record 23 grand slams. All told, his 2,130-con-
secutive-game streak led to his nickname, "the Iron Horse,"
and would be an inspiration for high and low in America,
among them novelist Thomas Wolfe, who would write in You
Can't Go Home Again:

> What visions burn, what dreams possess him, seeker
> of the night? The packed stands of the stadium, the
> bleachers sweltering with their unshaded hordes, the
> faultless velvet of the diamond, unlike the clay-baked
> outfields down in Georgia. The mounting roar of
> eighty thousand voices and Gehrig coming to bat....

Meanwhile, Ruth was only a shadow of his previous greatness during that 1925 season. His flashes of brilliance offered

a clue to how he would overshadow Gehrig, as he did every-one else for as long as he was a Yankee. Gehrig could be great, Gehrig could be consistent, Gehrig could be a perfect role model, but Ruth was larger than life. Not only was Babe an un-paralleled hitter, but he was also as outgoing and flamboyant as Gehrig was reserved and quiet.

"Lets face it, I'm not a headline guy. I always knew that as long as I was following Babe to the plate I could have gone up there and stood on my head," Gehrig would later say about playing with Ruth. "No one would have noticed the difference. When the Babe was through swinging, whether he hit one or fanned, nobody paid any attention to the next hitter. They all were talking about what the Babe had done."

Lou Gehrig would tell close friends that he never truly un-derstood Babe Ruth and that for that reason never felt close to him. Of course, that would come as a surprise to the thousands fans who saw them play together in the 1920s and 1930s, as well as to the millions who later immortalized the pair as symbols of friendship and bonded teammates.

Jimmie Reese, who played with Babe and Lou in 1930 and 1931, recalled:

> When I joined the Yankees, I imagined I would be coming into a clubhouse [with] the usual camaraderie you find on a team to be led by two teammates who were buddies, Ruth and Gehrig, for that's what you thought. But what did I really know? I'd been playing on the other side of the country, in California, with the Oakland Oaks of the Pacific Coast League. There was no major league ball played out west then, so

what we knew of Ruth and Gehrig was what we read in the papers and what we saw on the newsreels when you went to the movies. And the movies weren't real. They were stories on film with actors. So, looking back, there might not have been any reason to believe that the way Babe and Lou were portrayed in those newsreels was any more authentic. Boy, was I in for a surprise when I went to the Yankees. Babe was the life of the clubhouse, that was for sure. If you walked in, you heard him well before you saw him. You couldn't mistake the voice. But Lou, you might miss him because he was like just one of the other players in there. That's how dominant Babe's personality was, and Lou was nothing like that. Don't get me wrong. [Lou] was his own man. He commanded respect—a different kind of respect than Babe—but they weren't close buddies. Babe cut a big space everywhere, especially in the clubhouse, but Lou was nothing like that. Lou was a good teammate. I think he was happy playing that role and leading by the example he set."

For much as the Babe was bold, rash, and set upon being the Bambino, Lou was humble to a fault. That suit of humility was tailor-made for Gehrig, by Lou's domineering mother, Christina. In her memoir, *My Luke and I*, Gehrig's wife, Eleanor, wrote that Christina's relationship with her son seemed "borderline Oedipal," and she had broken up Lou's previous relationships. Christina almost succeeded in breaking up Eleanor and Lou, and failed only because her famous son managed the nerve to stand up to his mother for one of the few times in his life.

That was the consummate Lou Gehrig, however, a heroic man who chose to avoid confrontation when at all possible, be it with his mother or Babe Ruth. Perhaps the people who most readily saw this side of Gehrig were those who caught glimpses of him while the Yankees were on the road—stories from fans who got close sightings of Ruth and Gehrig while the players were on preseason barnstorming tours in the American South during spring training.

Baseball fans in Texas saw this side of Ruth and Gehrig during the 1929 spring training season, when the Yankees played exhibitions throughout the Lone Star State, playing in divided squads but coming together in Waco. It was the smell of cottonseed wafting up into his railroad car that awakened Babe Ruth one late morning as the train pulled into Katy Station, permeating his sleeper cabin even before the porter knocked on his door. Slits of sunlight peeked through the windows as Ruth groaned, wishing this extended spring training barnstorming had some breaks in the schedule. The Yankees had played in Fort Worth the day before, a Wednesday, and typically Babe had gotten little sleep in his hotel. On his tour through Texas, he was doing his sleeping on the train, undisturbed by either the fans or women admirers who often came knocking at his hotel room doors.

As Thomas Stephens, Ruth's porter recounted, he entered the Babe's berth. "Good mo'ning, Mr. Babe, 11:30 on the dot," the porter said as he stuck his head inside Ruth's car. "Gotcha some coffee and toast. You sleep all right?"

"Like a log."

"Well," said the porter. "You must have a clear conscience."

"Nah, I think it was the scotch," said Babe. "Are we here?"

"Just pulled in. Katy Station. Oh, and here's the mo'ning paper with your picture in it. They're expecting greats things. The whole region is here it seems."

"Are they indeed? We'll have to not disappoint."

Ruth handed the porter an enormous tip. "Much obliged, Mr. Babe," the porter said. "No hurry. You got about an hour 'fore we have to pull out."

Ruth quickly studied the headline in the *Waco Times Herald*: RUTH HEADS YANKEE INVASION OF WACO.

"So, keed, this is Whacko?" Babe asked the porter

"They might get mighty unfriendly, Mr. Babe, if you go and call it that," the porter said. "It's *Way*-co."

"I know," said Ruth. "It's just everything I've heard and what you were telling me when we left Fort Worth. You think all that's true? Was this really the bastion of the Ku Klux Klan in Texas?"

"For a fact, Mr. Babe," said the porter. "That hotel where you're gonna be staying, it's where the Grand Wizards and whatever they call themselves would meet to decide who was gonna get their votes."

"Power brokering, huh?" Ruth sat up, swigged some coffee, and examined the newspaper. "Well, keed, wait until they get a load of my power brokering." Then Babe let out a laugh, slapping the paper as he laughed. "Keed, I've seen it all. The writer they got covering us is named Jinx. Jinx! For God's sake, only a fucking sportswriter would use a name like Jinx. I haven't heard anyone named Jinx except a stripper in Baltimore!"

Sportswriter Jinx Tucker's story in the paper reported that the Yankees' stop in Waco had all the trappings of a presidential campaign, with residents from all the nearby central Texas towns pouring into Waco to catch an afternoon exhibition game between the Yankees and the local minor league team, the Waco Cubs. The anticipation had been growing for days and had heightened with the news that the full roster of the world champion Yankees would be on the field at Waco's Katy Park.

The Yankees had broken spring training in Florida and headed west across the Deep South, into Texas and the Midwest, before heading north to open the season in mid-April. They divided the fattened spring training roster into two squads, allowing more fans to see the greatest team of the national pastime. It also doubled the revenue from this barnstorming tour, making baseball's most profitable team even richer. However, it meant that most fans would either see Ruth or Lou Gehrig, each was the star attraction of his squad. On Wednesday Gehrig's team had played in Austin against the University of Texas baseball team, while Ruth's squad had competed in Fort Worth. In Waco, though, the Yankees would field their complete team. Gehrig's squad, fresh off a humiliating defeat by the Longhorns, had arrived an hour earlier and been greeted by a crowd that stormed the train station and then the Hotel Raleigh, where the Yankees were booked just four blocks from the stadium.

The Yankees were a team of all-stars, but it was obviously Babe Ruth who was the smashing draw, as it was everywhere he went. "Never since he began smashing out home runs has the Babe been seen in this city," wrote Tucker in that day's *Times Herald,* "so all Central Texas stirs uneasily on the eve of the appearance in Waco of the greatest array of diamond

all-stars the world has ever produced." There was no denying the Yankees were baseball's dynasty. From 1921 to 1928,
they had won six American League pennants; and they had
won World Series championships in three of those years, including the previous two. Their slugging lineup was known as
"Murderers' Row" and "Swat," anchored by the most famous
ballplayer of them all.

Thomas Stephens, the porter on the train, would later detail his conversation with Ruth that morning to Jefferson
Stephens, his cousin who worked at the Raleigh Hotel and
polished shoes at Jimmy's Shoe Shine on Austin Avenue in
Waco. Jefferson Stephens also recalled his cousin Thomas asking him what Gehrig had been like, since he had also seen Lou
arrive at the hotel.

"No impression," recalled Jefferson. "I told him Lou Gehrig
left no impression. He looked like a nice gentleman, but he said
nothing. Well, maybe 'thank you.' I helped him with his suitcase. *He don't say much,* I remember thinking. But that's not so
bad, my momma used to say. Silence isn't just golden, she used
to say, silence can sometimes be deafening."

5 Claire Ruth

"Get what you can while you're on top."
—Claire Ruth to Mickey Mantle

WHILE SHE WAS WITH TY COBB, FROM TIME TO TIME CLAIRE MERRITT Hodgson would hear the irascible Cobb for no apparent reason sink into profanity-laced tirades about Babe Ruth—on everything from the way Ruth ran the bases to the size of his genitals, which Cobb, sometimes in a drunken stupor, would attribute to his outlandish and unproven claim that the Babe was "a goddamn nigger." At the time that Hodgson and Cobb were dating, in the early 1920s, Cobb was in his mid-thirties and no longer baseball's greatest player, not to mention being the most despised man within the game. He was still among baseball's premier hitters, having hit .420 in 1911 and .409 in 1912, and still hovering near .400 in his thirties, the same years when Ruth was proving himself invaluable with the Red Sox. But in 1919, Ruth's unheard-of mark of 29 home runs suddenly propelled the game from Cobb's spikes-first, one-base-at-a-time baseball to one that celebrated the long ball, and Ruth's 59 home runs in 1921 catapulted him past everyone else.

There was no way for the ever-competitive Cobb to match the game's new darling. So both on the field and off, Cobb took every opportunity he could to disparage Ruth, whom he despised in a manner that Claire Hodgson saw as both comical and neurotic. She knew little about baseball other than what she had learned from Cobb, but she found his obsession with Ruth contagious. Her curiosity led her past newspapers' society pages to the sports sections, where she became fascinated with the attention commanded by Ruth, even in newspapers outside New York. Soon she was even inquiring of some of her socialite friends, did they know of this Babe Ruth? Did they know people in New York who knew him? Had any of them ever seen him play? What was his wife like? Why had she never seen a photograph of her, or of them together?

Never in her wildest dreams could Hodgson have imagined how different her life was from Ruth's. Claire Hodgson had been a child of privilege from the South. Her father, James Merritt, was a prominent Georgia lawyer who had handled the legal affairs of fellow Georgian Ty Cobb. Growing up in Georgia, she had been familiar with Ty Cobb's background. The local hero who came to be known as the "Georgia Peach," Cobb had grown up in a middle-class family with strong Southern values. He was the eldest son of a rural schoolmaster, who was well-respected even if he had taken a 15-year-old as his bride. Affectionately called "Professor," Cobb's father was elected mayor of his small town and later served in the Georgia state legislature. Hodgson later would say that she had seen some of that breeding in Cobb, especially in his traditional Southern manners.

Overall, Cobb had been a gentleman with Claire—except on those occasions when the subject of Ruth arose and he exploded in expletive-filled diatribes. By the middle of the 1921 season, when Cobb and Ruth competed on the field in a contest Babe dominated, Hodgson had heard and read so much about the object of Cobb's hatred and fears that she felt she was destined to meet him. After all, they both lived in the same big city, and it was not as if she were a stranger to meeting men.

She was a beautiful, slender woman who for a while had worked as a model for fashion illustrators and had caught the eye of stage producers. Hodgson had been in a show called *Tangerine,* and performed bit parts in silent movies and even in the famed *Ziegfeld Follies.* In addition to Cobb, Hodgson had known other men since moving to New York with her young daughter at the end of World War I. The people who knew her sensed that Claire was the daughter of privilege. She had a Southern maid, Marie Martin, who looked after young Julia along with the household at 219 West 80th Street, which by the early 1920s came to include her mother, Carrie, and her two brothers.

No one around Hodgson seemed to know much about how she managed to afford her lifestyle, but assumed that her financial independence came either from family money or from her late husband's estate. No one suspected just how close Hodgson was living on the edge. When she moved to New York, she had little knowledge of the city. Separated from her husband, she left Athens, Georgia, without even telling her parents, and immediately upon arriving in New York checked into the Waldorf Astoria Hotel, only because it was the only hotel in Manhattan that she had ever heard of. She was still being supported by her husband, Frank Hodgson, who continued to live in Georgia. Then in 1922, just months before meeting Ruth, Hodgson received news that her estranged husband had died. No one said so—they didn't have to—but the elegantly lovely and young Claire Merritt Hodgson was both of an age and at an age where, as a widow with a child in need of father, she was looking for a husband.

That Babe Ruth just happened to be the most exciting man in America may have said as much about Hodgson as it did about Ruth. Their relationship may have begun out of the need for security on Hodgson's part and acceptance on Ruth's part. In May 1923, when they met, Hodgson was on the road with a stage show titled *Dew Drop Inn*. It starred an actor named James Barton, whom Ruth knew through social circles in New York. Barton, who later starred in *Tobacco Road*, took Hodgson and a friend to a Yankees-Senators game in Washington, where Ruth saw his old drinking buddy and approached his box. Later that night, Ruth sent Hodgson a note at the theater, asking her to have dinner with him at his hotel room. She agreed to come only after Ruth agreed that she could bring her friend.

Teammate Joe Dugan, the Yankees' third baseman, was with Ruth the night after the day he met Hodgson, attending, at her insistence, a performance of her show with Babe. Dugan recalled that Ruth slept through part of the show, having to be nudged awake and finally perking up when Hodgson appeared on stage. "See that black-haired gal on the end?" Ruth asked Dugan. "She's coming to the hotel for dinner later. I want you guys to meet her."

Dugan assumed she was just another of Ruth's conquests, remembering that at some point, after Hodgson and her roommate showed up, Babe ordered him and several teammates who had tagged along out of the suite. For Babe, however, it was an off-the-field strikeout. Usually it was the women calling on him, agreeing to join him in his hotel room with the clear under-standing that they would be having sex. With Hodgson it was an entirely different set of rules. From the beginning, she made it clear that she was going to be in control of their relationship.

Years later, Yankee teammate and on-the-road roommate Jimmie Reese recalled that sometimes Ruth would reminisce about courting Hodgson, becoming misty-eyed and explain-ing with apparent genuine sincerity, "She was a lady, and if I could get someone like her to love me, I'd be one lucky son-of-a-bitch."

Claire Hodgson epitomized a kind of glamour that may have been unique to that time and perhaps seen later in finish-ing schools, where wit, wisdom, and charm were often forged from private tragedy, ambiguous privilege, and a deep, pow-erful sense of purpose. She also had the good fortune of be-ing naturally beautiful. Years later, Ruth's adopted daughter Dorothy, who never cared much for the woman who became her stepmother, was forced to concede that Claire looked like a brunette Jean Harlow. What greater compliment than to be compared to the consummate sex goddess of her generation? Hodgson had lush red lips, piercing brown eyes, skin like satin, and the figure of a movie star.

In her 1988 memoir, *My Dad the Babe,* Dorothy Ruth Pirone recalled that "Claire was only five feet two, but she looked taller; she always seemed to be up on a pedestal, look-ing down at the rest of the world. When she posed for photo-graphers, she would give come-hither looks, yet if you met her

on the street you would be struck by her aloofness." Those
who knew Hodgson described her inimitable voice as salty,
sly, incisive, and hilarious—perhaps a hint of her extraordinary
roller-coaster life: from a childhood in the South to a runaway
bride at the age of 14 to an early broken marriage that left her
a widow in her twenties. She had the air of a debutante, which
she had not been, and the knowing experience of having lovers
who agreed at her insistence to the utmost discretion.

From her earliest years, Hodgson had also acquired a trait
that made her highly sought-after as a confidant, everyone
from the obscure aspiring actress to the famous, as in the case
of Cobb. Hodgson was a wonderful listener, who like all marvelous listeners made one feel like he was the only person in the
room. At cocktail parties, she never looked over your shoulder
to see if there was someone more important or interesting to
talk to. She gave a person her complete attention. Even Ruth,
who could captivate a room as few others, later spoke about
how Hodgson had a way of making him feel great about himself. "When I talk to Claire," Ruth often boasted, "I felt taller,
stronger, and even smarter. Of course, the feeling never lasts
because I always went back to being myself!"

However, what may have set Hodgson apart from most
women, even in New York at the time, was her sense of style.
She loved high fashion and wore the straight silhouette that
broke with the shirtwaist-and-skirt look that had been in vogue
since the 1910s. Hodgson was among the trendsetters who in
the early 1920s had begun sporting long, straight shapes as daytime wear. These dresses featured a tubular bodice that draped
straight down to a dropped waist then a full skirt ending at
mid-calf or ankle. Later in the 1920s, Hodgson was also among

the first to be seen wearing wearing shorter dresses, many of them cut to the knee. This, of course, complemented Ruth's self-image. He had fancied himself a fashion-plate ever since he had started making good money and sometimes spent extravagant sums on clothes for himself and his friends. But often what he bought was loud and garish. Hodgson immediately noticed this and set about changing his ways.

She began with Ruth's underwear. The first time she saw him naked—the first time they had sex, some weeks after they met—she immediately noticed the cheap underwear he was wearing. The next time they were together, Hodgson presented Ruth a boxed gift: three pairs of silk boxer shorts. From that time onward, Ruth wore only imported silk underwear, and his tailor eventually began custom-making silk underwear that often was made from the same imported silk that lined his suits. On a couple of occasions, after Gehrig had become the Yankees' starting first baseman, Ruth introduced Lou to his preferred New York haberdashery and tried in vain to get him to upgrade his wardrobe, including his underwear. "That keed don't know what he's missing," he once told Louis Shapiro, his Russian-born tailor. "He'd add 20 points to his batting average!"

It was an emotional and psychological connection that developed between Claire and Babe. Ruth found that he could talk to Hodgson as he never had with anyone. And Hodgson wanted to hear it all, to know all there was to know about Ruth. She was not a person who could be easily surprised, nor was she given to be judgmental, which served her well in learning Babe's story firsthand.

Hodgson had been no fool. She knew that once she had given Ruth what he wanted that she would have to maintain his interest. She knew she could compete—in the bedroom and in charm—with the countless women who threw themselves at Babe each day and night. But those trollops were not her competition. Her competition was Ruth's wife, Helen, who by 1923 was living in Massachusetts with their adopted two-year-old daughter, Dorothy. As she saw it, her competition for Ruth's attention was the family that he often spoke of to newspapermen and which he celebrated with photographs that adorned his suite at the Ansonia Hotel. Hodgson was shrewd enough to understand that what Ruth needed was a nurturing family in New York, a family that could shower him with the affection and attention for which he obviously hungered.

In 1923, Hodgson's daughter, Julia, was already a first-grader and at an age when she could playfully interact with the American hero who loved children and, in some ways, remained a child himself. Each time Ruth visited Hodgson, she willingly shared him not only with Julia and her own mother but also her brothers Eugene and Hubert, with whom he sometimes played golf and at other times took on hunting trips. Within a short period of time, Claire Hodgson's family had become Ruth's family.

It was also not long before Hodgson's daughter began calling Ruth "daddy," and that he started looking upon Julia as his daughter, an older daughter with whom he could do many of the things he yet couldn't with Dorothy, who was still barely more than a toddler. "He taught me how to bowl, and how to dance," Julia remembered. Ruth also gave Julia an affectionate nickname that always gave her mother the shudders. Babe called his new daughter "Butch," a name that always made Julia light up. "Whatever Daddy did, he was good," she recalled.

Ruth also insisted on paying for Julia to attend all-girl, private schools in the New York area. When her friends from school would come to visit, they were all initially starstruck in Ruth's presence, but that would quickly pass. "The girls would come home to visit or spend the night, and right away they'd like him," Julia recalled with fondness years later. "Some of the younger kids were awestruck. But daddy was a lot of fun."

"Actually, except when we went out, he was like any other father," Julia said in an interview almost 70 years later. "We did a lot of the same things normal families did. In those days we listened to the radio, played cards or checkers. Whatever daddy did, he played to win. He didn't let you win."

Ruth was especially competitive playing cards. "Daddy didn't know the first thing about the rules of contract bridge," Julia said. "But he was a great bridge player. I'd say, 'Daddy, you can't bid that.' And he'd say, 'Yes I can.'... And he would."

Claire was particularly attuned to Ruth's connection to Julia and her family. Early in their relationship, Hodgson gently broached the idea of Ruth reconciling with his own family. Babe brushed the notion aside. He had never truly understood why his parents had sent him to St. Mary's, nor why they had effectively made him a ward of the school. Although he was not an orphan, he felt like one. He also had used an orphan's sense of needing to belong to drive himself. "No wonder he later demanded the attention and affection of the world," wrote biographer Robert W. Creamer. "Everything exploded into athletic genius and sexual hunger, and he was forever seeking approval and gratification."

Hodgson could appreciate both the athletic wonder and the sexual predator. She came from a family of athletes. Both her brothers had been athletes in school, and her Georgia cousin

Johnny Mize—only 10 years old in 1923—eventually developed
into a Hall of Fame baseball player, at one point a power hitter
with the Yankees. In the bedroom, Hodgson dealt with Ruth
by being submissive yet strong. In the years after her first marriage, Hodgson on her own as a single mother—unique among
her friends—had become self-empowered. She had learned that
sometimes giving men the feeling of power led to them wanting
to protect her and, in turn, put her in control.

The extent to which Hodgson soon controlled Ruth's life began to affect Babe's relationship with his wife. Always discreet
in the past, Hodgson seemingly encouraged Ruth to flaunt their
love affair publicly. On numerous occasions, Babe asked New
York reporters not to write about them, and he begged photographers not to take their pictures because the camera flashes
frightened "my good friend." But Ruth never made a serious issue of this, and Hodgson never nagged him about it. In fact, she
kept a scrapbook of the coverage in the twelve daily newspapers that existed in New York at the time. Hodgson knew that
even hidden away in Massachusetts, Helen was bound to hear
of her husband's latest ongoing affair and would see that it was
different than Ruth's past womanizing.

There were some superficial attempts at discretion. Ruth
and Hodgson still ate many of their meals in either her apartment or his hotel room. By her daughter's account, Hodgson
also was reluctant about hanging photographs of Ruth in her
apartment, fearing that a neighbor or a delivery boy might become the wiser. However, all that is outweighed by the fact
that Hodgson would rarely let Ruth out of her sight. Even
when Ruth took trips to Massachusetts to visit Helen and their
daughter in Sudbury, Hodgson would accompany Babe and

check into a hotel in downtown Boston, where she would insist that he return each evening to dine with her.

In return, she also was a woman willing to do whatever she
needed to do to please Ruth, especially given the incentive
that Babe had women admirers prowling the lobby of his hotel room and sometimes even paying off bellmen for his room
number. Ruth used to boast to some teammates that Hodgson
never allowed him to leave their home alone for any length of
time without "taking care of me." When Jimmie Reese was
asked about the story some 70 years after rooming with Ruth
on the road, the onetime Yankee second baseman confirmed
that it was true. Had Ruth meant that Hodgson never let him
leave home without first having sex? "Well," said Reese, trying
to phrase it delicately, "I think she just wanted him to remember what he had waiting for him at home."

At long last, orphaned emotionally and psychologically,
Ruth had a family and a home. It would become so comfort-
ing that Ruth would not only forsake his wife but also abandon the daughter he and Helen had adopted. When she was
seven, Dorothy was sent to a convent school in Wellesley Hills,
Massachusetts, where months would go by without visits from
her mother and at which Ruth never visited her. Babe was fully
immersed in his life with the Yankees and Hodgson and their
family in New York. Ruth denied Hodgson nothing, except
matrimony. Incredibly, given his long infidelity to his wife,
Ruth looked upon marriage as the most sacred of sacraments of
the Catholic faith that he otherwise practiced so poorly. "I'm a
Catholic, and Helen's a Catholic, and we can't get a divorce—
it's against our religion," was Ruth's stock answer whenever
Hodgson steered their conversations to the topic of marriage,

which came with increasing frequency after Babe and Helen legally separated in 1925.

The eternal optimist, Hodgson took solace in the fact that Ruth had married the first time. In 1914, when he was 19 and a wide-eyed rookie with the Red Sox, Babe fell for the first woman who paid any attention to him in Boston. Helen Woodford was a 16-year-old waitress from south Boston working at the Landers Coffee Shop, where Ruth happened to stop off for breakfast on his first day in town. Ruth liked to say that he courted Helen over large helpings of bacon and eggs, and it may well have been the extent of it. Boston soon shipped Babe to their minor league Providence team, some 40 miles away, which only increased Ruth's loneliness and his longing for Helen. After the season, Ruth couldn't face the prospect of returning to Baltimore and being even further away from her. So, barely three months after meeting, Ruth and Helen eloped to Baltimore, where they moved in with his father. As Babe was not yet the legal age of 21, his father had to give his permission for him to be issued a marriage license. Helen, who had recently turned 17, claimed on the marriage license application to be 18 (the legal age for women) and to be from Galveston, Texas. On October 17, 1914, they married in a small ceremony at St. Paul's Catholic church in Ellicott City, Maryland, and fittingly had a wedding reception at Ruth's father's apartment, above the bar that had led to the problems that forced Babe to be sent away to St. Mary's.

The marriage to Helen was little more than the result of Ruth's ill-spent youth, living an almost monastic existence at St. Mary's, where his experience with women had been limited almost exclusively to the nuns and other women who worked at the school. There is little indication of Babe having dated much, if at all, as a young man. It did not take much insight for a woman of Claire Hodgson's sophistication to see all this, and to recognize that Ruth's almost insatiable sexual appetite was a byproduct of incredible loneliness and insecurity. Neither was his marriage a typical one, especially given Ruth's career as a baseball player, away for most of the year, and given the youth and immaturity of both Babe and Helen.

Helen became even more removed from his life after his second full season with Red Sox, when they bought an 80-acre farm some 20 miles outside Boston. Soon Ruth was away much of the off-season as well, making those Hollywood movies that tried to exploit his new fame, playing golf in California, and attempting to trim off his fat in Hot Springs, Arkansas, each winter before reporting for spring training. When Ruth was sold to the Yankees for the 1920 season, their separations became even longer. Babe showered Helen with clothes, jewelry, and gifts during those long absences and tried to make her happy when he did spend time with her. But Ruth could not give her what both of them wanted after the first year of marriage. They wanted to have a baby and tried for several years with no success.

Hodgson, like the rest of New York and most of America, was well-acquainted with the story of how Babe and Helen had finally adopted a child. Dorothy was 16 months old when those stories broke in the New York newspapers late in the 1922 season, several months before Claire and Ruth met. The news caught everyone by surprise, and the explanations becoming fodder for reports, rumors, and gossip because Babe and Helen were reluctant to admit that the child had been adopted and that they were unable to conceive. In America in the 1920s and for much of the century, especially in the male subculture of sports, the notion of sterility was often associated with weakness and, incorrectly, with sexual impotence. As the widespread accounts of his sexual conquests indicate, Ruth was hardly impotent. However, Ruth's inability to conceive with Helen (and later Claire) suggests that he likely was sterile; so, too, the fact that despite the hundreds of women he slept with over the years, there were never any illegitimate children produced by those encounters.

Hodgson had no great interest in having another child. She wanted the financial security that marriage would bring; and she was willing to wait, either for Babe to forego his Roman Catholic opposition to divorcing Helen or the hand of Providence itself. She would soon have her faith rewarded. By 1926, Helen and Babe had separated. Ruth continued to live in Manhattan while Helen stayed at their farm and her cherished privacy outside of Boston. By 1929, Helen had quietly taken up with a dentist and moved into his home. Unfortunately, she was there alone on January 11 when she died of suffocation in a fire. Helen was 31.

Just three months later, at 5:00 A.M. on April 17, 1929, Babe married Claire in the St. Gregory the Great Church in New York on what was also scheduled to be the season's opening day at Yankee Stadium. Rain, however, forced a postponement of the game, allowing a wedding breakfast at the Ruth's 11-room apartment to go on late into the night.

Babe and Helen's daughter, Dorothy, who was eight at the time and was living at and attending a parochial school under an assumed name, was not told about her mother's death or Ruth's remarriage until months later. Claire's daughter, Julia, who was 12 years old, had spent the night at a girlfriend's house and only learned of her mother's marriage when she spied a wet newspaper on the sidewalk outside her school. BABE RUTH WEDS, the headline read. "I said, 'What are they talking about?'" Julia recalled years later. "When I got home, they could tell by my face I knew what happened. I think they said, 'Well, you must have expected that this was going to happen.'"

As a wedding gift to the masses, Ruth slugged a first-inning home run, smiling and waving at the Yankee Stadium crowd as he circled the bases before blowing a kiss to his new bride as he crossed the plate.

6 Eleanor Gehrig

*"I would not have traded two minutes of joy and the grief
with that man for two decades of anything with another."*

—Eleanor Gehrig

IF YOU HAD ASKED LOU GEHRIG WHAT HE CONSIDERED HIS GREATEST
accomplishment in living out the American dream as the son
of an immigrant couple, he probably wouldn't have said it
was his glorious baseball career. For Gehrig, an unabashed
romantic, he likely would have said it was marrying Eleanor
Grace Twitchell.

Her background was more that of a working-class American
princess than an immigrant's daughter—or so it seemed to
many who saw only the veneer of perfection Eleanor presented
to the public. Eleanor's father, Frank Bradford Twitchell,
traced his ancestry to the first governor of Massachusetts.
Frank Twitchell moved around the country and made his mark
in the gaming industry. He set the odds on horse betting. In
that sense, he was a self-made man who might have had more
in common with Babe Ruth than with his eventual son-in-law.
Eleanor's mother, Nellie Mulvaney Twitchell, was Canadian-
Irish and only 17 when she married Frank. On March 6, 1904,
on Chicago's South Side, she gave birth to Eleanor. Life took a

dramatic upward jump when Frank Twitchell became manager of Chicago's popular Heidelberg Café. Soon, after Frank was appointed the official concessionaire of the Chicago parks, the family relocated to the more affluent South Shore.

Eleanor Twitchell had a surprising toughness that would serve her well. She had her family to thank for hardening her to the realities of life. She was there when her mother learned from a newspaper headline that her husband was having an extramarital affair with an assistant. When Nellie considered getting a divorce, a lawyer talked her out of it. "What the hell do you want to divorce a guy like that for?" she later told friends the lawyer advised, and she returned home for reconciliation. It was before the 1920s in America, after all. But teenage Eleanor couldn't help but be affected. She wasn't much of a student, and got into trouble for truancy when she missed 21 straight days of school. She loved to ride horses, golf, ice skate, and often sneaked into the Palace or the Majestic to see the latest vaudeville show.

She owed her interest in baseball to her closest girlfriends, a pair of sisters who had married brothers. One of the sisters was married to a prolific professional gambler, and the other sister to the vice president of the Chicago White Sox. Through them Eleanor learned about professional sports at the racetrack and the ballpark. She also rubbed shoulders with people who had organized crime connections. One of her poker partners, in fact, was the wife of John "Papa Johnny" Torrio, an Italian American mobster who built the Chicago Outfit, a crime syndicate eventually inherited by his protégé Al Capone.

"I suppose, in the 1920s, you could say I fiddled while Chicago burned," Eleanor wrote in her memoir. "I was young and rather innocent, but I smoked, played poker, drank bath-tub gin along with everybody else, collected $5 a week in allow-ance from my father, spent $100 a week, made up the difference from winter-book jackpots at the racetrack that filled a dresser drawer with close to $10,000 at one point, and learned to be-come a big tipper."

Eleanor developed a party-girl lifestyle that she curbed only when her father hit the skids personally and professionally, losing his business and going broke. "The Twitchells were ahead of the times," she recalled. "We were going broke be-fore the Depression." Eleanor took stock of her own life, took a job as a secretary, and in 1931 met the love of her life. Later she would tell at least two versions of how she met Lou Gehrig. In one version, their paths crossed at a party in the fall of 1927. In another account, they met at Comiskey Park while she was at a ballgame with one of her girlfriends. However, her relationship with Lou didn't begin until 1931, when an-other girlfriend asked her to come over to her penthouse apartment for a drink, telling her that Gehrig would be there. "Big, handsome, successful, I thought. All those things," she remembered thinking about Lou. "And, as luck would have it, painfully shy."

On what amounted to their first date, Gehrig walked Eleanor home and, as she recalled, "abruptly said good night and disap-peared into the dark." The Yankees, he told her, had a midnight curfew, and he was one who followed the rules.

Eleanor was stunned by this display of affection—or lack of it—but few could mistake Gehrig's intentions when a week later a package arrived for Eleanor containing a dia-mond-cut crystal necklace that Lou had brought back from a postseason Yankees barnstorming tour in Japan. From there a correspondence ensued, blossoming into love over the next year. Of course, as there was with Ruth, stories about Gehrig inevitably begat different versions, even from Eleanor's own lips. According to a version in *Collier's* magazine, Gehrig nervously tried to propose while walking her home from dinner, but "began to stutter to himself, saying incoherent things."

"Honey," Eleanor finally chimed in, "I know what you're trying to say, and the answer is 'yes.'"

Then, in *My Luke and I,* Eleanor described their proposal in a more romantic fashion. Gehrig had felt so badly after a misunderstanding they had in a telephone conversation that he showed up outside her office window first thing the next morning, "motioning me with open arms and that mile-wide grin. I did a double-take and raced downstairs, and then, in front of the whole Century of Progress staff arriving for work, we kissed madly in the center of Grant Park. We went to the Drake Hotel for breakfast. I don't remember who proposed to whom. We just plotted and planned."

According to Eleanor, this proposal occurred during the baseball season, while the Yankees were in Chicago for a series with the White Sox. That afternoon she attended the ballgame at Comiskey Park. "You bet your life," she recalled, "he hit a home run, strictly following the script in the corniest way imaginable.... What he needed badly was confidence, building up. He was absolutely anemic for kindness and warmth."

Eleanor herself became a sensation in the news media, as the woman who had captured the heart of baseball's most eligible bachelor, the player whose unflinching devotion to playing every game of the season had earned him the nickname "the

Iron Horse." Her face became known to readers through the photographs alongside newspaper stories about her and their upcoming marriage. For Eleanor, some of the reports were fictitious, such the account that she had attended the University of Wisconsin, which she hadn't. Other stories continually referred to her as "a high-spirited socialite from Chicago" who had come from a wealthy family. And that was how the public came to think of her—not that Eleanor herself didn't enjoy her new image of self-importance.

"There were times when Eleanor was impressed with the fact that she was Mrs. Lou Gehrig," recalled Maye Lazzeri, wife of Yankees Hall of Fame second baseman Tony Lazzeri, who once felt the need to remind her to remember her place. "'Listen Eleanor,' I said, 'I'm only married to Tony Lazzeri. I have nothing to do with all the home runs and the honors. I'm just lucky I've got him. And the quicker you learn that you're not Lou Gehrig, the better off you're going to be.'... Looking back, I realize Eleanor was young and it was easy for her to lose perspective," she recalled.

Lost in the story of the Gehrigs' relationship was the fact that Lou was no young player but a grown man, 30 years old when he began courting Eleanor. In fact, Lou lived with his parents until that year. Until Eleanor, ostensibly, the only woman in Lou's life had been his mother, Christina. "He's the only big egg I have in my basket," Christina was fond of saying. About the only thing in her son's life that she didn't control was his love for baseball, which ironically became the family's salvation. According to biographer Sara Kaden Brunsvold, "The parents didn't chide baseball much after Gehrig used his signing bonus to pay off their mountain of medical bills. [When

Gehrig was debating whether to stay at Columbia until grad-
uation or sign with the Yankees, Pop was epileptic and Mom
had double pneumonia.] What was left of his bonus he used to
send them on their first-ever vacation. He made sure they received a cut of every paycheck he earned, ensuring they would
never have to work again. They got a particularly large cut of
his first paycheck—he bought them a house in a well-off part of
the city. This was an especially important accomplishment for
Gehrig; he had grown up sleeping in the kitchen of their two-
room apartment in one of the poorest sections of the city."

Gehrig often called his mom his "best girl." He could not
imagine life without her. His loving, strong-willed mother became the gatekeeper for everything in his life, controlling his
personal life as well as his own measure of self-worth.

In 1927, the year Ruth slugged 60 home runs, it was Gehrig
who stole the thunder with his 173 RBIs, 47 home runs, and
.373 batting average—even winning the American League's
Most Valuable Player Award. But Lou's numbers fell off in
1928, down to 147 RBIs, just one more than Babe produced;
meanwhile, Ruth hit 54 homers, twice the number of Lou's.
The Yankees went on to win a second consecutive World Series
championship, which further stamped the Ruth-Gehrig team's
greatness. As was his custom, Babe celebrated in triumphant
Ruthian fashion. He was 33 years old and showed no sign of
slowing. But for Gehrig, eight years younger than Babe at 25,
there were questions, not the least being the drop-off in his
power numbers.

Gehrig, few knew, was struggling with an issue far more important to him than home runs and runs batted in. His mom
was ill. "If I lost her," he said at the time, "I don't know what

I would do." His concentration was on life outside of Yankee Stadium. Gehrig even seriously considered sitting out the World Series against St. Louis. Fortunately, Christina Gehrig regained her strength. And Lou helped the Yankees overpower the Cardinals, marking the first time a team swept consecutive World Series titles. Gehrig crushed four home runs with nine RBIs in the Series, driving in as many runs by himself as the entire Cardinals team combined.

Even so, it was still Babe Ruth's team, as his World Series performance would underscore. Babe batted .625 as the Yankees crushed their National League opponent by a combined score of 27 to 10. Ruth also repeated what he had done against the Cardinals in the 1926 Series, smashing three home runs over the right-field pavilion in Sportsman's Park in Game 4, the only one to do it twice in a World Series. The way Ruth did it in 1928, though, befitted the Babe. Although he had homered early in the game, the Cardinals led 2–1 going into the seventh inning of Game 4. In the top of the seventh, the Cardinals' 21-game-winning southpaw, Bill Sherdel, had an 0-2 count on Babe. As Ruth turned to say something to catcher Earl Smith, Sherdel surprised him with a quick pitch, throwing without a windup. The pitch appeared to be strike three and a strikeout of the Babe. But the two leagues had separate rules, and "quick pitches" were legal in the National League but not in the American League—nor in the World Series. Umpire Cy Pfirman called "no pitch," touching off an irate protest from the Cardinals but leaving the count at 0-2. Babe took two balls, evening the count at 2-2, and then crushed his second home run to tie the game. Gehrig followed with his own home run that put the Yankees ahead for good.

They scored twice more in the seventh, and then Ruth slugged his third homer of the game in the two-run Yankees eighth inning. In the bottom of the ninth, Ruth caught the game's final out, a fly ball near the stands, where Cardinals fans pelted him with newspapers and programs. Unhurt, a laughing Babe Ruth showed off the ball in his outstretched arm as he ran toward the celebration in the Yankee dugout. "The biggest thrill of my career," Ruth said later, rubbing salt in the wound of the Cardinals and their fans.

The 1928 World Series was special to Gehrig because it symbolized his beloved mother's own struggle to recover her health. For that reason, he kept intact the specially designed Hamilton "Piping Rock" model wristwatches presented to the players from the 1928 championship team. Each watch was engraved with a player's name and featured backs specifically designed with an American eagle perched atop two intersecting bats, baseball-like stitching and the phrase YANKEES 1928 WORLD CHAMPIONS. The wristwatch was among a small but significant group of his mementos that was bequeathed by Lou's mother, Christina, to longtime family friend Ruth Quick upon her death in 1954. The watch remained in the Quick family until 2011, and was sold at auction in 2014. Most of Lou Gehrig's championship rings and other presentation jewelry were deconstructed and fashioned into an elaborate charm bracelet for Eleanor. That bracelet now resides at the National Baseball Hall of Fame in Cooperstown.

The 1928 championship wristwatch was also symbolic of the unresolved rift that later surfaced between Gehrig's mother and his wife. Their relationship was chilly from the start, exacerbated by Lou's refusal to consider his mother's second-guessing of Eleanor: "Mom is the most wonderful woman in the world," Gehrig told Fred Lieb. "She broke up some of my earlier romances, and she isn't going to break up this one."

Christina Gehrig did her best to keep her son from marrying Eleanor, who in turn tried her best to befriend her in-laws. Eleanor even agreed to move in with the Gehrigs in New Rochelle while she and Lou searched for an apartment; it was a disastrous turn of events. The Gehrigs seemingly went out of their way to make their future daughter-in-law feel uncomfortable. They would converse, even over dinner with Lou, in German, knowing full well that Eleanor neither spoke nor understood the language. Christina and Eleanor also clashed so much that the future Mrs. Lou Gehrig moved out and stayed with her aunt and uncle in the days leading up to their wedding, which was scheduled for the Saturday evening after the Yankees' next-to-last game of the 1933 season.

The feud between Christina and Eleanor continued, reaching a climactic end in an argument over curtains in the apartment where Lou and Eleanor planned to live. It was the day before their planned wedding, and Eleanor was left in tears. Then and only then did Gehrig finally stand up for the woman he loved. He called the mayor of New Rochelle, New York, who hurried over to Gehrig's apartment, where movers were delivering furniture and plumbers did last-minute repairs. There in the living room of their future home, the Honorable Walter G. C. Otto married Eleanor and Lou in the presence of a few family members and Yankees catcher Bill Dickey. Gehrig said his wedding vows in his shirtsleeves, while Eleanor still wore her apron. Christina Gehrig did not attend.

It was only after the short ceremony that Eleanor and Lou changed to have their picture taken. The mayor had arranged for a police escort to take Gehrig to that Friday's afternoon game at Yankee Stadium. Lou went hitless in four at bats as the Yankees lost to the Washington Senators 8–5. The Yankees finished the season in second place, seven games behind the American League–champion Senators. The previous season, the Yankees had won their seventh pennant and fourth World Series championship. That was a team with a record nine future Hall of Famers: Babe Ruth, Lou Gehrig, Earle Combs, Bill Dickey, Lefty Gomez, Tony Lazzeri, Herb Pennock, Red Ruffing, and Joe Sewell. However, 1933 would be the start of a three-year drought without an American League Pennant, which would end with the arrival of Joe DiMaggio in 1936. Lefty Gomez, one of the Hall of Famers from that Yankees team, would later perhaps sum it up best: "It was the end of an era, and what an era it was."

For Gehrig, though, it would be a time of transition—to a time when it would be his New York Yankees, not Babe Ruth's. To a time when he would pair up with another future baseball legend, Joe DiMaggio, for another run at greatness. And, finally, a transition to married life. Eleanor was his opposite: a partygoer, a drinker, and very outgoing. She would end up having a profound influence on his career in their eight short years of marriage. She took on the role of Gehrig's manager, agent, and promoter in an era long before every player had these positions on their payroll. She would also become a great source of strength during his battle with a debilitating disease.

For Christina Gehrig, sadly, it was a transition she would never accept. She would never forgive Eleanor for coming between her and her son. She would soon befriend Ruth Martin, a vivacious redhead from Elizabeth, New Jersey, whom Gehrig had dated before he met Eleanor and whose romance with Lou the overbearing mother cleverly wrecked. Not much about Lou's relationship survived the eight decades since their breakup beyond a 1930 Christmas card signed by Gehrig with an envelope addressed to Miss Ruth Martin. Their relationship didn't last, but Ruth Quick (see Martin) had made an impression on Lou's mother. "She rarely spoke about Gehrig," according to her only son, Jeffrey Quick, from her marriage to Herbert Quick, a salesman at an upscale Fifth Avenue furniture store. They married in 1934, only a few months after Lou's own marriage to Eleanor.

Jeffrey Quick was born in 1942 after Gehrig's death of ALS. To celebrate his birth, Christina took a Lou Gehrig Spalding first baseman's glove into the Yankees locker room and had it signed by the manager, Joe McCarthy, and her son's former teammates, including Red Ruffing, Joe Gordon, Tommy Henrich, and Bill Dickey. Christina Gehrig then gave the glove to the Quicks as a gift for their newborn son. It is the only piece of Gehrig memorabilia that he did not sell. "From what I understand, she did date [Gehrig] some," Jeffrey Quick told an interviewer in 2011, the year that he sold a huge stash of Lou Gehrig memorabilia for almost $1 million dollars. "Regardless of what happened with my mom and Lou, there was a lasting, and I'll say even perhaps a loving, relationship between my Mom and Christina."

Quick later recalled that his parents often took him to visit Lou Gehrig's parents, who, in turn, regularly came to the Quick's home in New Jersey or to their vacation cottage on the Delaware River in Pennsylvania. Christina Gehrig had had a change of heart over Ruth, to the point where young Jeffrey took a sentimental spot in her heart that might have gone to her own grandchild, had Lou and Eleanor had one. Among the photographs in the Quick family album would be one of Ruth and her husband sitting with Christina Gehrig on the front steps of her house in Westchester County—and a special one of a young Jeffrey Quick bathing in a washtub as Mom Gehrig sat smiling in the background.

"I remember her as outgoing and fun, a big woman, very pleasant," Quick said.

Not only did Christina and Eleanor Gehrig never make up, but they also continued to feud after his death over Lou's will. Gehrig had left behind the entirety of his estate—valued at $171,251 in assets—to Eleanor, who was executor of his will. To his parents he bequeathed the interest received from stock investments and monthly payments from a $20,000 life insurance policy. Christina and Heinrich Gehrig, however, felt cheated and, believing that Eleanor was withholding these payments, sued her in August 1943 for $5,188.53. They eventually settled out of court, but the feud between the Gehrigs and their daughter-in-law continued.

Christina took her bitterness to her grave. When she died in 1954, Christina willed her estate, including her own extensive collection of Lou's baseball possessions, to two friends, one of them being Ruth Quick, despite the fact that Eleanor Gehrig was still alive. In that collection were the wristwatch as well as a rare Gehrig game-used uniform that Jeffrey Quick once wore to a costume party; a baseball signed by the 1926 Yankees; a baseball cigarette lighter autographed by Gehrig, Babe Ruth,

Jimmie Foxx, and Connie Mack from a 1934 tour of Japan; and even personal items, such as Lou's grade school autograph book and a tooled leather wallet with Gehrig's name.

"As a Gehrig biographer, what's fascinating to me is this relationship," Jonathan Eig, author of the 2005 Gehrig biography *Luckiest Man* told the *New York Times* when the items went to auction in 2011. "Gehrig was so shy and inhibited he never had any interest in sharing his private life or telling his story. So I'd love to know more about this person able to charm him and charm his mother—and Christina Gehrig was not an easy woman to charm."

7   "Baseball's Gift to Women"

*"Not for you, $50,000,
or $250,000 will I give up women."*

—Babe Ruth

BABE RUTH COULD HAVE POPULATED A SMALL NATION. HE HAD affairs all over America. Some were one-night stands at most. Many were quickies on Yankees road trips, when women lined up outside his hotel room—and not for autographs. For a time in the 1920s, the New York Yankees front office received letters every week from different women claiming to have given birth to Babe Ruth's love child. The Roaring '20s were a time of sexual liberation, experimentation, and exploration. Having just won the vote, women were at the forefront of social causes and societal change. In spite of—or perhaps because of—Prohibition, the '20s were boom times. Young women attended college, flocked to major cities to find work, and lived on their own in numbers never before seen in the history of the nation.

And Babe Ruth wasn't just America's biggest sports star of
the time. He was its biggest sex symbol, and he loved it. He especially loved Hollywood, to which he was introduced even
before the 1920s. He had first gone there after the Boston
Red Sox's 1918 season, when he discovered that the streets
off Hollywood Boulevard were lined with apartments hous-
ing beautiful young actresses. Already having connections he
had made in Boston and in New York, Babe often spent time
around the Famous Players-Lasky Studios, at the time the most
important motion picture studio in the world. There he often
picked up either a young actress or a golf date. Sometimes both.
Babe quickly became a regular at the golf course at Griffith
Park, where golf shop attendants often took messages for him.
In fact, Ruth was playing a round there just after Christmas
1919, when he learned that he had been dealt to the New York
Yankees. Babe's immediate response was to proclaim his love
for the Boston area, his farm there, and the Red Sox fans.
"Will not play anywhere but Boston. Will leave for the East
Monday," he angrily wired back. The Yankees then had manager Miller Huggins cut short his Christmas with family and
dispatched him to Los Angeles, where he personally tracked
down Ruth at Griffith Park. Huggins, who had invested two
seasons in trying to turn the Yankees into a winning team, believed Babe was the missing link he needed.

"Babe told me he might have made a bigger stink than he did
about going to the Yankees had it not been for Miller Huggins,"
Ruth's friend Johnny Grant recalled. "[Huggins] had managed the Yankees against Babe in 1918 and 1919. He knew
what Babe could do, and he kept saying to him, 'Babe, you
hit 29 home runs with the Red Sox last year. Come play with

the Yankees, and you'll hit 50. You'll play half your games at the Polo Grounds. It's 258 feet down to the right-field fences.' Imagine: 258 feet was almost 50 feet shorter than right field in Fenway. And that started going round and round in Babe's head. He was a pull-ball hitter to right field. All those fly-ball outs within 40 feet of dead right in Fenway would become home runs in the Polo Grounds, where the Yankees played in New York at the time. Babe said that was what did it, and he was right. In 1920, Babe's first year with the Yankees, he hit 54 home runs. In 1921, Babe's second year in New York, he hit 59 home runs."

By late 1919, Ruth was also head over heels about a young, green-eyed beauty named Juanita Jennings, who was trying to break into the movie business in California. Her given name was Juanita Grenandtz, but she had changed her surname to Jennings, believing that would broaden her casting chances. Her background has been a mystery. In Los Angeles, an aspiring actress by her name was known to have been of Hispanic ancestry, with a claim of having been the granddaughter of onetime Mexican president Francisco Madero. Madero was the son of one of the wealthiest families in his country and came to be known as the "*caudillo de la Revolución* [leader of the Revolution]". His assassination in 1913 is one of the factors credited for paving the way for the Mexican Revolution. Madero's family took refuge in Cuba, and Juanita Grenandtz was said to be a Cuban national when she arrived in Hollywood.

Some reports later claimed that she had met Ruth while he had been barnstorming with a team in California. According to Johnny Grant, Babe told him he had met Juanita at the Players-Lasky Studios. At the time, Ruth's primary reason for being in

Hollywood was for the making of a low-budget exploitation film titled *Headin' Home*, a fictional biography of Babe aimed at capitalizing on his growing popularity. The 29 home runs he had hit in 1919 was still an unheard-of number to a country accustomed to the lowly homer numbers of the dead-ball era. Ruth had been talked into making the film by Hollywood director Raoul Walsh, who promised him $50,000 to appear in the picture. Babe received only $15,000 of his money, and it was the worthless check for the remainder that he carried around in his wallet to pull out as a conversation prop. It remains unclear why Walsh reneged on paying Ruth. But it's certain that cinema lost no matinee idol in Ruth, though critics have come to hold Babe blameless to the hustler mentality of Hollywood, as one reviewer would note:

> In 1920, the year the silent film *Headin' Home* was released, Ruth was only recently acquired by the New York Yankees. At this point he was merely "a really good baseball player." An odd film with little story, *Headin' Home* has a big place in sports history, offering an early look at Ruth before he developed his trademark belly. It's also something of a landmark because starring in a film is a sign that a sports star has hit the big-time. *Headin' Home* takes Ruth's biography and skews it to the point where it's comical. He's a Paul Bunyan figure who marches into the woods and makes his own bats out of trees that he's cut down. He also consoles young girls and imagines dogs being put into meat grinders. It's surreal stuff made all the more strange when you notice the caked

on white makeup on Ruth's face that makes him look like a clown (the powder was common practice in films at the time but it still looks odd, particularly on someone not normally connected to movies).

Director Walsh went on to make a name of his own in Hollywood. He played John Wilkes Booth in D.W. Griffith's epic *The Birth of a Nation* and also served as an assistant director on the film. He later discovered John Wayne, who had been a prop boy named Marion Morrison. Over the course of his career, he directed many of Hollywood's biggest names: James Cagney and Humphrey Bogart; John Wayne and Roy Rogers; George Raft and Ann Sheridan; Ida Lupino and Errol Flynn; Marlene Dietrich and Clark Gable. But wherever he was, he always went out of his way to avoid Babe Ruth, who had vowed to use his head for batting practice. Perhaps that is because Walsh may have been on the hook for even more money. The Baseball Hall of Fame Archives has a photograph of "Babe Ruth signing a movie contract for $100,000 with W.A. Shea and T.W. Walsh, two film company executives" in 1919. Shea was one of the producers of *Headin' Home,* and T.W. Walsh was Raoul Walsh's father. So it seems Walsh may have actually run out owing Babe $85,000.

In late 1919, the only barnstorming that Babe was doing in Hollywood was in Juanita's bed. It was not until the 1920s, after he had joined the Yankees, that Ruth said his business manager, Christy Walsh, began organizing barnstorming tours so that fans across the country could come out and see him and other baseball stars. And the deal that would take him to the Yankees, he soon came to understand, presented a unique opportunity to have Juanita nearby in New York during the baseball season. This would never have been possible in Boston, where Babe's wife, Helen, was comfortably ensconced on their farm in rural Massachusetts. So Ruth relented and accepted his sale to the Yankees in a deal that would alter the game forever, dramatically changing the fortunes of baseball's two storied franchises and creating the legend of the game's greatest player. For Boston, the impact of the deal would come to be known as "the Curse of the Bambino." The Red Sox, who had won five of the first 16 World Series played between 1903 and 1919, would not win another pennant until 1946, or another World Series until 2004. For the Yankees, Ruth's impact would be equally as dramatic. They had not won an American League title before acquiring Babe. After the deal, they would win seven pennants and four World Series championships with Ruth and go on to lead baseball with 40 pennants and 27 World Series crowns in their history.

By the start of the 1920 season, Juanita Jennings was living in New York in an apartment kept for her by Babe Ruth. Years later, Babe told Johnny Grant that Juanita's New York apartment was part of his new deal with the Yankees, who were eager to have him and the potential he held for the future. In all, Ruth had played six seasons with the Red Sox, leading them to three World Series victories. On the mound, Ruth pitched a total of 29⅔ scoreless World Series innings, setting a new league record that would stand for 43 years. He was fresh off a sensational 1919 season, having broken the major league home run record with 29 and led the American League with 113 RBIs and 103 runs. In addition to playing more than 100 games in left field, he also went 9–5 as a pitcher. With his prodigious hitting, pitching, and fielding skills, Ruth had surpassed the great Ty Cobb as baseball's biggest attraction.

Red Sox owner Harry Frazee tried to make it appear that he had gotten the better end of the deal. "The price was something enormous, but I do not care to name the figures," Frazee told the *Boston Globe.* "It was an amount the club could not afford to refuse. I should have preferred to have taken players in exchange for Ruth, but no club could have given me the equivalent in men without wrecking itself, and so the deal had to be made on a cash basis. No other club could afford to give the amount the Yankees have paid for him, and I do not mind saying I think they are taking a gamble. With this money the Boston club can now go into the market and buy other players and have a stronger and better team in all respects than we would have if Ruth had remained with us. I do not wish to detract one iota from Ruth's ability as a ballplayer nor from his value as an attraction, but there is no getting away from the fact that despite his 29 home runs, the Red Sox finished sixth in the race last season."

Aware of his value, Ruth had demanded a salary raise, and New York agreed to negotiate a new contract with terms that would satisfy their new slugger. The sale was contingent on Ruth signing a new contract, which was quickly accomplished. Babe agreed to fulfill the remaining two years on his contract but was given a $20,000 bonus, payable over two seasons. "When I made my demand on the Red Sox for $20,000 a year," he said in an interview, "I had an idea they would choose to sell me rather than pay the increase, and I knew the Yankees were the most probable purchasers."

New York may also have been the one American city that could deal with the outsized Ruth persona. For if sportswriter Glenn Stout's alternative theory in *The Selling of the Babe* on why the Red Sox dealt away Ruth is to be believed, all of his excessive drinking, womanizing, and gambling were about to explode in Boston, as if ballplayers of the dead-ball era had been mostly saints. Of course, this is the Ruthian Babe that came to be accepted by fans who in 1920 packed into the Polo Grounds in record numbers, making the Yankees the first team to surpass the one million-attendance mark in a season. Yes, Babe Ruth didn't just make news, he made bold banner headlines. As the *New York Times* was to observe looking back on Ruth, "The city's 18 newspapers covered him like a character in a lurid soap opera and indeed, his escapades became bigger, flashier, noisier under the news media glare. Appropriate nicknames were coined to exploit his new currency, among them Bambino, the Big Bam, the Sultan of Swat, and, courtesy of the *Times,* the Caliph of Crash." In New York, in his first season in 1920, Ruth's 54 home runs boggled the collective American mind. Consider that only five years earlier, the Boston Red Sox as a team slugged only 14. The legendary slugger called "Home Run" Baker never hit more than a dozen homers in a season, the most any player hit between 1904 and 1918.

Forgotten perhaps in Babe Ruth's move to New York was none other than his wife, Helen, who didn't care much for city life and could now place some distance between herself and the man she had married. Helen Woodford Ruth had kept to herself after their marriage. Not much would ever be known about her. The *New York Times* would even use the mystery

surrounding Helen to bash Leigh Montville's otherwise entertaining 2006 biography, *The Big Bam*. "What's missing here,
however, is any exploration of Ruth's inner conflicts and de-
mons," the *Times* reviewer wrote. "Time and again, Montville
sidesteps critical issues with a device he calls 'the fog.' Often,
when some aspect of the Babe Ruth legend falls outside his research, the fog rolls in. This is especially frustrating with respect
to Ruth's family history, as well as his mounting medical problems. His first wife, Helen Woodford, also remains shrouded
in myth."

Among the few tidbits of information ever published in
newspapers at the time was Helen's claim that her family was
from Nova Scotia, which it may have been. However, in an
affidavit she signed for her marriage license when she married Babe in Maryland on October 17, 1914, she stated she was
born in El Paso, Texas, in 1896. According to that document
she would have been 18 when they wed, though she may have
been as young as 15. The only birth certificate filed in Texas
for a Helen Woodford showed that infant to have been born
in 1899. So who was she, and how old had she actually been
when she married Babe? For years, Helen would avoid news
media scrutiny about her and her family. Not much would be
known about Helen until the tragedy that would take her life.
And in her life, she was comfortable remaining in the shadow
of a husband whose personality and image towered over everyone around him.

That was fine with Babe, who in 1920 cruised into New York
as its new prince of the city, and no one questioned who it was
that he was keeping in lavish princess fashion in the Upper West
Side of Manhattan. Such was the outsized persona of Babe Ruth

and the media's obsession with him that Juanita Jennings often accompanied him about town without raising any suspicions. Some may have confused her with Helen Ruth. She was petite, beautiful, green-eyed with olive complexion, and she dressed and carried herself with the blithe spirit of many carefree young women in the Roaring '20s. At other times, Babe had any number of friends who were always at his beck and call to help out for things such as escorting Juanita to social engagements to which Ruth absolutely could not arrive with her. One of them, Charles Ellias, the head accountant for Harry M. Stevens, America's first great ballpark concessionaire, would eventually even marry Juanita.

It was rare when Babe wasn't out on the town. If ever there was a player for whom day baseball was tailor-made, it was Babe Ruth, who rarely ate dinner at home whether the Yankees were playing in New York or on the road. Record crowds throughout the American League flocked to see the Yankees and their new star. Ruth was hitting so many home runs that they all wanted to see the Babe hit another. When the Yankees played the Browns in St. Louis, three cowboys waited outside the Yankees' clubhouse to tell Ruth that they had ridden on horseback three days to reach a Wyoming railroad station, from which they took a train to Missouri. "Baby Ruth," the *St. Louis Post-Dispatch* quoted one of the cowboys telling Ruth, "I'd have ridden on horseback all the way to St. Louis to see you hit them home runs." In Washington, D.C., one fan reportedly became so excited seeing Ruth slug a home run that he suffered a heart attack and dropped dead. In New York, the Yankees were regularly selling out the Polo Grounds as Ruth slugged a record 12 home runs in May. On May 16 alone, the

Yankees drew 38,600, a record for the ballpark, and had to turn away another 15,000. By midseason, Ruthmania was so feverish in New York that the Yankees felt a need to hold a "Babe Ruth Day" July 9 at the Polo Grounds, where he received a diamond-studded watch from the local Knights of Columbus chapter. Fittingly, Babe slugged a home run.

Babe basked in the adoration. He once told Jimmie Reese that, while he loved baseball, he got a special thrill playing in front of women. "I loved seeing their faces when I cross the plate after running the bases when I hit a home run—it's like seeing the face of a woman who's just been freshly fucked by me," Reese recalled Ruth saying. "I guess that's how come I love fucking so much. I enjoy it, for damn sure, but the look of a woman after we've fucked, well, I can't put it into words except to say that it's like having just hit a home run and knocked the ball to kingdom come."

Too often Ruth's 1920 home run explosion has been solely credited to the arrival of the so-called live-ball era. The manufacturing of baseballs used in the major leagues changed that season when the A.J. Reach Company began using a more efficient machine to wind the yarn around the core of each baseball. Al Reach, a former player and founder of the Philadelphia Phillies franchise, owned what was then the largest manufacturer of sporting goods in the United States in the late 19th and early 20th centuries. He was a pioneer, always on the lookout for new developments that would improve the game—and he may have been ahead of his time. In 1900, his company developed a prototype batting helmet that players and teams refused to use. He also published an annual publication, the Reach Guide, which was regarded as one of the most important sources of information on baseball through the 1930s. But in 1934, Al Reach sold his company to his main rival, Albert Goodwill Spalding's sporting goods company, which replaced the Reach name on baseballs and other merchandise. The Reach Guide merged with the Spalding Guide, which was eventually replaced with *The Sporting News'* guide.

Ruth may have also benefitted from two other developments taking place in baseball in 1920. Baseball was gradually abolishing the use of the spitball, and the games incorporated more new baseballs. The impact of all these changes quickly became evident in 1920, when major league players hit 183 more home runs than in the previous season. By midseason, on July 15, Babe hit his 29th home run of the year, tying his own major league record of 1919. He broke his record four days later, hitting two home runs in the second game of a doubleheader. By the end of the month, he had hit 37 home runs.

But then the Yankees' fortunes changed. The Yankees struggled the rest of the season and finished in third place behind the Cleveland Indians and Chicago White Sox as baseball reeled from the worst black eye of its history. The scandal that had been brewed around the White Sox's World Series defeat the previous fall exploded just as the 1920 season was ending. On September 28, as a grand jury convened, White Sox stars Eddie Cicotte and Shoeless Joe Jackson confessed their participation in rigging of the 1919 World Series. Shoeless Joe Jackson and other implicated players were suspended, and the White Sox lost the American League pennant to Cleveland.

For Babe Ruth, his first season as a Yankee would be gloriously bittersweet. His record-shattering 54 home runs would take some of the sting from the shame of the Black Sox scandal.

But in the final weeks of that season, life began touching Babe as never before. After finishing the month of July with 37 home runs for the season, Babe Ruth would hit only 17 home runs in August and September. Why had Ruth slumped? Had all the partying gotten the better of him? Had the pressure of playing in New York worn him down, as it would to so many others? Or had it been something more common to the most mortal of men when they know their life will soon change?

In August 1920, Babe Ruth learned that Juanita Jennings was pregnant with his baby. The Babe was about to be a father.

8   The Yankees' Team Mom

"Every Yankee loved Mom Gehrig, and none more than Babe Ruth—
except, of course, Lou."

—Jimmie Reese

BASEBALL SPRING TRAINING CAMPS HAVE ALWAYS HAD THEIR anecdotes of strange happenings and even stranger bedfellows. As Gehrig biographer Jonathan Eig later wrote, it was "a time for loose curfews and easy women, mornings full of baseball and afternoons full of fishing." Certainly, one of the most curious sights must have been that of Christina Gehrig at Yankees spring training in the 1920s, after 22-year-old Lou became its regular first baseman. In 1926, when the Yankees were training at St. Petersburg, Florida, Gehrig was the only member of the team who arrived accompanied by his mother, for whom he rented a room at the Del Prado Hotel. Not only would Lou dine with and entertain his mom every evening, but they would also converse entirely in German, Christina's native tongue.

"Half a dozen writers' wives, including mine, would be there, three or four other writers and Mom Gehrig," beat reporter Fred Lieb later wrote in *Baseball As I Have Known It*. From Lou's perspective, he was simply still taking care of his mother, trying to make her life easier after all her hard work and sacrifices in raising him. He felt his mother had earned the comfort of traveling south from New York in a fancy Pullman railroad car. Mom Gehrig, as she was called by the Yankees, often accompanied her son to spring training or on short road trips or even to the World Series. Fred Lieb described coming home from a road trip with Gehrig and being met at the train station by his Christina. "Mom and Louie kissed and hugged for fully 10 minutes, as though they had been apart for years."

Curiouser and curiouser. Or perhaps Lou Gehrig, Mom Gehrig's son, was just the most boring major league baseball player the world had ever known. He was certainly among the nicest, and possibly the consummate American immigrant son—who just happened to achieve greatness in the national pastime. Early in his career, there was criticism of Lou being too laid back, unwilling or unable to assume a leadership role after taking over the first base job from Wally Pipp. Some felt he failed to get angry when the moment called for it.

The best example may have been the 1926 World Series, when the Yankees took the National League–champion Cardinals to a deciding Game 7. There, with the Yankees trailing 3–2 in the ninth inning, Ruth committed possibly the worst mental mistake of his illustrious career. With two outs, legendary pitcher Grover Cleveland Alexander, pitching for the second day in a row, walked Babe and created an opportunity for the Yankees to tie the game or win the World Series outright. It brought to the plate slugging outfielder Bob Meusel, the cleanup hitter who had batted .315 hitter that season with 78 RBIs in just more than 100 regular-season games (he had missed almost a third of the season with a broken bone in his left foot). More important, Meusel had gotten two extra-base hits (a double and triple) off Alexander in Game 6. He also had an ulterior motive for wanting to deliver in that moment: he had dropped a key fly ball with one out and the bases loaded in the fourth inning that opened the door for the Cardinals to score all their runs. The moment was made for Meusel's redemption. Alexander would have to retire his nemesis of the previous day, with the prospect of facing the young Lou Gehrig should he choose to walk Meusel as he had Ruth.

Then, as Alexander threw his first pitch to Meusel, Babe Ruth had a brain freeze. He surprised everyone at Yankee Stadium by breaking for second base on a delayed steal attempt. Meusel swung and missed, but Cardinals catcher Bob O'Farrell didn't. Farrell, the National League's MVP for the 1926 season, threw a strike to second baseman Rogers Hornsby for the easy World Series–clinching put-out. "[Babe] didn't say a word," Hornsby would recall. "He didn't even look around or up at me. He just picked himself up and walked away."

Kneeling in the on-deck circle, Gehrig clutched his bat and took a long walk to the clubhouse. He showed no emotion and, though he may have been the only player who could have said something to Ruth about his bone-headed base running, he didn't. Then again, Ruth had no equal at the time. He could do what he wanted to do with little consequence on his team. But this had been a squandered opportunity of epic proportions.

Lou Gehrig's great disappointment in not winning the 1926 World Series may have been that he had only $3,417.75 in the losers' share to bring home to his mom. He returned home that off-season to his parents' Morningside Heights home, where he gorged himself on his mom's cooking. Mom was No. 1 in Lou's world. What she thought, virtually about anything, never failed to register in her son's mind—and that included baseball. In fact, it had been one of her criticisms of Lou's play in a 1924 game that had a resounding impact on his on-field decorum. In 1924, the Yankees had taken a long look at Gehrig in spring training and decided he needed more seasoning. He was assigned to play in the Hartford minor league team, as he had the previous season, where Lou's offensive production—a .369 batting average with 37 home runs, 40 doubles, and 13 triples in 134 games—earned him a call-up to the Yankees in September. Lou had only a dozen at-bats but hit .500 and drove in five runs that year. Christina happened to watch her son in a game against the Detroit Tigers, in which Lou delivered a two-run single to right field. Gehrig, though, rounded first base too aggressively and got caught by the throw from the outfield. Lou extended an ensuing rundown long enough for centerfielder Ty Cobb to get involved, and he swore at Gehrig as he tagged him. The usually cool tempered Gehrig swore back and continued screaming at Cobb as he walked off the field and from the steps of the Yankees dugout. Even a warning from the umpire failed to calm Gehrig, and he was soon ejected from the game. Later, Gehrig attacked Cobb in the tunnel between the dugout and the clubhouse, and escaped the clutches of his team-mates, including Ruth, to take a swing at Cobb, who had a repu-tation as the meanest man in baseball history. Gehrig missed with his punch, stumbled, and fell, hitting his head on the hard con-crete floor and momentarily knocking himself unconscious.

Gehrig felt foolish when he regained consciousness, and even more so when his mother offered her opinion later that night. His temper, she told him, made him look silly and hurt the team. The Yankees were swept in that three-game series with the Tigers and ultimately ended up losing the pennant by two games to the Washington Senators. Christina didn't have to lobby too hard or too long with her son to make her point. Lou sensed that the incident had been beneath him and learned in the coming days from Babe and other teammates that he was only the latest major league ballplayer who had allowed himself to be drawn into a fight with the irascible Ty Cobb. Cobb would tell his biographer Al Stump that getting under the skin of opposing players had been a trick he had long used and with which he often succeeded in getting opponents to lose their focus.

"Babe Ruth was one of the few who I couldn't rattle," Cobb said. "For Babe, baseball was always a game, a game he loved to play, but it wasn't life or death to him. He took everything in stride. I think that's one of the things that helped him be as great as he was. He never got too high, and he never got too low. Now Gehrig, that was an entirely different matter. He wore strikeouts and losses on his face. Everything got to him, especially in his early years with the Yankees. He could be a hothead when he was young, but he got it under control. I don't know if it was Babe or [Miller] Huggins, but somebody sure did a job in roping him in."

Ty Cobb had no idea it had been Christina Gehrig. She was, as it would turn out, her son's best and closest friend. In most biographies, that title has been bestowed on Bill Dickey, the Yankees catcher who understood that what many saw as stand-offishness in Gehrig was simply shyness and self-conscious-ness. In his early years with the Yankees, Lou dreaded doing interviews, so concerned of saying the wrong thing that he feared that "I would just about shit my pants." The art of the traditional baseball player's interview, of saying the most mun-dane of things, wasn't something that the conscientious Lou

Gehrig could have embraced. Lou may have been four years older than Bill Dickey, but he was far less mature.

Dickey, however, didn't join the Yankees until late in 1928 and only became the starting catcher the next season. It was easy for Dickey to feel intimidated on a team that had won the World Series in 1927 with the already legendary Babe Ruth having hit 60 home runs. Dickey first tried to model his game on the Babe's, until Manager Miller Huggins pulled him aside. "We pay one player here for hitting home runs and that's Babe Ruth," he told Dickey. "So choke up and drill the ball. That way, you'll be around here longer." The first teammate to make him feel at home in the clubhouse was Lou Gehrig. In the years ahead, Dickey and Gehrig would become roommates on the road after the Yankees released Lou's first roommate, Joe Sewell. Later, Dickey was the first teammate to learn that Gehrig was ill, and he was the only active player to play himself in *Pride of the Yankees*.

William Malcolm Dickey was born on June 6, 1907, in Bastrop, Louisiana, one of seven children born to John and Laura Dickey. John Dickey worked as a brakeman for Missouri Pacific Railroad and was part of a baseball family. He was a semipro pitcher and catcher. Bill's brother Gus played second base and pitched. Younger brother George "Skeets" Dickey was a major league catcher for six seasons with the Chicago White Sox and Boston Red Sox. Bill spent his childhood in Kensett, Arkansas. His family moved to Little Rock when he was 16, and he maintained a home there until his death. He played second base on his hometown team when he was young and pitched in high school. In New York, as a Yankee, he became a regular guest at the home of Christina and Heinrich Gehrig, who regarded him as family, much as they did Babe Ruth.

Dickey also became a mainstay of the Yankees dynasty that ruled over the American League between World Wars I and II. He would be rated by many as the finest all-around catcher in the history of the sport. In his 17 years as a player, from 1928 until 1946—all with the Yankees and all at catcher—Dickey would play in eight World Series, winning seven championships. "He was a great catcher, great hitter, and a great man to have on the ballclub," Joe McCarthy, the manager of the Yankees during most of Dickey's career, once said. "The records prove Dickey was the greatest catcher of all time." In 1,789 games, the left-handed-hitting Dickey compiled a batting average of .313, with 202 home runs and 1,209 runs batted in. In 11 seasons he batted .300 or better, with a career high of .362 in 1936. A Hall of Famer, Dickey was a member of the New York Yankees as a player, manager, and coach spanning four decades. In 1949, Dickey returned to the Yankees as a coach under new manager Casey Stengel and helped turn Yogi Berra into the field marshal of World Series–championship teams in the coming decade. As Berra would famously tell sportswriters, "Bill is learnin' me his experience." The Yankees would later retire the uniform No. 8 Dickey wore and which was later worn by his catching protégé Berra.

Elston Howard, who succeeded Berra behind the plate, was more articulate about how much Dickey had helped him. "You've got to have Bill work with you to understand how much he can help you," said Howard, the first African American player on the Yankees roster, who was also the American League's Most Valuable Player in 1963. "The year

I came to the Yankees from Toronto, I wasn't as good as a lot of semipro catchers. Bill took me over and he talked to me. Then he worked with me. We'd go off in a corner and practice. Without Bill, I'm nobody. Nobody at all. He made me a catcher. Now when I start to slip and get careless, there's old Bill to give me a hand."

Could Bill Dickey have been the greatest catcher of all time? Hall of Famer Bob Feller, the great fastball-throwing pitcher of the Cleveland Indians, thought he was, without any question. "Bill Dickey is the best [catcher] I ever saw," he said in an interview. "He was as good as anyone behind the plate, and better with the bat. There are others I'd include right behind Dickey, but he was the best all-around catcher of them all. I believe I could have won 35 games [a season] if Bill Dickey was my catcher."

For Gehrig, though, Bill Dickey's greatest influence may have been off the field: assuring him that none of the Yankee ballplayers had any opposition to his mom's presence at ballgames. Often when the Yankees were home, Christina Gehrig hosted half the ballclub's roster for dinner. Not the least of them was Babe Ruth, who regularly left his teammates listening to the radio in the Gehrig living room to join Ma Gehrig in the kitchen, where he picked at the food she was preparing.

"Babe said he envied only one thing that Lou had—his mom," Johnny Grant recalled of their long talks. "He said she was the greatest cook in the world and a great mom. He said, 'They say boys need a father if they're going to make it in life, but that's a bunch of baloney. They need a mom far more.' You could tell that Babe was hurt, resentful, and embittered, that he hadn't had that kind of relationship with his mother.'"

9   Pre-Yankees Babe

"A man who knows he's making money for other people ought to get some of the profits he brings in. It's business, I tell you."

—Babe Ruth

YANKEE STADIUM MAY HAVE BEEN "THE HOUSE THAT RUTH BUILT," but in the 1920s all of baseball was synonymous with the Babe. There was no other player like him. He was a man of mythical proportions, and his image extended far beyond baseball. His nicknames alone suggested someone unreal: the Bam, the Big Bam, the Great Bambino, Colossus of Clout, the Prince of Pounders, and the Sultan of Swat. His popularity and fame exceeded that of presidents and national heroes, and he came to epitomize the America of the 20th century the world over, even overseas. In World War II, almost a decade after his retirement, Japanese soldiers who charged American troops in the fighting in the Pacific were heard to scream the battle cry, "To hell with Babe Ruth!" Quite simply, Ruth was "a unique figure in the social history of the United States," wrote Robert Creamer in *Babe: The Legend Comes to Life.* "For more than any other man, Babe Ruth transcended sports, moved far beyond the artificial limits of baselines and outfield fences and sports pages."

What was it Ty Cobb had said of the national pastime? "Baseball is a red-blooded sport for red-blooded men. It's a contest and everything that implies a struggle for supremacy, a survival of the fittest." Yet Ruth's years with the Yankees scarcely exhaust the epic story of his life, which was stuffed with high drama. From his troublesome youth and time in a religious orphanage to his own battle with a deadly disease, Ruth's life was so tumultuous that it cannot be described in broad strokes. The Babe embodied an enduring archetype of the American dream. An unwanted child who discovers an uncommon ability in the national pastime, recreates himself, and succeeds beyond anyone's wildest dreams. His transformation from Baltimorean Oliver Twist to the savior and king of his sport offers both a gripping personal story of redemption and an unexpected reflection of the important emerging years of America between world wars.

"Probably nowhere in all the imaginative field of fiction could one find a career more dramatic and bizarre than that portrayed in real life by George Herman Ruth," the *New York Times* wrote in its obituary of the Babe. "A creation of the times, he seemed to embody all the qualities that a sport-loving nation demanded of its outstanding hero." At a future time, he would have been the dream of every fantasy league player. A dozen times he led the American League in homers, 11 times he hit more than 40, four times more than 50. From 1920 to 1933, he slugged 637 homers, an average of 45.5 per season. From 1926 to 1931, from ages 31 to 36, when he was presumed to be past his prime after a subpar 1925, he averaged 50 homers, 156 RBIs, 147 runs, and a .354 batting average.

Yet baseball purists might have credited him for the game's salvation for his achievements in only the first couple of seasons following the Black Sox scandal. The full scope of the "throwing" of baseball's Fall Classic weren't felt until the end of the following season, when the stunning suspensions of Shoeless Joe Jackson and other White Sox players became an embarrassing black eye for the game.

Baseball was already a multimillion-dollar business for major league owners, and the scandal caused panic and fears of lost fortunes. As baseball braced for an uncertain 1921 season, the scene was ideal for a rescue of epic proportions. Ruth's second season in New York proved to be even better than his first, quickly solidifying his reputation in helping put scandal aside. As a catchy tune of the time put it, "Along Came Ruth." Even team owners hummed the ditty.

"Inside of a fortnight the fandom of the nation has forgotten all about the Black Sox, as they had come to be called, as its attention became centered in an even greater demonstration of superlative batting skill by the amazing Babe Ruth," the *New York Times* reported. "Home runs began to scale off his bat in droves, crowds jammed ballparks in every city in which he appeared, and when he closed the season with a total of fifty-nine circuit clouts, surpassing by five his own record of the year before, the baseball world lay at his feet."

Yet the legend of Babe Ruth, the slugger who saved baseball, might never have reached that had it not been for the decision years earlier made by one Ed Barrow. Barrow's name would become linked with the front office management of the great

Yankee teams of the 1920s, but it was what he did while with the Boston Red Sox that had its signature in Babe Ruth. A career baseball man, Barrow was already 50 when he became manager of the Red Sox in 1918. By then, Boston had lost many of its top players during World War I. Barrow convinced team owner Harry Frazee to buy a handful of stars from the Philadelphia Athletics. Barrow had also concluded that Babe might be more valuable as an everyday position player than as a pitcher. It was not an easy decision to make. As a pitcher, Ruth had been 18–8 in 1915 and 23–12 in 1916, leading the league with a 1.75 earned run average and nine shutouts. He won a World Series game to lead the Red Sox to that year's championship, including a 14-inning performance that remains the longest postseason complete-game victory. Ruth was arguably the best pitcher in the game. But Ruth's hitting was also difficult to ignore. especially since the crowds were also larger when Babe played.

While Barrow would be credited for his "vision" in turning Ruth into an everyday player whose prolific home run power would change the game, it idea may not have been his idea alone. Harry Hooper, the Hall of Fame right fielder on four separate Red Sox teams that won World Series titles, was instrumental in talking Barrow into converting Babe Ruth from a pitcher to an outfielder. "I was the team captain by then," he told Lawrence Ritter for the baseball history *The Glory of Their Times*. "I ran the team on the field, and I finally talked Ed into converting Ruth from a pitcher into an outfielder."

Hooper was a rarity for his time. He was a college graduate with an appreciation of both baseball management and finance. Hooper "reminded Barrow that his sixty-thousand-dollar investment in the [Red Sox] was only as sound as Boston's ability to draw fans to the park," Paul J. Zingg wrote in *Harry Hooper: An American Baseball Life*. "Why not give them one of the game's top gate attractions on a more regular basis?" In a 1973 interview, Hooper recalled that "Babe wanted to play every day. Barrow said he would be the laughing stock of baseball if he put the best left-handed pitcher in the league in the outfield. I told him that the crowds were turning out to see the Babe hit, not pitch."

It was only the beginning of the Babe Ruth mania of which Harry Hooper would have an early front-row seat, as he would say in another interview. "Sometimes I still can't believe what I saw," he said. "This 19-year-old kid, crude, poorly educated, only lightly brushed by the social veneer we call civilization, gradually transformed into the idol of American youth and the symbol of baseball the world over—a man loved by more people and with an intensity of feeling that perhaps has never been equaled before or since."

On May 6, 1918, Babe Ruth appeared on a major league starting lineup in a position other than pitcher, starting at first base for the injured Dick Hoblitzell, who was often assigned to room with Babe when the team traveled. Ruth ushered in the change by hitting a home run, and followed that with another round-tripper the next day. The only problem was that Babe's defensive play was a work in progress. Ruth wanted to remain at first base, but Barrow had doubts about him being able to handle the position's demands, especially should he fall into a slump. Barrow had even predicted that when that did happen, Ruth "would be down on his knees begging me to pitch." So Barrow made Hooper responsible for turning Babe into an outfielder and got immediate results. A month into the experiment, Ruth was leading the league in batting at over .400, half his hits going for extra bases. In 1919, Babe would hit a record-breaking 29 home runs while driving in an equally un-heard-of 113 runs.

But that is only part of the story. The making of Babe Ruth, the home run hitter, had brought with it the explosion of a gargantuan personality that would have been intolerable if not for his God-given ability to slug a baseball out of the park like no one else.

For its part, Boston's management was complicit in failing to adequately discipline Babe in a way that would have made an impression on its problem child. The reason, of course, was that Ruth was too valuable as a left-handed pitcher for those outstanding Red Sox teams of the mid-1910s. "He didn't drink when he came to Boston," recalled Hooper, "and I don't think he'd ever been with a woman. Once he found out about [drinking and women], he became a bear."

Ruth's outlandish behavior—and his getting away with it—particularly upset Chick Shorten, a veteran outfielder for the Red Sox who also happened to be the unfortunate player that Babe displaced. "You'd see Babe only at game time," Shorten later said. "As soon as it was over, he'd take off for a party and have more fun. It never seemed to affect his ability and there was a saying among the Sox that, 'He does everything right on the field and everything wrong off it.'"

In 1917, while pitching, Ruth physically threatened an umpire who had called four straight balls in favor of the game's leadoff hitter. Babe stormed off the mound and yelled at the home plate umpire Clarence "Brick" Owens: "If you'd go to bed at night... you could keep your eyes open long enough in the daytime to see when a ball goes over the plate." When Owens warned that he would toss him from the game if he persisted, Ruth bellowed out, "You run me out and I will come in and bust you on the nose!" Babe was ejected, and as the *Boston Globe* reported, "Then in rushed Ruth. [Red Sox catcher] Chester Thomas tried to prevent him from reaching Owens, who had not removed his mask, but Babe started swinging both hands. The left missed the arbiter, but the right struck him behind the left ear, knocking down the umpire. Manager Barry and several policemen had to drag Ruth off the field. All season Babe has been fussing a lot. Nothing has seemed to satisfy him."

Ruth's only punishment was a 10-day suspension, a $100 fine, and an apology he had to make to the umpire. As for the Red Sox in that game at Fenway Park, they would get an extraordinary relief effort from Ernie Shore, who at 6'4" and 220 pounds was one of the most physically imposing pitchers of the era. Before Shore even retired a batter, he was presented a gift. Senators base runner Ray Morgan, the leadoff hitter Ruth had walked, was thrown out trying to steal second base by catcher Sam Agnew. The backup, Agnew had replaced starter Chester Thomas, who was ejected along with Ruth. With the walk that started the fracas wiped off the bases, Shore settled in to what essentially became an emergency start. He retired the next 26 Senators in a 4–0 Red Sox triumph to record with Babe the first combined no-hitter in major league history, and almost a perfect game. (At the time, it was ruled to be a "perfect game" because Shore had been on the mound for all 27 outs. But in the 1990s, Major League Baseball downgraded the pitching performance to simply a combined no-hitter.)

Ruth's behavior, in fact, was one of the reasons the Red Sox turned to Barrow to manage the team in 1918 and inject his brand of discipline. "We called him Simon Legree [after the cruel slave master in Harriet Beecher Stowe's *Uncle Tom's Cabin*]," said Harry Hooper. "He was a strong disciplinarian and merciless with people who didn't produce."

Barrow even went so far as to hire former minor league player Heinie Wagner as a Red Sox coach whose only duty was to babysit Babe, though from time to time Ruth was able to entice his chaperone to join him drinking and carousing. Babe was simply uncontrollable. Wagner did protect Barrow when the manager and his star slugger almost came to blows in the dugout one day. "The whole fuss was started over a play in the field," Ruth explained to reporters. "I hit at the first ball and [Barrows] said something about it being a bum play. Then we had words, and I thought he called me a bum, and I threatened to punch him. He told me it would cost me $500, and then I made a few more remarks and left the club." Perhaps Ruth should have left it there, but he further infuriated Barrow by bragging to the *New York Herald*, "I got mad as a March hare and told Barrow then and there that I was through with him and his team. I knew I was too mad to control myself, but suiting the action to the word, I did leave the team and came home."

Barrow was livid, and Red Sox players wasted little time in siding with the manager. They also were furious that team owner Harry Frazee had just rewarded Babe with a big midseason bonus and promised him another $1,000 if the Red Sox won the American League pennant. As the *Boston Post* reported, "Not a single player on the team is in sympathy with him and the Red Sox first and last are disgusted with the actions of a man whom they say has his head inflated with too much advertising and his effectiveness impaired by altogether too much babying."

Ruth responded by temporarily reining in his behavior. Like most of Babe's attempts to change his ways, it didn't last long. He was the Babe, and it seemed as if baseball needed him as much, if not more, than he needed the game himself. There was also the threat of war looming over America, making times and the future uncertain for all businesses.

The impact of the war is sometimes overlooked in context of the time leading up to the Black Sox Scandal. During the tumultuous summer of 1918, the Great War raged in Europe. It cast an ominous shadow over the game, as it did throughout America; enlistments and the draft wreaked havoc with the roster of every team. Baseball club owners shut down most of their farm team operations in 1917 but continued with their full major league schedule for 1917 as just a handful of players were immediately drafted into the military. However, in 1918 the major leagues lost an average of 15 men from each team to either the draft or enlistment, opening the rosters to many rookies and inexperienced players. The New York Giants were virtually eliminated from any realistic shot at the National League pennant race while the Chicago Cubs were made contenders, all because the war ravaged the pitching staff of the former while leaving it relatively intact for the latter.

Although some players were accused of getting preferential treatment by the military, clearly there were those who paid a dear price. Tragically, the war would cost major league teams the lives of five men who died in battle, among them

Harvard-educated veteran infielder Eddie Grant, who had retired in 1915 to open a law practice in Boston. Grant was one
of the first men to enlist when the United States entered the war
in April 1917, and he became the first Major League Baseball
player killed in action. On the front lines in France, the great
pitcher Grover Cleveland Alexander was exposed to German
mustard gas and sustained traumatic injuries from a shell that
exploded near him. It caused partial hearing loss and triggered
the onset of epilepsy. After the war, the man who had once
been the game's best pitcher suffered from shell shock and was
plagued with epileptic seizures that only exacerbated a drinking problem. Christy Mathewson, who had won 94 games over
his previous three seasons before the war, was also exposed to
poison gas in a defense drill and was never the same. His health
deteriorated, and he died of tuberculosis in 1925 at the age of
45. Ruth registered for the World War I draft but was never se-
lected. As a married man, he was also given a deferment. (Babe
had been married to Helen Woodford since the end of the 1914
season.) In the WWI draft, you could avoid being drafted by
working in an essential industry; the most famous baseball
player to do this was Joe Jackson.

As the war continued in Europe, players and owners in
America engaged in bitter fights over contracts and revenue, for
the previous years had made the national pastime big business.
So much so that major league ballparks had become magnets
for gamblers. Many players felt that they were underpaid and
shortchanged by the owners, and the conditions were ideal for
anyone bold enough to buy off players to fix any ballgame, even
a World Series. Most ballplayers, after all, were getting paid nowhere what Ruth was already earning in salary and bonuses.

But Ruth was showing his value in 1918, a season shortened because of the war from 154 games to 140. Boston rebounded from its previous year's disappointment with a banner season, even with Ruth being the only Red Sox hitter with a batting average over .300. He led the league with 11 home runs, the first of his home run titles, though he actually hit 13 out of the park. Baseball's arcane rules at the time dictated that when a game was decided in extra innings, only the winning run would be counted. That season, Babe won two extra-inning games with what years later would be considered walk-off homers. Under the rules, he was credited with game-winning RBI triples by the official scorers.

The war brewing between owners and players was fomenting, and even threatened the 1918 World Series between the Red Sox and Chicago Cubs. Had the owners shortchanged the Red Sox and Cubs? It was easy to see how players on both teams felt that way. In the past, the profits from the World Series had gone to only the two teams playing for the championship. However, the game's national commission, the governing body of organized baseball, had changed the rules so that each league's second, third, and fourth place teams would also share in the World Series revenues. The Red Sox and Cubs players learned of the change at the 11th hour, when they were told that their shares for either winning or losing would be significantly less than what they imagined. Owners were preparing to slash the revenues paid to players while holding the line on ticket prices and also increasing gate receipts, especially when the Cubs' home games were moved to the much larger Comiskey Park. The payout to players in the 1918 World Series would be the lowest ever: $1,102 for each winner's share, $671 for each loser. Players were so outraged that both teams refused to take the field, and the Series was almost called off.

Only an appeal from American League president Ban Johnson, who reminded the players that Americans were dying in Europe, got players to drop their threatened boycott. Players also knew there had been talk that this could be their last baseball paycheck for a while. If the war continued into 1919, according to rumors at the time, owners might have to scuttle the major league schedule for the coming season as they had for the minors.

Ruth didn't need reminding that one of his oldest friends on the Red Sox wasn't playing in this World Series. Ernie Shore, the pitcher who hurled the no-hitter when Babe had been kicked out of the game in 1917 for attacking the home plate umpire, missed the Red Sox's 1918 world championship season because he had enlisted. Shore had known Ruth since their minor league days, when both of them pitched in Baltimore. Shore was the better pitcher at the time and the player the Red Sox wanted most when they made the deal to get both of them. Of course, Ruth quickly changed the pecking order once the two got to Boston. Babe compiled an 18–8 record in 1915, followed by two 20-plus-game-winning seasons—23–12 in 1916 and 24–13 in 1917. The Red Sox fell short of winning the pennant in 1917 but were world champions the next season, when Babe pitched and won two games against the Chicago Cubs, and also extended his World Series record to 29.2 scoreless innings. As it turned out, the 1918 series would be Ruth's last hurrah as a pitcher. That season would also be the Red Sox's last world championship until 2004, when they broke the infamous

Curse of the Bambino, the supposed jinx on the team for selling Ruth to the Yankees.

Ernie Shore also went to the Yankees in that sale, though he was all but forgotten in the newspaper accounts, which focused their attention on Babe. To his credit, Shore was no slouch. He had his best season in 1915, when he won 19, lost eight, and compiled a 1.64 earned run average. He also had a 3–1 record in World Series action in 1915 and 1916.

Shore, though, was never again the same pitcher he was before the war, leaving the game with no regrets, nor bitterness toward Ruth. "Hell, I roomed with him in 1920 when we were both with the Yankees," Shore later said. "I was the only one he would listen to. He was the best-hearted fellow who ever lived. He'd give you the shirt off his back."

10   The Eastern Babe

*"We won the Series in 1926, and I sometimes wonder
if the only reason is that Gehrig didn't get to bat in the ninth inning."*
—Rogers Hornsby, St. Louis Cardinals player/manager

IN THE YEARS AHEAD, NO PLAYER BETTER UNDERSTOOD BABE RUTH'S
place in the game than Lou Gehrig, his fellow slugger, with
whom he formed the marrow of their Murderers' Row Yankee
teams. Ruth, of course, was already his larger-than-life self as
player and celebrity when Gehrig became a starter in 1925.
So it was natural that Lou held back and often deferred to the
Babe. "At first the two dissimilar men formed a mutual admiration society, despite the fact that Ruth was an outrageously
undisciplined man in every facet of his life except home-run
hitting, while the modest, insecure Gehrig was never much
taken with flamboyance or empty boasting," wrote biographer
Ray Robinson, author of *Iron Horse: Lou Gehrig in His Time.*
"Ruth and Gehrig should have grown closer with the passing
years. Instead, they pulled apart, their sharp differences of personality and character souring their relationship."

It did not start out that way. From afar, while a student
and player at Columbia, Gehrig had looked up to Ruth—an

admiration that had caused him to be awestruck in Babe's presence when he met him at Yankee Stadium in 1923, which continued for the next few years. As far back as his early days at Commerce High School, Lou had relished the comparisons sometimes made of him to Ruth, who was then a member of the Boston Red Sox as both a pitcher and hitter. It had been Gehrig's ninth-inning grand slam in a 1920 intercity game at Chicago's Wrigley Field that led some sportswriters to liken him to Babe. And though his last name was misspelled in one newspaper account, Gehrig didn't seem to mind. The feat brought him to the attention of the athletics department at Columbia, which encouraged him to enroll. It was the beginning of the nickname that, uncomfortable as it was for young Gehrig, would stick with him for a while: Columbia Lou. Later, a few sportswriters tried giving Lou the nickname "Buster," But that didn't stick either. Some had overheard Babe calling him that during his tryout in 1923, though Ruth had used it only because, as usual, he had forgotten Lou's name as quickly as he had been introduced.

Gehrig, as a newly signed rookie, was hardly on anyone's mind. After signing his contract, Lou spent the rest of 1923 playing for the Yankees' farm team, the Hartford Senators of the Class A Eastern League. He was barely 20. But quickly made an impression with the team's front office, which in 1924 promoted him to start the season with the Yankees. It was a decision they may have been too hasty in making. For all his promise, Gehrig was destined to spend much of the season riding the bench, being primarily employed as a pinch hitter. Veteran Wally Pipp, after all, was still the team's starting first baseman. Ideally, Yankee front office executives concluded,

Lou should be sent back to the minors for more seasoning and regular playing time. But they realized that they had created a problem for themselves in having Gehrig start the season in New York. To move a player from a major league roster back to the minors required a player to clear waivers, meaning that every other team would have to waive its right to claim Gehrig. Ordinarily, there was an unspoken collusion among teams to protect prized prospects. But Gehrig was clearly a phenom and no ordinary prospect, as he had shown at Columbia and in the minors. No fewer than five teams refused to let the Yankees clear waivers with Gehrig. All of them thought they could find a place for Gehrig on their roster, if not in their starting lineup. The Yankees were almost forced to keep Gehrig on the big team's roster before lengthy negotiations with those other five teams finally allowed him to clear waivers.

In the coming months, back in the minors, Gehrig showed all the promise that other clubs had feared. Lou slugged 37 home runs, batted a sizzling .369, and earned yet another nickname: the Eastern Babe—after the Eastern League, whose pitching he tore up that season. If you had read the myth building of Gehrig in the *Hartford Courant,* you would have thought the sportswriters were watching Babe Ruth himself. Various accounts claimed that Gehrig had learned to swing a bat when he was just a toddler, that he shattered windows at his elementary school with his playground home runs, and that he could be better than Ruth. The Bambino indeed! By the end of summer, locked in a pennant race with the Washington Senators, the Yankees called Lou back to the majors. Gehrig signed a contract that would pay him $800 a month from August 30 until the end of the Yankees season, which came when the Detroit

Tigers heartbreakingly defeated them in a crucial series that gave the pennant to the Senators.

Even so, Gehrig's time in Hartford had redeemed his initial experience in 1921. That year, before his freshman year at Columbia, Lou had attended a tryout at the Polo Grounds, where he had hoped to land a professional contract to help his financially strapped parents. In batting practice, Gehrig pounded out six straight home runs, but his fielding was so bad that it had led Giants manager to angrily tell his coaches, "Get this fella outa here! I've got enough lousy players without another one showing up!"

Gehrig then did something he shouldn't have done. He signed on to play the rest of 1921 with the Hartford Senators, while apparently trying to hide his identity to maintain his amateur collegiate standing. Lou played at least a dozen games as a professional under two different assumed names, Lefty Gehrig and Lou Lewis. Did Gehrig know that he was breaking collegiate rules by playing professionally, especially since he was doing so under a false name? Was he that naive? Gehrig defenders have long insisted that he either didn't know, or that the agent who arranged the deal had misled him. Fortunately for Gehrig, the person who discovered the ruse was Columbia baseball coach Andy Coakley, who acted quickly to correct what could have been a horrendous and embarrassing mess. He contacted coaches in the Ivy League and other rival schools, pleading for special dispensation for what he called an "innocent mistake." Eventually Coakley was able to negotiate a deal in which Gehrig wasn't expelled from collegiate competition permanently but only suspended for one year.

Then Gehrig did something curious. He risked his amateur eligibility all over again. In the summers of 1922 and 1923, using another fictitious name, Gehrig played professionally in Morristown, New Jersey, for a baseball team that wasn't affiliated with any major league club and played only on Sundays. "Whether from stubbornness, the need for extra money or love for the game, Gehrig didn't learn his lesson," recalled Morristown native Joe Connor, reminiscing about stories his father had told him. "For parts of the next two years, while still at Columbia, he played for the Morristown town team under the name Lou Long.... While it was widely known locally that Lou Long was really Gehrig from Columbia, no one spilled the beans." That Gehrig played in Morristown was widely known. An old photo of him in a Morristown uniform even hangs in a local bar named Hennessey's. Possibly because the team played only on Sundays, it could have been considered semipro—though he was still being paid. No one is sure whether Columbia failed to find out about the indiscretion or whether they knew and decided to ignore it.

All this was a distant memory by June 2, 1925, when by fate, luck, or the hand of Providence, Gehrig stepped into the first base position that had belonged to Wally Pipp and took possession for a ride into history. That day the Yankees were hosting the defending World Series champs, the Washington Senators, in the second game of a four-game series. The Senators had dethroned the three-time defending American League champion Yankees and then beaten the New York Giants in the 1924 World Series. Just days earlier, at a ceremony at the White House, President Calvin Coolidge had bestowed a gold watch on Stanley "Bucky" Harris, the Senators' second baseman, who as a rookie manager had guided Washington to the World Series title.

It seemed as if Bucky Harris' team had discombobulated the Yankees, whose slide into second place in 1924 had continued in the new season. The Yankees were now on a five-game losing skid and only a half-game ahead of the last-place Boston Red Sox. So for this game, Yankees skipper Miller Huggins shook up his lineup, benching several slumping starters. Catcher Wally Schang gave way to rookie Benny Bengough, second baseman Aaron Ward sat down for Howie Shanks, and Pipp was replaced by Gehrig. Babe Ruth, who had missed action in April and May suffering from influenza or stomach problems, was also back in the lineup for the first time in the season. One news account reported that he appeared "slimmer and weaker, his face drawn and his legs so feeble that they could hardly carry him over the ground." Still, Babe's weakened condition aside, in their first game together, Gehrig and Ruth both got hits and led the Yankees to an 8–5 triumph that snapped the team's losing streak. Even so, it would be a miserable year for the Yankees, and at 69–85 (.448) their worst since their seventh-place finish in 1913. It was also the first time the Yankees had finished below .500 since 1918.

Gehrig's rookie season, though, lived up to his own expectations. At spring training in 1925, the New York pitchers agreed that the youngster "hits the ball as hard as Babe Ruth." That season, Lou hit 20 home runs, drove in a respectable 68 runs, and missed batting .300 by five percentage points—all on a team that was among the worst. In fact, they were all better batting numbers than Babe's, except that Ruth slugged five more homers than Gehrig. Further, it signaled the arrival of Lou Gehrig as a force on the team, if only the Yankees could get past the poisoned season. It would be too easy to blame the debacle of 1925 on Ruth and whatever his ailments may have truly been. Had it been influenza, as was often written? Was it a digestive problem, the famous Ruthian bellyache, as others believed? Could it have been all the fast living, the drinking, the all-night womanizing? Or was Ruth finished as the player he had been in his first years as a Yankee?

After the 1925 season, it was hard to find a sportswriter—or anyone, for that matter—who didn't think Ruth's career over. Babe was now 31 years old—an "old 31," as sports columnist Fred Lieb put it that season. He'd also had a career unlike any other hitter in the game: 356 career home runs, more than 1,000 career RBIs, and a batting average of .345. He likely was already assured of having a spot in the pantheon of baseball's legends. So how could Ruth turn it around? Or could he still? For his first few seasons in New York, manager Miller Huggins' tough discipline on the rest of the team may have had some impact on Ruth. Perhaps the secret was to get to Babe's die-hard Catholic guilt, which had helped in making him want to follow up disappointing seasons with better ones. This would be what ultimately created the Murderers' Row teams, beginning in 1926, when Babe would have been a candidate for Comeback Player of the Year, had that honor existed then. The Yankees indeed regrouped, and it would be 40 years before they would finish below .500 again.

In 1926, Ruth played all but two games and produced 47 home runs while driving in 153 runs and batting .372. In winning their fourth pennant, the Yankees had a 91–63 record. Had it not been for the disappointment of ultimately losing the World

Series against the St. Louis Cardinals, the year would have been considered an extraordinary redemption for both the Yankees and the Babe. As it was, Ruth was having a spectacular Series, mythologized beyond what it already had been by the writers who were following Babe. Before Game 4, Ruth had visited a New Jersey hospital and promised to hit a home run for a sickly boy named Johnny Sylvester. Babe then went out and delivered on the promise by hitting three home runs to carry the Yankees to a 10–5 victory. Suddenly, writers reported, Little Johnny's condition miraculously improved. (Imagine what those journalistic giants would have written about Lazarus.) Baseball historians have disputed Ruth's healing miracle, though it remains one of the most famous anecdotes in baseball history. At that point Babe was already the leading contender to be the Most Valuable Player of the Series. He had hit four home runs, with six walks in 20 at-bats, with a .516 on base percentage. Too bad for Babe and the Yankees that the World Series didn't end with Johnny's healing. Instead, the conclusion came suddenly and far less dramatic—on an embarrassing base-running mistake by Ruth in the bottom of the ninth inning of a one-run Game 7 that would also go down as one of the greatest bonehead blunders in the annals of baseball. Babe had drawn a two-out walk and represented the tying run.

"Of course Bob Meusel was the next hitter. He'd hit over 40 homers that season and would mean trouble," the Cardinals' Grover Cleveland Alexander recalled. He had won two games in the series, including Game 6, and had come in to relieve in the seventh inning of the finale. "If Meusel got hold of one, it could mean two runs and the series, so I forgot all about Ruth and got ready to work on Meusel. I'll never know why the guy did it, but on my first pitch to Meusel, the Babe broke for second. He probably figured that it would catch us by surprise. I caught the blur of Ruth starting for second as I pitched, and then came the whistle of the ball as [Cardinals catcher Bob] O'Farrell rifled it to second. I wheeled around, and there was one of the grandest sights of my life. Hornsby, his foot anchored on the bag and his gloved hand outstretched, was waiting for Ruth to come in. There was the Series."

Years later, talking to former radio reporter Johnny Grant in Hollywood, Ruth offered a previously untold explanation of why he tried to steal second base and why he had never spoken about it. Ruth's story told another side of the man, a compassionate side not often seen. It had to do with Alexander, a pitcher whose great career had been shortened by the injuries in World War I that exacerbated his epilepsy and worsened his drinking problem. In June 1926, when the Chicago Cubs had given up on Alexander, the Cardinals had grabbed him off waivers, hoping he had some pitching life still left in him. As it turned out, he did—and he helped get St. Louis into the World Series, even if he hadn't beaten his alcoholism. Then in the World Series, Alexander shut down the Yankees in Game 2 6–2—retiring the last 21 batters he faced. In Game 6, Alexander had saved the Cardinals from elimination by cooling off the Yankees and beating them 10–2. Naturally, he had gone on a celebratory drinking binge and shown up for Game 7 not seriously expecting to pitch. But in the seventh inning the Yankees loaded the bases, and Cardinals starting pitcher Jesse Haines developed a blister on a finger of his pitching hand. The dire situation led to St. Louis manager Roger Hornsby to gamble once more on the 39-year-old Nebraskan who had been born in the first term of President Grover Cleveland. The bet paid off. Alexander responded by getting the Cardinals out of the bases-loaded jam, retiring the Yankees in order in the eighth inning and getting two outs in the ninth before giving up a full-count walk to Ruth.

"Babe told me that 'Big Pete'—that's what he called Alexander 'Big Pete'—was on his last leg and barely holding on," Grant later said in an interview. "He said, 'Big Pete came into the game with the bases loaded, so he pitched from a full windup to get out of trouble in the seventh and pitched from a full windup again in the eighth and the ninth until I got on base. And so he was having to pitch from the stretch for the first time all afternoon, and in his condition, well, I'd been there. And from the stretch, Big Pete is going to take an awful long time delivering the pitch to the plate, so I figured I could get a good jump on him. And you figure, three things can happen if I break for second, and two of those things are good for us. I get a good jump and I steal second. Or I get a good jump and, especially hungover as he is, he's so surprised that he breaks from the stretch and balks, which also puts me on second. I just never thought he would hold it all together and make a pitch quick enough for his catcher to make a perfect throw. But that's what it was. On that day Big Pete was perfect.'

"Babe said he'd never talked about that play like that before because he just wasn't going to show up Big Pete Alexander by talking about how he was thinking he could capitalize on his condition. As he said, 'Big Pete showed he was in good enough condition to beat us.'"

Lou Gehrig was on deck when that World Series ended. Disappointed, he took away a big lesson about the inevitability of humility in the game and that no matter how great a ball-player you are, you will still make mistakes when you least expect to. "In the beginning I used to make one terrible play a game," he would later say. "Then I got so I'd make one a week and finally I'd pull a bad one about once a month. Now I'm trying to keep it down to one a season."

11   The Making of Gehrig
and Ruth

"It's a pretty big shadow. It gives me lots of room to spread myself."

—Lou Gehrig

BABE RUTH'S GREATEST SEASON, AND ARGUABLY LOU GEHRIG'S as well, didn't begin well. On January 22, 1927, weeks before the start of spring training, Ruth was arrested in Long Beach, California. It was a bullshit arrest. There is no other way to describe it. Regardless of having blown the Yankees chance of winning the World Series just months earlier, Ruth was still the most famous man in America. And in California, an ambitious politician was trying to make a name for himself by charging Babe with violating child labor laws. He might have had a better chance of accusing Ruth of violating underage women because Babe spent each night in Hollywood having sex with a string of young gorgeous women, some of whom at least looked young enough to make one wonder about how old they were. Babe was known for indulging all his excesses, including sex, particularly while traveling, and this was the consummate road trip. Ruth was in Southern California preparing to star in a Hollywood baseball movie, *The Babe Comes Home*, about a famous home-run hitter who played for the then–minor league Los Angeles Angels.

Since his days with the Red Sox, Ruth often spent several weeks and sometimes months in Los Angeles during the off-season. He played golf several times a week and often spent time signing autographs at restaurants. It wasn't long before Babe was lured into stage shows built around his personality that packed theaters wherever he performed. Since November, he had been on a 12-week Pantages Circuit single-act vaudeville tour that concluded in late January in Southern California. "Ruth has good stage presence, a winning smile, and he gets away with the singing part," a *New York Times* review reported. Babe was earning $8,333 per week during the full run of the show, making in a week more than what all but a few baseball players were paid for an entire season. For that matter, no one could remember a performer of that day ever making that kind of money—not W.C. Fields, not Al Jolson, not even Fanny Brice. But then, perhaps Babe Ruth had had more practice, in front of much larger audiences during the span of his career to that point. Baseball, after all, was the country's biggest form of entertainment. And Ruth's natural showmanship was exactly what had been packing stadiums.

It made sense that a showman with a gargantuan ego would find success in a vaudeville revue in which he could engage with audiences the way he had with baseball fans, exchanging light banter and laughs, kissing babies, hugging grandmothers, and shaking grown men's hands. Babe Ruth up close and personal. Babe loved the adulation—no, he needed it. He reveled in it. Ruth's shows included a variety of skits and songs and ended with him inviting kids up on stage, where he offered them tips on hitting and playing baseball and finished by giving each one an autographed baseball as a souvenir. In Long Beach, where he was set to appear in three shows at the old State Theater, an arrest warrant had been issued. The official who filed the charge was Stanley M. Gue, the deputy State Labor Commissioner. Ruth's crime, according to this state labor official, was that he had allowed a child actress onstage without first obtaining work permits for her. "They forget how much I've done for kids," Ruth told a newspaper reporter when he learned his arrest was imminent. "I've done nothing that would harm them. I've only tried to give them a little bit of sunshine."

State authorities had not only issued a warrant for Babe's arrest but also sent police officers to Long Beach to apprehend him before his scheduled show that day. Ruth was soon on his way to San Diego, where the charges had been filed, to be booked and then allowed to post his $500 bail in cash, counting out 25 crisp $20 bills. A magistrate scheduled a court date for February 11 in San Diego. Three weeks later, a judge acquitted Ruth, ruling, in effect, that the child in question was not a member of the cast for Babe's show and that no labor law had been breached. Babe didn't even have to attend the hearing.

Babe took this passing crisis as a good omen for the 1927 season, for which he had been preparing since the World Series. He had spent part of October barnstorming. At one stop in Montreal, according to a report in the *South Bend Tribune*, Ruth hit so many home runs into a nearby river that the game was called for lack of baseballs. Yes, he would be ready for 1927. Every day, Babe could be seen running three to five miles along Hollywood Boulevard before returning to his room at the Hollywood Plaza Hotel. There Ruth was given a massage and rubdown from Artie McGovern, a New York trainer to the stars whose clients included boxer Jack Dempsey, golfer Gene Sarazen, and composer John Philip Sousa. But it was Ruth, whose 1926 comeback he helped orchestrate, that made McGovern's reputation. The stomach problem that required surgery had left Babe a physical wreck. "Ruth weighed 254 pounds," McGovern said years later. "His blood pressure was low and his pulse was high. He was as near to being a total loss as any patient I have ever had under my care. His stomach had gone back on him completely. His eyes had been affected. The slightest exertion left him short of breath. His muscles were soft and flabby."

Ruth spent the off-season working out under McGovern, losing 44 pounds in six weeks and dramatically improving his health and physical conditioning for 1926. By the end of that year, though, Ruth had once again put on weight. Hoping to have an even better season in 1927, he called on McGovern once more to join him on the road while he completed his vaudeville tour. No comeback, Ruth insisted, was complete unless it included winning the World Series.

As spring training neared, all he needed was a contract. He had already rejected the Yankees' offer to pay him $52,000, the same salary he had earned in 1926. Salary negotiations at the time were far different than they would be later. Multi-year, high-dollar contracts were virtually unheard of. Besides, Ruth disdained any contract that would bind him too long, believing he could best negotiate on a year-to-year basis by producing big results on which to bargain. Yankees owner Jake Ruppert upped the offer to $55,000 in early February, but Babe still refused to budge. He had heard that the aging Ty Cobb, now with the Philadelphia Athletics, was going to be paid $75,000, and he thought he should be paid more. Of course it wasn't true, not anywhere close. Still, Ruth thought he could wait out the Yankees. Could they survive if he chose to sit out the season, or retire altogether? Babe was spoiled into thinking he could continue making his enormous money outside baseball without remaining in it. The touring show had just paid him $100,000 for three months of work. In 1926, he had earned an estimated $200,000 outside baseball from endorsements of cars, milk, and home appliances, as well as income from movies, stage shows, and barnstorming. It all augured well for outside income, but Ruth was smart in his business dealings. He knew people loved him first of all because he was a ballplayer—the greatest ballplayer in the game. When negotiations with the Yankees bogged down and spring training near, Babe accepted the team's offer on the table—$70,000 for the season—and called it a triumph. Ty Cobb hadn't been making the money he was rumored to earn. More important, his new salary was $5,000 more than that of baseball commissioner Kenesaw Mountain Landis. Babe celebrated by signing his new deal at the brewery owned by Yankees owner Jake Ruppert, who loved the publicity of Ruth's annual contract negotiations. "You can say for me that I'll earn every cent of my salary," Babe told reporters who had gathered outside Ruppert's office. "There'll be no more monkey business from me."

On the contrary, Babe's contract signing became the final linchpin in the 1927 team. The Yankees had been forced into negotiations with most of their other starters, including pitcher Herb Pennock. He received a three-year deal worth $60,000 that made him the second highest-paid Yankee at the time. Meanwhile, Gehrig proved to Yankee management that he would be the consummate team player, especially when it came to money. When he received his contract from the Yankees, offering him $8,000 for the upcoming season, he signed it without questions or hesitation and mailed it back.

And if the Yankees had any continuing doubts about Lou—there had been reports they were thinking of trading him—they would be gone soon after the season began. The Yankees started with a six-game winning streak, including a season-opening sweep of the Philadelphia Athletics, who had been picked by most of the writers to win the American League. And although this was still Babe's Yankees team, it quickly became evident that someone else was the early-season difference. "[Manager Miller] Huggins knew what he was doing when he benched the veteran Wally Pipp in favor of the former Columbia University player," reported Joe Vila of the *New York Sun*. "Gehrig today is first class in his position. He is faster on his feet and thinks quickly. As a hitter, he ought to lead all of the first basemen in the American League." Arthur Mann of the *New York Evening World* took the praise of Gehrig even higher, writing: "This giant of a youth is heading fast for a prominent place among baseball's great players. No one on the team has more chance of playing all 154 games than Gehrig."

And yet the season was only two weeks old. It would be only another month before the Age of Ruth and Gehrig would be officially christened. "Babe Ruth and Buster Gehrig, the home run twins of the Yankees, put on their specialty act this afternoon." the *New York Times*, America's newspaper of record, announced on May 24.

The silly Buster moniker wouldn't last long, as Gehrig quickly gained a widespread respect among the writers that few other players had ever earned. Years later, reminiscing about Lou, Babe would tell Hollywood personality Johnny Grant that by midseason in 1927 he found himself answering as many questions about Gehrig he did as about himself. "It got to be like having a brother I was having to answer for," he said. "Whadaya think of the ball Lou hit? Does it make it easier on you having Lou hit behind you? Are ya seeing better pitches because they know they have to face Lou after you?"

Soon, Ruth sensed the Yankees weren't just celebrating their 25th season but that it was a special team, a feeling that was shared by players, fans, and writers. This was also the first year the Yankees sported the team name on their uniforms, albeit only on their grey road uniforms. (Their home uniforms were pinstriped but without any logo on them.) Soon the Yankees were the talk of the country, as Ruth and Gehrig were enjoying unprecedented seasons. Ruth was chasing his own home run record of 59, which he had established in 1921, and no one was more surprised than Babe himself. "I don't suppose I'll ever break that 1921 record," he told writers early in the season. 'To do that, you've got to start early, and the pitchers have got to pitch to you. I don't start early, and the pitchers haven't really pitched to me in four seasons. I get more bad balls to hit than any other five men... and fewer good ones."

Of course, early that season, Babe hadn't counted on Gehrig having his own marvelous year and, by batting immediately behind Ruth, pitchers weren't anxious to walk Ruth. "Pitchers began pitching to me because if they passed me they still had Lou to contend with," Babe said, looking back to 1927. Then, as the season wore on, Lou continued his remarkable hitting. He, too, was challenging the home run record, and some papers, such as the *New York World-Telegram* went so far as to anoint Gehrig the favorite. "The most astonishing thing that has ever happened in organized baseball is the home run race between George Herman Ruth and Henry Louis Gehrig," observed writer Paul Gallico, who became obsessed by the competition to break the home run record.

> Gehrig, of course, cannot approach Ruth as a showman and an eccentric, but there is still time for that. Lou is only a kid. Wait until he develops a little more and runs up against the temptations that beset a popular hero. Ruth without temptations might be a pretty ordinary fellow. Part of his charm lies in the manner with which he succumbs to every temptation which comes his way. That doesn't mean Henry Louis must take up sin to become a box-office attraction. Rather one waits to see his reactions to life, which same reactions make a man interesting or not. Right now he seems devoted to fishing, devouring pickled eels, and hitting home runs, of which three things the last alone is of interest to the baseball public. For this reason it is a little more difficult to write about Henry Louis than George Herman. Ruth is either planning to cut loose, is cutting loose, or is repenting the last time he cut loose. He is a news story on legs going about looking for a place to happen. He has not lived a model life, while Henry Louis has,

and if Ruth wins the home run race it will come as a great blow to the pure.

September would ultimately turn the homer record race in Ruth's favor. On September 5, the battle was tied at 44 home runs apiece with 23 games remaining in the season. A new record seemed out of reach. But the next day Babe hit three homers in a doubleheader and then two more the following day, putting him at 49. At the same time, Gehrig slipped into a slump. He would bat a disappointing .275 with only two home runs and 14 RBIs in the last 22 games of the season. Had the long season and mounting pressure gotten to young Lou? It seemed like a reasonable conclusion, though writer Fred Lieb reported that Gehrig's focus been had been stolen by his mother's failing health. Christina Gehrig had developed an inflammation of the thyroid and needed surgery. "I'm so worried about mom," Lou told Lieb, "that I can't see straight."

Babe, meanwhile, slugged an astounding 17 home runs in September. On September 29, Ruth tied his own single-season record of 59 with two home runs. The next day, with one on and one out in the eighth inning of a tie game at Yankee Stadium, Babe broke the record off Washington southpaw Tom Zachary. Only an estimated 8,000 fans were in attendance to witness the momentous at-bat, which the *New York Times* reported for history: "The first Zachary offering was a fast one, which sailed over for a called strike. The next was high. The Babe took a vicious swing at the third pitched ball and the bat connected with a crash that was audible in all parts of the stand. It was not necessary to follow the course of the ball. The boys in the bleachers indicated the route of the record homer. It dropped about halfway to the top.... While the crowd cheered and the Yankee players roared their greetings, the Babe made his triumphant, almost regal tour of the paths. He jogged around slowly, touched each bag firmly and carefully, and when he imbedded his spikes in the rubber disk to record officially, Homer 60... hats were tossed into the air, papers were torn up and tossed liberally, and the spirit of celebration permeated the place."

That home run would be only his 28th hit at home that season, dismissing critics who claimed his record had been padded at Yankee Stadium's short right-field porch. It was his third homer of the season off Zachary, who had joined the Senators in a midseason trade from the St. Louis Browns. "We all knew he was going for a record," Zachary would say years later. "And the first time he came at bat I yelled at him he'd better start swinging at everything because he wasn't going to get a good pitch all day. I cussed at him and he cussed me back. There's a ballgame that has to be won and I don't want to walk him if I can help it. I threw him the best pitch I had, with the most on it. Well, it was a big wallop. It went up and out but close to the line. As soon as I saw it, I started hollering 'foul'—it was too late to do anything else. I've been wishing ever since I'd stuck that pitch in his ear."

In a letter written in 1965, Zachary revealed some still-brewing anger at giving up the home run. "I threw him a curve, but I made a bad mistake," he wrote. "I should have thrown a fast one at his big fat head. Lost game, 4–2. It was a tremendous swat down right field foul line. At that time there were just bleacher seats in right field with foul pole. But since [at first] it went so and far up in bleachers that it would be difficult to judge it accurately. I hollered "foul ball" but I got no support, very little from my team mostly so it must have been a fair ball—but I always contended to Ruth that it was foul."

The next season, Zachary became Ruth's teammate when he was traded to the Yankees, for whom he compiled a perfect 12–0 record in 1929. Zachary, though, continued to insist that Babe's historic home run deserved an asterisk. "I used to tell Ruth that it was a foul ball," he said in a 1961 interview, "and he always insisted that it was fair." Zachary saw the Babe one final time, when he was invited to the farewell ceremony at Yankee Stadium in 1948 honoring Ruth, who was dying of throat cancer. "The Babe came up to me afterwards, so hoarse he could hardly talk, and said, 'You left-handed SOB, you still think that was a foul ball?'" Perhaps because of the moment at the time, Zachary told Ruth the ball hadn't been foul. "But close, I reckon." Then in 1961, when the Yankees' Roger Maris broke Ruth's home run record, Zachary appeared on *The Ed Sullivan Show*, on which he again insisted that that the Babe's 60th homer had sailed foul. Zachary, who had a solid career, winning 186 games in 19 seasons, died in 1969 at the age of 72.

For Ruth, this was the 416th home run of his 714 career total. Forty-year-old Joe Forner, a truck driver from the Bronx, corralled Ruth's home run ball in the right-field bleachers. After the game, he was introduced to the Babe in the Yankees clubhouse, where he signed, dated it, and noted it was the ball he hit for his 60th home run. The ball eventually came into the possession of hat concessionaire Albert "Truly" Warner, who reportedly paid Forner $100 for it. In 1964, Warner's family donated the baseball to the National Baseball Hall of Fame in Cooperstown, New York.

"Sixty, count 'em, 60!" Ruth boasted as his greatest season came to a close. "Let's see some son of a bitch match that!"

The Yankees finished 19 games ahead of the Philadelphia Athletics, their record of 110–44 breaking the previous American League mark of 105 that had been set by the 1912 Boston Red Sox. Then they swept the Pittsburgh Pirates in the World Series.

Ruth had one of the greatest seasons in the history of the game. In addition to the 60 home runs, his triple slash line read .356/.486/.772/1.258 with an OPS+ of 225 (12.4 WAR), 417 total bases, 165 RBIs, 158 runs scored, 192 hits, and 29 doubles. One of Ruth's homers was an unusual dinger—a memorable one on July 8 in Detroit's Navin Field, later Briggs Stadium and Tiger Stadium. "I hit an inside-the-park home run!" he told his teammates, who cheered and laughed at the sight of the exhausted Babe returning to the dugout. "I beat it out! Can you believe that?"

But as great as Ruth's 1927 season was, he didn't win the American League's Most Valuable Player Award, which didn't really exist as it came to be known in modern-day baseball. The equivalent in the American League at the time was known as the League Award, instituted in 1922 to honor "the baseball player who is of the greatest all-around service to his club." The major drawback to the League Award was a player could not win it more than once in his career. Since Babe had won the award in 1923, he was ineligible, no matter how many home runs he might have hit. (The National League had no such restriction.) As a result, Ruth won only one MVP Award, though it is conceivable that the Babe would have won the MVP in 1920, 1921, 1923, 1925, 1927, 1928, and 1930. (The League Award was

The young Babe Ruth was such an outstanding pitcher for the Boston Red Sox that he might have become the greatest in the game, had his hitting not forced him to become a full-time position player. After going 18-8 in his first full season in 1915, Ruth amassed a 23–12 record in 1916, leading the league with a 1.75 ERA and nine shutouts. He also started and pitched all of Game 2 of the World Series that year, winning 2–1 in 14 innings. Ruth's pitching performance is still the longest postseason complete-game victory. (AP Photo)

Lou Gehrig is all smiles in Yankee pinstripes on June 12, 1923, the day he joined the team after having signed straight out of Columbia a month earlier. Gehrig, still just 19, made his Yankees' debut three days later as a ninth-inning defensive replacement for first baseman Wally Pipp. It would not be the only time that Lou Gehrig replaced Wally Pipp. (AP Photo)

Babe Ruth, about to hit the prime of his career in 1923, changed the fortunes of the New York Yankees. That season the team opened Yankee Stadium, which was christened "The House that Ruth Built." (AP Photo)

Three New York Yankee legends—Tony Lazzeri, Babe Ruth, and Lou Gehrig—pose before a mid-season game in 1927. All three are in the Baseball Hall of Fame. (AP Photo)

They were called "Murderers' Row"—the 1927 Yankees, widely considered one of the best teams in history. They went 110–44 that year, winning the American League pennant by 19 games and sweeping the Pittsburgh Pirates in the World Series. That Yankees team batted .307, slugged .489, scored 975 runs, and outscored their opponents by a record 376 runs. Lou Gehrig and Babe Ruth are, respectively, first and third from the left on the back row. Manager Miller Huggins is at the center, middle row. (AP Photo)

Lou Gehrig's swings and misses were almost as dramatic as his prodigious home runs, as he shows here at the 1932 Yankees spring training camp at St. Petersburg, Florida. (AP Photo)

No sooner had Babe Ruth and Lou Gehrig led the Yankees to the 1927 World Series championship than they were out on the road barnstorming across America with their two exhibition teams, the Bustin' Babes and the Larrupin' Lous, who routinely packed stadiums and ball fields. Ruth and Gehrig regularly barnstormed with their teams, both before and after the regular seasons. (AP Photo)

Lou Gehrig, left, and Babe Ruth prepare for their final season together in 1934, photo-graphed here at the Yankees' spring training camp. Gehrig was in the middle of his historic Iron Horse playing streak and would not miss a game that year, but it would be one of the longest seasons for the Babe. He would have an un-Ruthian farewell season, batting only .288 with 22 home runs and 84 RBIs. (AP Photo)

One of the strangest sights in baseball was seeing the great Babe Ruth, who made the New York Yankees the greatest franchise in the game, in a uniform that was anything but Yankee pinstripes. In 1935, having outlived his usefulness to the Yankees ownership, Ruth left the team—giving up his dream of becoming its manager—to sign with the near-bankrupt Boston Braves. The experiment was a disaster and would mark the end of Ruth's career. This was one of the happier moments of that year, Babe with his former teammate Lou Gehrig, before a spring training game. (AP Photo)

The onetime friendship of Lou Gehrig and Babe Ruth turned chilly in Babe's final years with the Yankees, and their feud simmered and never really healed. What brought them together for this historic photo was the July 4, 1939, game at which the Yankees honored Gehrig, whose games-played streak had just ended. Moments after Gehrig delivered his famous farewell speech, Babe dramatically flung his arms around Lou in one of the most memorable moments in sports history. (AP Photo)

When Lou Gehrig died on June 2, 1941, 17 days before his 38th birthday, he had already won his place among baseball's demigods. Babe Ruth was among the mourners at Christ Episcopal Church in the Bronx. Lou was buried at Kenisco Cemetery in New York, next door to Gate of Heaven Cemetery where Babe Ruth was buried in 1948. (AP Photo)

The original Monument Park in the old Yankee Stadium was in front of the wall in center field where, on April 19, 1949, the monument to Babe Ruth was unveiled, with his widow, Claire, doing the honors. Standing next to Mrs. Ruth is her stepdaughter Dorothy Helen Ruth Pirone, who was the biological daughter of Babe Ruth and his mistress Juanita Jennings. The two monuments with flower wreathes are those of Lou Gehrig and Miller Huggins. (AP Photo)

ultimately dropped, and in 1931 the Baseball Writers Association of America adopted the format the National League used and presented the first modern-day MVP Award after the season.)

In 1927, Gehrig won the League Award, and some argue that he might have been more worthy than Ruth anyway, regardless of the honor's restrictions. Lou himself hit 47 home runs, and no one except Ruth had ever hit as many. Gehrig also beat Ruth in runs batted in, establishing a new record of 173 RBIs in a season. It was an even more incredible accomplishment considering that Lou went to bat 60 times after Babe cleared the bases of runners with a home run. Gehrig also had a higher batting average than Babe, .373 to .356. His triple slash line for 1927: 373/.474/.765/1.240 with an OPS+ of 220 and 11.8 WAR. He had 447 total bases, a league-leading 52 doubles, 18 triples, 47 home runs, 173 RBIs, 218 hits, and scored 149 runs.

Lou Gehrig had more than held his own with Babe Ruth, the American legend—and Lou was still only 24. Until the end of 1927, sportswriters of that day too willingly emphasized that Gehrig seemed content to live comfortably in Ruth's shadow. That storyline would now begin to change, and even Babe acknowledged that Lou was about to break out on his own. Even in the Yankee clubhouse, talking to reporters just half an hour or so after hitting his 60th home run, Ruth pointed to Gehrig at his locker nearby and suggested that there was a new media darling in the making. "Wait till that bozo over there wades into them again," Ruth said, "and they may forget a guy named Ruth ever lived."

12 The Gehrigs and Ruth

"He's the only big egg I have in my basket.
He's the only one of four who lived,
so I want him to have the best."

—Christina Gehrig

IN THE LATE SPRING OF 1928, FEW PEOPLE STROLLING PAST THE four-bedroom house at 9 Meadow Lane, a corner lot atop a gentle slope of grass in New Rochelle, New York, would have guessed that sitting at the dining table on any night were two of the biggest names in America, being personally waited on hand and foot by the home's proud new owner. For Christina Gehrig, a German immigrant who spoke little English, the home symbolized her vision of the American Dream realized by her devoted son. Lou Gehrig, the star first baseman and slugger of the New York Yankees, bought the house for his parents only weeks after his breakthrough 1927 season. The tremendous success of Murderers' Row resulted in the Yankees tripling Lou's salary from $8,000 a year to $25,000. He also had a World Series–winner's share of more than $5,000, and he wasted little time in splurging on mom. He put the house in his mother's name, taking over an existing mortgage of $10,000, according to 1927 records. Gehrig then spent the off-season remodeling the house so that the three of them—Mom, Dad, and Lou—could move in shortly after Christmas. Lou had brass fixtures installed, along with galvanized steel wiring. There was also new clapboard siding, parquet floors, and a screened-in porch added.

"Not a bad joint, is it?" Gehrig was quoted in a story published in the *New York Sun* on January 9, 1928. "Not a new place, but it will be as good as new when I get 'er all dolled up. It was a Christmas gift to my mother."

The new Gehrig house was only 13 miles north of Yankee Stadium, and soon after spring training in 1928 it became Babe Ruth's own second home as well. Babe was already living in Manhattan with Claire and her daughter, and these days allowed him to enjoy some time away with the Gehrigs. In Christina's new formal dining room, Babe spent long evenings with Lou, devouring his mom's homemade bratwurst and schnitzel under exposed wooden beams that reminded Ruth of an authentic German restaurant, especially when several teammates would join them. "Mom Gehrig," he recalled in one interview, "would try to cook enough pigs knuckles for all of us." Christina sometimes would go overboard in catering to Babe. She would prepare a quart of pickled eels to tide over Ruth on doubleheader days. Babe would spend the time between games eating the pickled eels with chocolate ice cream.

Over the course of the Yankees' historic 1927 season, Ruth and Gehrig bonded easily, largely because of their mutual success. Their eight-year difference in age naturally led to Lou assuming a little brother role at first. They had then barnstormed for a few weeks after the season concluded, and later they traveled to spring training together. Ruth quickly found a welcoming presence at the house, just as he had at the previous Gehrig home. It was nothing short of a godsend for someone who had been virtually abandoned by his family as a child. Babe also loved Christina's home cooking. "It was one of the rare tastes of home life I ever had," Ruth said.

Surprisingly, the straitlaced Gehrigs showed a great tolerance for Ruth's lifestyle. Just days after the Yankees swept the Pittsburgh Pirates in the World Series, Lou and Babe were joined by their respective loved ones on an October morning at New York's Penn Station, from where they would depart on a barnstorming tour. There, as they waited for their train, stood Lou with his mother, talking to Babe and the two call girls with whom he had spent the night. As their departure time neared, Ruth paid the call girls, bidding them farewell, while Lou kissed his mom good-bye. Babe then turned and hugged Momma Gehrig, assuring her he would look after Lou and make sure he wrote to her daily.

Christina Gehrig called Ruth "Judge, a corruption of Jidge—itself a version of George, Ruth's given name; it was also how his teammates often referred to him. When Babe gave Christina a Chihuahua, she felt she had the perfect name for the playful new puppy; she called him Judge, too. Babe eventually became closer to the Gehrigs than he had ever been with any other family. Christina loved listening to the stories Babe would tell about places he had gone and people he had met. He was always careful with his language and about leaving out any off-color details of his tales. A typical mom, Christina was especially taken by Ruth's accounts of his visits with his daughter Dorothy, who would turn seven that summer. At the time, Dorothy was living at a parochial school in Wellesley, Massachusetts, under an assumed name.

Christina felt close to Ruth's young daughter and urged him to allow her to visit soon. For him, though, the visits to the Gehrig home allowed him the freedom he needed away from his own home. It was also acceptable to Claire, who had slowly curbed Ruth's wayward behavior. She liked Lou Gehrig's innocent personality and suspected he could quietly be a positive influence on Babe. In her time with him, Claire had slowed Ruth's drinking and eating marathons as well as his extravagant spending, sometimes tipping as much as $100 for a ham sandwich. Claire had also taken over the household finances, limiting Babe to the $50 checks she wrote when he needed pocket money for haircuts and cigars. It was Claire who had insisted on Ruth committing himself to losing weight and getting in better shape the last three off-seasons.

"In a lot of ways, she was rather strong-willed," Claire's daughter Julia wrote of her mother in her memoir, *Babe Ruth: A Daughter's Portrait.* "But she had to be to keep Daddy in tow. And she did it in a way that Daddy didn't mind. If she would say, 'I don't think we should do such and such,' he wouldn't argue. He'd say, 'All right.' I think he felt she was a better manager of the house, social life, and things like that than he was."

To understand just how much Claire was able to change Ruth's lifestyle, one has to especially consider how extremely ravenous Babe's sexual appetite had been in the past. Perhaps to some it says enough that Ruth loved prostitutes and their brothels. It wasn't as if Babe had any difficulty finding women; they usually found him. They were attracted to his fame and to his power—not just his ability to hit home runs but the command he had over other men because of his popularity and stardom. He was more popular than the president, he often boasted, and made more money as well. But Ruth disdained exhibiting the romance and interest required of even a short relationship, especially since he was married.

He also knew that he was a prime target for being shaken down. In 1922, a teenage employee at a Manhattan department store slapped Ruth with a breach-of-promise lawsuit for $50,000. Dolores Dixon, who claimed she was carrying Babe's love child, alleged he had raped her and later promised to marry her. She also claimed they'd met numerous times for liaisons in his car. The case went to trial in 1923, and Babe was vindicated when the young woman withdrew her lawsuit and admitted making up the allegations. In Babe's book, that was a nod for prostitutes. They didn't complicate sex—and that alone was what Babe found most attractive about women. He also wasn't above bragging that many of his sexual conquests were women whom he had paid. He would boast about being a regular at "the House of the Good Shepherd" in St. Louis whenever the Yankees would visit to play the Browns. If you assumed that Ruth, being a Catholic, meant he was going to church, the joke was on you. The House of the Good Shepherd was actually the name of a brothel. In Philadelphia, according to one of Babe's teammates, it was not unusual for him to go through all the girls at one brothel the two consecutive nights the Yankees were in town. At that time, most brothels had a dozen or so women on duty on any given night.

The brothels at least were somewhat safer for Ruth in one sense. Stories abound of a nearly naked Babe being chased through a train by an angry woman brandishing a knife, threatening him when she discovered he was cheating on her. Similar scenes were reported of a half-clothed Ruth running out of a hotel room where a gun-toting, angry husband had discovered him having sex with his wife. Sportswriter Fred Lieb later maintained that Ruth, who was famously well-endowed, had an obsession with his penis and loved to pepper his speech with phallic allusions. "I can knock the penis off any ball that ever was pitched," he would say. Or that an object was "as big as my penis." Lieb claimed that when Ruth got older, he confided that, "The worst of this is that I no longer can see my penis when I stand up."

Of course, this was not the kind of talk Babe used when he visited the Gehrigs. He thought of Christina literally as Mom Gehrig, a surrogate mother. It had its benefits for both. Christina knew that Babe's presence as a regular visitor meant that Lou had all the more reason to stay home, near her. The Gehrigs' new home may also have been just what Lou, Ruth, and the Yankees all needed. This was a crucial crossroads for Murderers' Row, who faced the same challenges that always threaten to derail championship teams from repeating. In 1928, the only major change to the team was the retirement of pitcher Urban Shocker, whose increasing heart illness apparently led him to take his life before the year was over.

The team, though, remained solid. In one stretch early in the season, the Yankees won 34 of 39 games. By July 1, they had a 13½-game lead in the American League standings. Babe Ruth, it seemed, was once again headed to a record-breaking season, having slugged 30 home runs by late June. Then the season got away from the Yankees. By the first week of September, the Philadelphia Athletics had caught the Yankees and taken a half-game lead over the Yankees with a big four-game show-down between them looming. Fortunately, the Yankees could always seem to rely on the magic of playing at the stadium. They won three of four and went on to repeat.

Ruth and Gehrig, however, couldn't repeat their individual success of 1927. How could they? Those were once-in-a-life-time seasons. Still, Babe finished 1928 with an almost off-the-charts stat line: 323/.463/.709 with 54 homers, 380 total bases, 137 walks, a 206 OPS+, and 10.1 rWAR. Gehrig followed his breakout year with these numbers: .374/.467/.648 with a best-in-the-league 47 doubles, 13 triples, 27 homers, 364 total bases, a 193 OPS+, and 9.4 rWAR, second only to Ruth.

The Yankees had struggled with injuries during the second half of the season, which may have been why the National League–champion St. Louis Cardinals were favored in the World Series. The most serious setback was a problem that forced second baseman Tony Lazzeri out of the lineup and led to the acquisition of the feisty Leo Durocher, whom Ruth never liked. Could the Cardinals repeat their mastery of the Yankees from the 1926 series, especially since Murderers' Row had struggled so much just to get there? Ruth had fallen into a horrible slump in the final three weeks, though he kept his head high. As historian Lee Allen described him at the time, he was: "a large man in a camel's-hair coat and camel's-hair cap, stand-ing in front of a hotel, his broad nostrils sniffing at the prom-ise of the night." When the Yankees clinched the pennant in Detroit, Babe demanded a piano for their riotous celebration only to be told the hotel didn't have one. So Ruth bought one and had it delivered.

The 1928 World Series would become one of the greatest showcases in baseball's Babe Ruth–Lou Gehrig era. It began innocently enough in the first inning of Game 1, when Ruth and Gehrig hit back-to-back doubles, leading the Yankees to a 4–1 triumph at Yankee Stadium. In Game 2, Gehrig again struck in the first inning with a three-run blast off 1926 Series hero Grover Cleveland Alexander, who failed to make it past the third inning. In Game 3 at Sportsman's Park in St. Louis, Gehrig smashed two more home runs in a 7–3 Yankees victory. In Game 4, Ruth hit an early home run off St. Louis starter Bill Sherdel—a 21-game winner during the regular season— who nevertheless carried a 2–1 lead into the seventh inning as the Cardinals tried avoid a sweep. But then the tide turned— on a quick pitch, of all things. Sherdel tried to catch Babe off guard by quick-pitching him. He threw a strike, but apparently didn't realize the World Series rules. Quick pitches were allowed in the National League but not the American, and they had been outlawed for the World Series. So when the umpire declared the apparent strike on Babe to have been a non-pitch, Sherdel and the Cardinals bench exploded in protest. Ruth remained patiently at home plate, watching the argument with a wide grin on his face. Once the storm subsided, Ruth settled matters by slugging another home run off Sherdel. Gehrig then followed with his own home run, his fourth of the series. In the next inning, facing Alexander, who had relieved Sherdel, Ruth slammed his third homer of the game, the second time he had done it in World Series competition, both times against the Cardinals.

In repeating as champs, the Yankees became the first team ever to sweep consecutive World Series. Ruth and Gehrig combined for a whopping .593 batting average (16-for-27), with seven home runs. They also scored 14 runs and knocked in 13. They carried the Yankees; the other New York hitters collectively batted just .187. Ruth and Gehrig's numbers for the four-game sweep:

Lou Gehrig: .545/.706/1.727, 6-for–11, 2B, 4 HR, 6 BB, 2.433 OPS

Babe Ruth: .625/.647/1.375, 10-for–16, 3 2B. 3 HR, BB, 2.022 OPS

Ruth topped off the pennant-clinching celebration by ordering four bushels of spare ribs, side dishes, and plenty of booze for the train ride from St. Louis to New York. Fans joined the celebration along the route. Every time the train passed through a small town, hundreds if not thousands showed up and cheered Babe and the Yankees. Ruth stood at the back of the train at each appearance, as if this were a political campaign and he were running for president.

Later that October, Ruth celebrated by dressing as a cowboy and riding a jeep decorated to look like a steer. Another cowboy, Gehrig, was alongside the jeep.

13   The Bottom Falls Out

"Heroes get remembered, but legends never die."

—Babe Ruth

UNTIL 1927, THE YANKEES HAD BEEN AN OUTSTANDING TEAM, breaking through to win pennants from 1921 to 1923 as well as 1926. But there was only one World Series title to show for the ballclub built by brewer Col. Jacob Ruppert. He had assembled a brain trust of manager Miller Huggins and general manager Ed Barrow, but none of them in their wildest dreams could have imagined the breakout that would happen in 1927, when the Yankees assumed the mantel of greatness. That Yankee team went wire-to-wire, never spending a day out of first place, and coasted to a 110–44 season, a .714 winning percentage, and breaking the AL record of 105 victories that had been set by the 1912 Boston Red Sox. It would be 27 years before another American League team surpassed this total. When Murderers' Row followed with the team's fifth pennant in seven years and back-to-back World Series championships, it served as the crowning moment of the New York Yankees baseball dynasty. It seemed, after the devastation of the Cardinals in 1926, that the Yankees' reign could last for years.

Who would have thought that the dynasty was already behind them?

The first sign of problems came early in 1929. On January 11, 1929, a tragic house fire in the Boston suburb of Watertown, Massachusetts resulted in the death of a 31-year-old woman known by her neighbors as the wife of Dr. Edward H. Kinder, a dentist. No one knew that she was actually Babe Ruth's wife, Helen. The events surrounding Helen Ruth's private life and her relationship with Babe would soon engulf Ruth in the most serious personal crisis of his life to that point. Babe's longtime separation from his first wife had been no secret, and neither had his ongoing relationship with Claire Hodgson. But little had been publicly known about Helen, and the developments of the coming weeks would be so shocking as to make the entire episode distasteful. Babe learned of Helen's death when an old friend named Art Crowley, son the Boston police superintendent, tracked him down and called him at a party at the home of teammate Joe Dugan, who had just recently been released by the Yankees. Upon hearing the news, Babe broke down crying and had to be consoled so that he could hurry to Penn Station to catch the last train to Boston.

"Is it true, Arthur?" Ruth demanded when he met Crowley at Boston's Back Bay Station. "It can't be true! Where's my little girl? I've got to see her." Crowley assured Babe that Dorothy was safe back at her school. Babe looked disheveled after his six-hour train ride, but he insisted on going to nearby Saint Cecilia's Church to pray for Helen. All throughout Mass, Babe could be heard reciting the rosary in a deep monotone as his fingers fumbled with his rosary beads, all the while sobbing. Afterward, Crowley took Ruth back to the Brunswick Hotel, where he had reserved Babe's old suite, Room 574. Concerned about Babe, Crowley had called two of Ruth's old friends, attorney John P. Feeney and realtor Thomas G. McEnaney, to help him settle down the Bambino. While Ruth slipped into a brief nap, the men tried to prepare a statement to give to the press. Babe read it when he awoke, and allowed one reporter into the suite to see him. He broke down crying again and told the reporter that he wouldn't be answering any questions.

"My wife and I have—" Babe started to cry again and then got hold of himself. "My wife and I have not lived together for the last three years. During that time I have seldom met her. I have done all that I can to comply with her wishes. Her death is a great shock to me."

Ruth then wadded up the sheet of hotel stationery from which he had read the statement and threw it into the fireplace in the suite. He locked himself in the bedroom, refusing to come out to talk to either his friends or Helen's sisters, Catherine and Nora, who had come to the hotel to discuss funeral arrangements. It was not until later in the day that Babe finally came out of the bedroom and went to the Watertown morgue, where he confirmed that the body of the woman found at the burned house was his estranged wife, Helen.

Babe had barely begun mourning Helen when the story of her death took an unexpected, even sadder twist. Fans were coming to grips with the revelations and didn't know what to make when the dead wife of a Watertown dentist turned out to be Mrs. Babe Ruth. Then one of the New York papers upped the scandal with a headline reading MRS. BABE RUTH DIES IN

LOVE NEST FIRE! Helen's brother, Thomas, a former police-man, stepped in to defend his family's name, telling the *Boston Globe* that reports that his sister "was carrying on a love af-fair with Doctor Kinder are a lot of rotten lies." But another brother of Helen's, attorney William J. Woodford, came forth with information that shed more negative light on her. "Helen was a good girl, but she was secretive," Woodford said in one interview. "For a long time my mother and my sisters won-dered what was the matter with her. But now I guess I have the key to those words she said to me, 'I found a doctor who will give me opium tablets.'" Helen, it seemed, had an opiate addic-tion and just four months earlier had been hospitalized for a nervous breakdown. Suddenly, Ruth was inundated with calls demanding an explanation of things he had never known about.

Two days after Helen's death, Babe found himself con-fronted by a horde of reporters in his hotel suite. "I'm in a hel-luva fix, boys," he began, nervously clenching and unclenching his fists. "All I want to say is that... it was a great shock to me." It was an emotional public moment, and Babe was barely holding on but still crying, tears running down his big cheeks. "Please, let my wife alone. Let her stay dead."

It might have ended there, except that Helen's family, having seen their loved one's memory sullied, suddenly tried to turn the tables on Ruth. Helen's sister Nora told one interviewer:

> In my opinion my sister did not die as a result of an accident. Three weeks ago I went to New York with my sister. It was December 10 or 17, maybe. She said she wanted me there as a witness. We went to the offices of [Ruth's agent] Christy Walsh, and he was

there with the Babe. The Babe said, "I've got to have a divorce." He said he wanted to marry this other woman. My sister said, "I'm willing to get a divorce quietly in Reno in order to keep things out of the newspapers... but I won't do this unless you give me $100,000 to protect Doc and myself and pay my expenses to Reno." Then the Babe got mad and said, "I won't give you another cent, but I want a divorce." He told her to go to hell because he'd given my sister enough money already. They couldn't come to any agreement, and they said goodbye. Of course, this meeting didn't end until after about two hours of quarreling, and during that time the Babe was very mean to Helen. Mr. Walsh tried to settle the argument but he didn't have much luck... And there's one other thing... the Babe threatened Helen with the gun while they were at the Sudbury farm about three years ago. He chased her all over the farm at the time and said he would shoot her. I don't know what the trouble was about that time.

Babe was dumbstruck by Nora's allegations, vehemently denying them. A lawyer for Helen's family also disassociated the Woodfords from the accusations, though Helen's mother continued to claim the fire had not been an accident. The Boston district attorney's office had little choice but to investigate Helen's death since it was splashed all over the newspapers. Meanwhile, the press had a field day examining Babe Ruth's life, not the heroic image that the media itself had helped create but rather the secrets and private lives of Babe and Helen.

Babe was getting little sleep in these days, and he sensed there could soon be a custody battle with his in-laws over Dorothy. Finally on January 16, the medical examiner confirmed that Helen Ruth had died in the house fire caused by "accidental overloading frayed electric wires." An autopsy performed on her body also found no evidence of narcotics or poison. More than 1,000 people attended Helen's rosary service, almost all of them there to catch a glimpse of the Babe. From the emotional toll the services took on Ruth, no one would have suspected he had hardly seen or spoken to his estranged wife in years. In his book, biographer Kal Wagenheim painted a pained, grief-stricken widowed husband:

> [Ruth] knelt at the bier, holding the rail in front of the bronze casket and making the Sign of the Cross. Then he began to moan, and his shoulders shook convulsively. Beads of perspiration rolled down his forehead. His right arm trembled as he took the rosary beads from his coat pocket. For about five minutes he moaned and cried. When he tried to rise he collapsed, and friends reached for him, carrying him toward the door past the weeping members of the Woodford family. Strong arms propped him against the wall, and John Feeney pinched his cheeks and said, 'Babe, everything is arranged for the funeral in the morning. You won't have to wait. We're going to take you away now.' Opening his eyes, Ruth blurted, 'What funeral?'

Ruth, it could be argued, would never be the same old Babe again. The same could have been said about the America that had been celebrating Ruth for more than a decade as a symbol of Roaring '20s boom times.

American culture was roaring in terms of style and social trends, as was the economy in a time of tremendous prosperity. After World War I, the industrial might of the United States had been unleashed as the country transitioned from wartime to peacetime production and produced an unprecedented consumer culture that stimulated economic growth. New York became the cultural epicenter of the country, during which time the media focused on famous celebrities, Babe Ruth being at the forefront. Cities cheered wildly for their home teams, and newly built theaters and sports stadiums resembled cathedrals. America was enjoying one of its greatest periods of economic expansion, making new millionaires overnight. The number of automobiles sold in the country more than tripled in a decade to more than 23 million in 1927. Radio sales, which had been 60 million in 1922, increased to 425 million. Then there was the stock market, once the haven of only the rich, which suddenly found itself attracting almost a million speculators. The most famous of these was baseball great Ty Cobb, who became independently wealthy by investing in Coca-Cola.

But there were signs and warnings. "By 1927," wrote F Scott Fitzgerald, "a wide neurosis began to be evident, faintly signaled, like a nervous beating of the feet." Still, the '20s though, roared on.

The 1929 season proved to be a disappointment and a tragedy for the Yankees. They finished 18 games behind the Philadelphia Athletics. The Yankees dynasty was undone primarily by lousy pitching. The team's top five pitchers were all almost 30, and no one had stepped in to pick up their slack. The offensive production was down from the past three seasons, but it was still strong. Ruth led the league with 46 home runs, and Gehrig hit 35. Babe Ruth drove in 154 runs, Gehrig 125, and Tony Lazzeri 106. Lazzeri led the team in batting with a .354 average. The Babe, now 34, batted .345 appearing in just 135 games, the fewest since he had become a Yankee with the exception of the suspension year and the bellyache season. Gehrig's batting average plunged to .300, 74 points below what he had hit in 1928. But pitching was the Yankee Achilles' heel.

Under the legendary skipper Connie Mack, the Athletics clinched the pennant on September 19. The next day, the Yankees got more bad news. Manager Miller Huggins, who had been ill for weeks, checked himself into the hospital, where doctors diagnosed a rare skin infection called erysipelas. The infection had unfortunately reached his bloodstream. Huggins was given four blood transfusions over the next few days, but on September 25, 1929, he succumbed to blood poisoning. Huggins was 51. Ruth had had a roller coaster relationship with Huggins—he had once dangerously dangled his manager off a moving train, according to reports—but he broke down and wept in the clubhouse upon hearing the news. One tragic death had started off a year for Babe that had been the end of an era, and now another death was closing it.

"Baseball men," Ruth lamented, "don't come any smarter than Miller Huggins."

As disappointing as the 1929 season was for the Yankees, it would begin an even more beleaguering time for America. On October 24, 1929, barely three weeks after the end of the baseball season, the stock market dramatically crashed on what would come to be known as "Black Thursday," when 16 million shares of stock were quickly sold by panicking investors who had lost faith in the American economy. By the height of the Depression in 1933, nearly a quarter of the nation's total work force, almost 13 million people, were unemployed. The Great Depression, the worst economic slump in U.S. history, would spread to the entire industrialized world, lasting for about a decade.

Many factors played a role in bringing about the depression. However, the main cause was the combination of an exaggeratedly unequal distribution of wealth and the extensive stock market speculation that took place during the latter part that same decade. The misdistribution of wealth in the 1920s existed on many levels. Money was distributed disparately between the rich and the middle-class, between industry and agriculture within the United States, and between the U.S. and Europe. This imbalance of wealth created an unstable economy. The excessive speculation in the late 1920s kept the stock market artificially high, but eventually led to large market crashes. As a result, the American economy capsized.

For the Yankees' rising star Lou Gehrig, the Great Depression could not have caught him at a worse moment. Like Ruth, he had hoped to capitalize on his fame and had been approached by financiers about off-season employment that could be mutually beneficial. A Columbia man, Lou had the educated manner and low-key personality that would have seemed ideal for the financial world. As soon as the season ended, he had begun working as a stockbroker at Appensellar, Allen & Hill. He was reconnecting with Walter Koppisch, his All-American football teammate at Columbia, with whom he shared a brokerage office. Though Gehrig was photographed for promotional purposes in a three-piece suit reading tickertape stock prices, Lou's stockbroking career was short-lived. Koppisch went out of business in the weeks after the stock market crash, and Gehrig soon returned to his baseball job exclusively.

There were dramatic changes in store for all of America, including the New York Yankees. "If Babe Ruth was the perfect hero for the glorious days of prosperity," biographer Jonathan Eig wrote, "Gehrig—durable, dependable, and dignified—was the man for hard times."

14   The Early 1930s

"The ballplayer who loses his head,
who can't keep his cool, is worse than no ballplayer at all."

—Lou Gehrig

DOROTHY RUTH WAS NOT TOLD ABOUT HER MOTHER'S DEATH
until months later, when she learned about Babe's marriage
to Claire on April 17, 1929. For most of her life, Dorothy
was led to believe that she was the child of both Ruth and
Helen. It was not until 1980, when she was 59 years old, that
she would learn that her natural mother was Juanita Jennings,
a woman she had grown up knowing and loving as a close
family friend. Dorothy would eventually be told the full
story—that she was the biological daughter of Babe Ruth and
his mistress Juanita—by Helen, the woman she came to accept as her natural mother just two weeks before her death.
Even Claire Hodgson didn't know that Dorothy was not
Helen's daughter, or that Juanita Jennings, the woman who
would soon became one of her closest friends, was Dorothy's
mother. Claire would eventually adopt Dorothy—and Babe
would legally adopt Claire's daughter, Julia—with the court
process completed on October 30, 1930.

By then, Babe Ruth's legacy as a ballplayer already seemed secure, though he would continue to add to it. From 1930 to 1934, Babe and Lou Gehrig would solidify their status as the most dynamic duo to ever play the game. Their statistics in those years were staggering. Ruth's yearly home run totals: 49, 46, 41, 34, 22; his batting averages: .359, .373, .341, .301, .288; his RBIs: 153, 162, 137, 104, 84. (And, remember, Babe was 35 in 1930 and almost 40 in 1934.) In that period, Gehrig's numbers were even better. Lou's yearly home runs: 41, 46, 34, 32, 49; his batting averages: .379, .341, .349, .334, .363; his RBIs: 173, 185, 151, 140, 166.

But for all those offensive fireworks, in those five years the Yankees could win only one pennant and one World Series championship, in 1932. In 1930, the Yankees slipped to third place with a record of 86–68, 16 games behind the Philadelphia Athletics. The 1931 Yankees finished with a record of 94–59, coming in 13½ games behind the Philadelphia Athletics. That Yankees team is notable for holding the modern-day major league record for team runs scored in a season: 1,067, or a 6.97 runs-per-game average.

Gehrig set an American League record in 1931 by driving in 185 runs, breaking his own record of 173. The total, which was six short of Hack Wilson's all-time record of 191 set the previous year and which still stands as of the end of the 2017 season. In 1933, the Yankees put up a record of 91–59, seven games behind the Washington Senators. Then, in 1934, the Yankees posted a record of 94–60, again seven games behind the pennant winners, the Detroit Tigers.

In a sense, after their great run of the 1920s, the Yankees didn't collapse so much as the American League caught up to them with their own power hitters. Stars such as Jimmie Foxx, Hank Greenberg, Earl Averill, and Charlie Gehringer gave other teams offenses to match the Yankees. In 1932, Foxx belted 58 home runs and drove in 169 runs while batting .364; he kept this up for most of the decade. Meanwhile, the pitching talent pool had aged or dried up for the Yankees, who could no longer count on buying pitchers from other teams, especially the Red Sox. Baseball was also evolving. The Cincinnati Reds installed lights and ushered in night baseball. In 1933, baseball introduced the All-Star Game and soon created the Hall of Fame—which would not be built until 1939, but whose first five inductees would be Babe Ruth, Ty Cobb, Honus Wagner, Christy Mathewson, and Walter Johnson.

Sadly, by 1935, Ruth would be gone from the Yankees, closing out his career with the Boston Braves that season. Meanwhile, led by manager Joe McCarthy, who had taken over the team in 1931, the Yankees won four World Series in a row starting in 1936 to close out the decade. Babe wasn't a part of those teams, but it was impossible to overlook his impact on the game, both in his swan song years and for the future.

Babe knew his value, even in hard times or perhaps especially in bad times. He had begun 1930 by asking the Yankees for a contract paying him $100,000 a season. Gehrig had already signed to play the next two years under a pair of one-year, $25,000 contracts. The Yankees quickly turned down Babe's $100,000 offer. When word got out, Ruth was asked by reporters to explain his exorbitant demand in the wake of what the country was going through.

"Say, if I hadn't been sick last summer," he said, "I'd have broken hell out of that home run record! Besides, the president gets a four-year contract. I'm only asking for three."

That just upped the ante, and reporters pressed him on what made him think he was worth more than the president of the United States. "What the hell has Hoover got to do with it?" Babe countered. "Anyway, I had a better year than he did." The country was in such horrible shape economically that no one could argue that point with Babe for long.

On March 8, 1930, as if Ruth defied the depression that had struck America, Babe signed a new two-year contract for $160,000 with the Yankees—at $80,000 per year, becoming then the highest paid player of all time and, yes, earning more money than the president of the United States. "No one in baseball," declared Yankees general manager Ed Barrow, unable to foresee the billion-dollar image of the game in the future, "will ever be paid more than Ruth."

Meanwhile, Lou Gehrig assumed his growing role with the Yankees the same way he quietly accepted life, even when he didn't agree with the decisions or the direction. He wasn't sold on the hiring of former teammate Bob Shawkey to succeed the late Miller Huggins as manager in 1930. Shawkey, the Yankees' franchise pitcher in the 1920s, had never managed in the major leagues and faced an uphill task all season in directing an aging team on the verge of collapse. More importantly, he soon lost the confidence of his most stable player when Shawkey disappointed Lou by trading away several of his friends in the lineup, among them mainstays Mark Koenig, Bob Meusel, and Waite Hoyt.

The cruel irony for the Yankees was that it was the pitching—Shawkey's bête noire as a player—that betrayed the team. Though in fairness to Shawkey, the Yankees' pitching troubles dated back to 1929, under Huggins' watch. Any significant changes to the existing pitching staff likely would have caused some resentment. Some players loyal to Ruth also felt that Babe should have succeeded Huggins. He had wanted to manage the Yankees and had pleaded with general manager Ed Barrow for the job. Several teammates even voiced their public support for Babe as their next manager, and Ruth might have even agreed to manage the Yankees with little or no increase in his salary. But Barrow instead chose to hire Shawkey, whose quiet, easygoing manner may have given his players too much latitude. An incident involving Ruth in late May showed how absurdly ridiculous he could become in making a joke of the game.

On May 21, 1930, Babe homered in his first three at-bats against the Athletics at Shibe Park in Philadelphia. At the time, only two other major league players had hit four home runs in a game, and no one had since 1896. On his fourth at-bat, Ruth came to the plate with a chance to make history. Babe, though, made a mockery of the opportunity. He decided to bat right-handed—against a right-handed pitcher at that. No one knew why. Then, after taking two called strikes, he turned around to bat left-handed. Maybe he truly believed that line he often used, that "every strike brings me closer to the next home run." This time, the two strikes batting right-handed left him no closer to his next dinger, righty or lefty. He struck out. What had been going through Ruth's mind? The story has been retold for decades. Did it ever happen? The *New York Times'* game story makes no mention of Ruth attempting to bat right-handed, and neither does *The Sporting News* recap.

Several years ago, Yankees fan and blogger J.G. Preston undertook an extensive examination into the story, concluding that it may just be indicative of whoppers created about Babe. He traced it back to Marshall Smelser's *The Life That Ruth Built: A Biography*, and surmises that the author was told the story by one of Ruth's ex-teammates. The book, though, is no lightweight castoff. Published in 1975 by the Quadrangle, a New York Times Book Co., *The Life That Ruth Built* was praised by *Kirkus Reviews* as "inclusive and definitive.... A tome statistically superior to Robert Creamer's personable *Babe: The Legend Comes to Life.*" Perhaps it all only underscores what was happening to the Yankees in the looking glass of the Great Depression: curiouser and curiouser.

"Baseball always has been and always will be a game demanding team play," Ruth had observed in 1929, almost as a poignant signal of the problems the next season's Yankees would have. "You can have the nine greatest individual ballplayers in the world, but if they don't play together the club won't be worth a dime."

Management wasn't happy with the post–Miller Huggins Yankees and decided to reload. As the 1930 season's end neared, Jake Ruppert and Ed Barrow set their sights on a new manager and signed Joe McCarthy almost immediately after he had been fired as manager of the Chicago Cubs. Unfortunately, the way the Yankees bosses made the change was both classless and unethical. Shawkey was still under contract. In fact, he only learned of his firing when he showed up at Yankee Stadium, where he saw firsthand all the fanfare over McCarthy becoming the new manager. "I have the highest regard for Shawkey," Ruppert told Movietone cameras that were on hand that day. "He was one of the first players we purchased after I became interested in the club. I think he did very well this year. He was in a tough spot, and I doubt that any manager could have done better. I am going to try to help him get a place as a manager somewhere in the minor leagues. I believe that with a little more experience he will make a great manager."

Joe McCarthy's hiring was a brilliant coup for the Yankees, but also a shot to the heart of Babe Ruth's dream—a dream that had become an obsession in the weeks and months following Miller Huggins' death in late September 1929. Babe wanted to be the manager of the Yankees. To many, the idea of the Babe Ruth of the early and mid-1920s managing a baseball team was absurd. He couldn't manage himself, everyone would say, so how could he possibly manage a team of 25 grown ballplayers? The Yankees players all respected Babe's incredible talent for hitting home runs and drawing fans into Yankee Stadium and everywhere else they played, but were they ready and willing to follow his lead as a manager? Could Ruth be trusted by either players or management to control his emotions, his drinking, and his womanizing? Of course not. But that was the old Ruth, or at least that was his argument and that of his agent Christy Walsh. They pointed out that Babe had gotten himself into good playing shape in recent years, and his behavior on and off the field had improved. Besides, hadn't all the great ballplayers of the past been given a chance at managing, greatness being in their baseball genes? Tris Speaker, Ty Cobb, and Rogers Hornsby—they had all been player-managers in their time.

Babe also believed that he had gone through a tremendous personal change in 1929 because of the circumstances that had tested his character. Helen's death had brought about a new appreciation for life, and his marriage to Claire Hodgson had solidified his home life with two young daughters and the guidance of a loving new wife. Ruth, though, was still paying for the image and reputation he created earlier in his career, nowhere more than where he least expected—in getting the public support and endorsement of teammate Lou Gehrig. Little of what Babe Ruth did, especially what he did in public, didn't embarrass Lou Gehrig. The tirades against the managers. The incessant showboating. The ongoing self-congratulations with the media. Why couldn't he just focus on baseball—on *winning* baseball? As great as Ruth was and had been in the past, Lou couldn't help but wonder how much greater Babe might have been had he focused and dedicated himself more.

Even Ruth might have had trouble making a case for himself as a player-manager over McCarthy, who had made a splash turning around the Chicago Cubs. Chicago had been mediocre during the early 1920s and had hit rock bottom, going through three managers to a last-place finish in 1925. But in four seasons, McCarthy's Cubs scratched their way out of the cellar to the National League pennant in 1929. The Cubs lost the 1929 World Series to Connie Mack's Philadelphia Athletics, and McCarthy was let go at the end of the 1930 season. The Yankees and the Red Sox got into a bidding war, and Ruppert and Barrow won, agreeing to pay McCarthy $30,000 a season. "The coming of McCarthy to New York is one of the biggest achievements of the American League since Colonel Ruppert engaged the late lamented Miller Huggins twelve years ago," one New York newspaper announced. "McCarthy is a figure of national importance. He is enjoying the friendship and sympathy of millions of fans who want to see him vindicated."

Joe McCarthy, who had managed the Cubs for the previous five seasons, was a disciplinarian who imposed a strict dress code and a rigorous exercise regimen on the Yankees. He had his own "Ten Commandments for Success in Baseball" that he used to preach to his teams, including "No. 4: Keep your head up and you may not have to keep it down." He immediately made it clear that his players had to be well conditioned or they would be benched. It seemed to be a message directed at Ruth. As for Gehrig, the new manager appeared to see him as the role model for the new New York Yankees. By the time McCarthy took the helm on Opening Day of 1931, Lou had already played in 888 consecutive games. "There is no excuse for a player not hustling," Lou was fond of saying. "I believe that every player owes it to himself, his club, and to the public to hustle every minute he is on the ballfield."

"His ballplayers play the part of champions at all times," *The Sporting News* wrote about McCarthy's teams. "Their dress and deportment in hotels and on trains was always McCarthy's concern and so successful were his methods that it was always easy to pick out a Yankee in a crowded lobby, even in Boston."

Joseph Vincent McCarthy would eventually become one of the greatest managers of all time in baseball. He was the first manager to win pennants in both the National and American Leagues, earning a total of nine league titles overall and seven World Series championships—a record equaled only by Casey Stengel. His career winning percentages of .615 in both the regular season and .698 in the postseason (all in the World Series), are the highest in major league history. His 1,460 career victories are the most by any Yankees manager. During his peak period, from 1936 to 1943, the Yankees won seven pennants in eight seasons. McCarthy had long idolized Connie Mack of the Philadelphia Athletics, considering him the game's greatest manager. He had noticed that Mack never yelled at his players in public, and adopted that trait himself. "Some likened manager McCarthy to a kind of Buddha figure on a ballfield," Alan Levy wrote in his biography *Joe McCarthy: Architect of the Yankee Dynasty.* "He sat quietly and saw absolutely everything. All matters flowed through him."

He did it all without ever playing in the majors, one of a handful of successful major league managers at that time with that distinction. After attending Niagara University in 1905 and 1906 on a baseball scholarship, McCarthy spent the next 15 years in the minor leagues, mostly as a second baseman with the Toledo Mud Hens, Buffalo Bisons, and Louisville Colonels. His big-league chance came in 1916, when he signed to play with the Brooklyn Tip-Tops of the Federal League— which existed for three seasons and was considered a third major league—but it folded before he could play a game with them. In 1968, organized baseball recognized its major league status, and with good reason. The National and American Leagues had effectively caused the Federal League to collapse and forced a landmark federal lawsuit, *Federal Baseball Club v. National League*, in which the U.S. Supreme Court ultimately ruled that the Sherman Antitrust Act did not apply to Major League Baseball. Another of the Federal League's legacies was Wrigley Field, which was originally built for the league's

Chicago Whales and has been the famous home field of the Chicago Cubs for more than a century.

McCarthy also had a penchant for one-liners. After a player was thrown out trying to steal home with one out, he told writers after the game, "The kid is the greatest proof of reincarnation. Nobody could get that stupid in one lifetime." Another time, after a reporter asked him if the great Joe DiMaggio could bunt, McCarthy turned to him and deadpanned, "I'll never know."

In his 16 seasons as skipper of the Yankees, McCarthy led one of the greatest collections of talent and personality baseball has ever seen—including Ruth, Gehrig, DiMaggio, Bill Dickey, Lefty Gomez, Tony Lazzeri, and Red Ruffing. Early on, Gehrig was highest on his list, and they developed a close friendship. In 1931, McCarthy's first season with the Yankees, the team improved to 94 wins, but they were outdistanced to the pennant by the Athletics' 107 victories. Gehrig came through as McCarthy imagined he would. Lou batted .341 and led the American League in hits, runs scored, and total bases. He also broke the American League RBIs record, driving in 185 runs, a mark that still stands today. His 46 home runs tied him with Ruth to lead the league in the area that Babe had long dominated.

Gehrig actually hit 47 homers that season and should have been the league home run leader alone. On April 26, 1931, a homer Gehrig hit against the Washington Senators was disallowed on one of the most freakish plays in history. Lou belted a two-out, two-run homer that should have scored Yankees teammate Lyn Lary, who had been on first base. The ball cleared the right-field wall and then caromed back toward the outfield and into right fielder Sam Rice's glove. Lary apparently wasn't watching the ball and never saw it go out—and, as he headed to third base, assumed the ball had been caught for an out. Trotting out his homer, Gehrig didn't see Lary leave the base path after crossing third base and stepped on home plate believing he had hit a two-run homer. Instead, he was called out for passing the runner and credited with having hit a triple. In the uproar that ensued, it turned out that the person most at fault was someone you would least expect. It was the responsibility of the third-base coach to prevent such blunders, and Joe McCarthy himself had taken over third-base coaching duties during the game. Where was he at the time? Apparently jumping up and down cheering Gehrig's home run with his back momentarily to the field. The two disallowed runs, Lary and Gehrig, would be the difference in the Yankees' 9–7 loss. Even Joe McCarthy was human.

Despite his connection with Gehrig, the Yankee who is perhaps closely identified with McCarthy is the phenom he most helped mold, Joe DiMaggio. "Joe did everything so easily," McCarthy later said of DiMaggio. "You never saw him fall down or go diving for a ball. He didn't have to. He just knew where the ball was hit and he went and got it."

A single play in DiMaggio's 1936 rookie season may best show how McCarthy was able to use his baseball knowledge and attention to detail to help shape an already outstanding but sensitive young player into the great one that DiMaggio became. In the ninth inning of a game that season, DiMaggio tracked down a deep fly in left-center field, wheeled in one motion and lasered a throw to home plate, nailing a runner. When the next batter grounded out to end the game, DiMaggio was greeted by a thunderous ovation when he ran from the outfield to the dugout. McCarthy was unmoved. He allowed Joe time to soak in the cheering before taking him aside. Then the manager explained to his young star that the proper way to make the play was to throw the ball on one bounce to the catcher because the skid would get there faster and closer to where the tag would be made on the runner.

"You'd be surprised by the lift a rookie gets from the McCarthy treatment," DiMaggio later said. "It impressed you right off the bat that you're a professional now. You're in the majors, and it's up to you to act like a major leaguer, not only on the ballfield but away from it. He stresses dignity, which may sound out of place among ballplayers, but which is definitely a morale lifter. Never a day went by that you didn't learn something from Joe McCarthy."

15   Called Shots

"While he was making up his mind to pitch to me,
I stepped back again and pointed my finger at those bleachers,
which only caused the mob to howl that much more at me."

—Babe Ruth

BABE RUTH GLANCED AT THE HEADLINE IN A COPY OF THE
New York Times that had been specially delivered to his
suite at the Edgewater Beach Hotel in Chicago and snapped
the newspaper with the back of his fingers and handed it to
Claire. ROOSEVELT HAILED BY CHICAGO THRONG, the headline read. The Bambino let out a roar as he chugged the last of
his orange juice and finished dressing to get to the ballpark.
The next president of the United States was in Chicago, Babe
now knew, but he wasn't there to campaign. True, the election
was still a month away, but most of the country must have felt
that Franklin Delano Roosevelt had a better lock on knocking
Hoover out of the White House than the Yankees did of winning the 1932 World Series—and the Bronx Bombers were already two games up on the Cubs. Babe was so pumped that
he couldn't wait to take batting practice. *Whoosh!* He took a
practice cut there in the living room, the drapes opened to the

private beach below and Lake Michigan beyond. Roosevelt, the sitting governor of New York and Democratic nominee for president, was in town—and he was there to see the most famous man in America hit a home run. Of course. *Whoosh!* Babe took another imaginary cut at the ball. He would have to do something special for FDR. It all would serve President Herbert Hoover right. When Ruth had been asked to pose with Hoover during the 1932 campaign, the Babe adamantly refused. Four years earlier, Hoover's campaign had been notable for its anti–Roman Catholic rhetoric against his opponent, New York Governor Al Smith. The Babe was a Catholic himself, and attacking his religion was an affront he did not forgive.

It was a crisp fall day in Chicago, the first of October, with the skies slightly overcast. A stiff wind was blowing out toward right field, whipping the American flag on top of the pole in dead center field. Babe was in a good mood. He had heard that Roosevelt would be throwing out the ceremonial first pitch. In pregame practice, whenever a fly ball was hit toward Ruth, Cubs fans in the bleachers peppered the outfield around Babe with lemons that he threw back. He shut them up in batting practice with a spectacular show of power. *Whoosh! Whoosh! Whoosh!* He lofted one ball after another into the right-field seats. Babe belted nine balls into the stands, Gehrig seven. "He knew he had the trick for the day," wrote sportswriter Westbrook Pegler of the *Chicago Tribune.* "I'm telling you that before the game began the Babe knew he was going to hit one or more home runs."

As he followed Ruth in the batting cage, Gehrig shook his head, laughing as he talked to a writer looking on. "The Babe is on fire," Lou said. "He ought to hit one today, maybe a couple."

Ruth took a couple of steps in the direction of the Cubs dugout and exchanged insults with the National League pennant winners. "I'd play for half my salary if I could hit in this dump all the time," he yelled at his opponents. There was bad blood between the two teams, and for the moment between Cubs fans and Babe, too. The Yankees had arrived to find that thousands of people had crammed into the LaSalle Street Station to greet their beloved Cubs and to jeer their New York opponents with an unexpected nastiness that surprised the Yankees players. Babe, accompanied by Claire, was the target of much of the fans' vitriol. They had to fight their way to a freight elevator and then to a cab. From there, motorcycle police had to clear the way for the Yankees team. Then, when Ruth and his wife entered the Edgewater Beach Hotel, a woman spat on them. "The Cub fans," wrote John Drebinger in the *New York Times,* "simply would not believe how severely or decisively their champions had been manhandled by the mighty Yankees in the East."

Ruth contained his anger. He still had a World Series to win. But he was going to savor every moment of it. "You mugs are not going to see Yankee Stadium anymore this year. The World Series is going to be over Sunday afternoon, four straight."

Some autograph seekers had gathered along the third-base barrier to the box seats, and Babe obliged. "Did you hear what I told them?" he asked the fans. "I told them over there? I told them that they ain't going back to New York. We lick 'em here, today and tomorrow."

As if they needed any motivation, the Yankees wanted to whip the Cubs as payback for their manager Joe McCarthy, who had been unceremoniously fired by Chicago, and for beloved former teammate Mark Koenig, who had been a big contributor to the great Yankees teams of 1926 to 1928 and was now playing against them. McCarthy intentionally stayed below the radar in the World Series, trying not to draw more attention to himself than necessary. Unknown to most, the Yankees manager had already made a smart but important contribution to his team's chances against the Cubs. As a former National League manager, he was keenly aware of the slight difference between the baseballs used by the two leagues. At the time, there were no standardized specifications on baseballs used by the leagues, and McCarthy knew that the National League used a distinctly less lively baseball than the American League. So as his team headed toward the World Series, where the National League balls would be used at Wrigley Field, McCarthy "bought a supply of National League baseballs so the Yankees could do some batting practice and get used to any subtle differences each player might see," according to his biographer Alan H. Levy.

Meanwhile, Yankees players were upset by reports that the Cubs had cheated Koenig by voting to give him only a half share of their World Series earnings. "They're chiselers," Ruth said in defense of his friend, "and I tell 'em so." During the games, Babe had hollered across the field, "Hey, Mark, who are those cheapskates you're with?" Koenig had been a late-season acquisition, but he had batted .353 in 33 games for his new team and picked up the slack after the Cubs' brilliant young shortstop, Billy Jurges, had been shot and wounded by his girlfriend in a Chicago hotel in midseason. The Cubs had been 3½ games out of first when Koenig came on board, and his hitting and defense helped them win the pennant by four games. Still, he was understandably upset that the Cubs only gave him a partial World Series share and that the team had given him only "six tickets for the games, and they were all behind posts."

"The Cubs appear outclassed," Grantland Rice wrote after the Yankees won the first two games in the Bronx, 12–6 and 5–2. "In bull markets and bear markets, in times of luxury and times of want, the Yankees continue to maul."

Nearly 50,000 people packed into Wrigley Field for Game 3 of the World Series, with Ruth quickly making some wonder if it hadn't been unrepentant Yankees fan Franklin Roosevelt who tossed him a fat pitch instead of the Cubs' 15-game win-ner Charlie Root, who had won a staggering four games during the last month of the season. "With a step forward, a lurch of his massive shoulders and sweep of his celebrated bat, Ruth drove the ball high into temporary bleachers that had been erected beyond the right-field fence," the *New York Herald Tribune* wrote of Babe's first-inning three-run homer that put the Yankees ahead. "Upward and onward the ball flew, a white streak outlined against the bright blue sky." In the top of the third, with the Yankees leading 3–1, it was Gehrig's turn to jump on a Charlie Root mistake, a change-up that he drove for a solo shot into the right-field bleachers. The Cubs then came back to tie the game 4–4, going into the top of the fifth with Ruth due up.

A chorus of boos, hisses, and jeers greeted Ruth as he paced his way to the plate, and several lemons thrown from the stands rolled around him as he swung three bats before stepping into the batter's box. Babe grinned at the Cubs' heckling, noting that pitchers Guy Bush and Bob Smith, both seated at the top of the dugout steps, were leading the storm of abuse.

Root's first pitch sailed by Ruth for a called strike. Ruth stepped out of the batter's box, holding up one finger as he looked into the Cubs dugout to indicate strike one. "Wait, Mug," he yelled at Guy Bush who continued shouting abuse. "I'm going to hit one out of the yard." Then he turned to Chicago catcher Gabby Hartnett and said, "It only takes one to hit it."

Babe took two pitches for balls before watching a second called strike. The heckling and booing grew louder as Ruth held up two fingers and yelled to the Cubs, "That's only two strikes, boys. I still have one coming."

"Then, with a warning gesture of his hand to Bush, he sent the signal for the customers to see, as if to say, 'Now this is the one, look,'" the *Chicago Tribune* reported.

Was the fabled Bambino calling his shot or has it all been a created myth, as some have speculated? John Drebinger of the *New York Times* left no doubt in what he reported: "In no mistaken motions the Babe notified the crowd that the nature of his retaliation would be a wallop right out of the confines of the park."

Paul Gallico in his column in the *New York Daily News* was even more emphatic: "He pointed like a duellist to the spot where he expected to send his rapier home and then sent it there. He went so far out on a limb with his gestures and his repartee and his comportment at the plate, that if he had missed he would never have been able to live it down.... The Babe now held up two fingers and shook them so that they seemed to reach right into the Cub dugout. And this time it was probably the most daring gesture ever made in any game. Because it meant that he intended to knock the next one out of the park."

Bill Corum rested his legendary reputation as a sportswriter and radio commentator on recalling how Ruth called his shot. "Words fail me," he wrote in the *New York Evening Journal*. "When he stood up there at bat before 50,000 persons, calling the balls and strikes, with gestures, for the benefit of the Cubs in the dugout and then, with two strikes on him, pointed out where he was going to hit the next one, and hit it there, I gave up. The fellow's not human."

On a 2-2 count, Root tried to fool Babe with his change-up. "There was a resounding report like the explosion of a gun," wrote Richards Vidmer of the *New York Herald-Tribune*. "The ball soared on a line to center field. Straight for the fence the ball soared on a line, clearing the farthest corner of the barrier, 436 feet from home plate."

"The ball just went on and on and on," Babe recalled in his 1948 autobiography, "and hit far up in the center-field bleachers in exactly the spot I had pointed to."

The silence in the Cubs' dugout was deafening, and the crowd seemed transfixed by what it had just witnessed. Not only could Babe Ruth predict their defeat, but he could also pick the spot where he would deliver the death blow.

"Before Ruth left the plate and started his swing around the bases," wrote Vidmer, "he paused to laugh at the Chicago players, suddenly silent in their dugout. As he rounded first, he flung a remark at [Cubs manager Charlie] Grimm. As he turned second he tossed a jest at [Cubs coach] Billy Herman. His shoulders shook with satisfaction as he trotted in."

Even years later, Root would remember the pitch as if he had just thrown it. "It was a change-of-pace ball, low and out-side," Root told an interviewer. "If it had been a fastball, I wouldn't have been surprised. But he picked it out and sent it on the line to center field. That convinced me of the power he has in his swings."

As Babe crossed home plate, taking Gehrig's congratulatory handshake, his teammates spilled out of the dugout, jumping and hollering as if they had just won the World Series. They hurried to congratulate Ruth and pat him on the back. Moments later, having barely sat down, they heard another loud crack from the direction of home plate. Gehrig followed Babe's called shot by slugging a hanging curveball into the right-field bleachers for his own second homer of the game, padding the Yankees' lead, 6–4.

In a late edition the same day of the game, the *New York World-Telegram*, evoking billiards terminology, headlined its story, RUTH CALLS SHOT AS HE PUTS HOME RUN NO. 2 IN SIDE POCKET. The Yankees would win the game, and the World Series the next day. The big hitter in the title-clinching contest was neither Ruth nor Gehrig but Tony Lazzeri, who belted two two-run home runs during a late Yankees rally that broke up a close game for a 13–6 victory.

And although Ruth's "called shot" is the moment the 1932 World Series would be most remembered for, it was Lou Gehrig who quietly stole the thunder. Gehrig went 9-for-17 with a .529 average, three home runs, scoring nine runs and eight RBIs. Catcher Bill Dickey batted .438, Earle Combs .375, and Joe Sewell and Ruth both .333. Babe's called shot would also be his last World Series home run, and this his 10th and last World Series.

The Cubs, that team of romantic misgivings and ambitions of greatness, would be denied a long-sought World Series championship, a dream that would go unfulfilled for another

84 years. The bad memories and frustration would linger in Chicago, similar to what fans in Boston felt in its long championship drought after the sale of Babe Ruth. Red Sox fans would wallow in blaming the so-called Curse of the Bambino, and perhaps Cubs fans, too, looked to Ruth as someone to blame, especially since what lingered so long from that 1932 World Series was Babe's called shot, the greatest home run in baseball's history. Or, as many Cubs fans would long insist, the imaginary greatest home run in memory.

Was Babe Ruth's home run in the fifth inning a called shot? Or was it "romantic fiction," as *Chicago Tribune* writer Jerome Holtzman maintained in a 1987 reexamination, created "because people gild lilies and sometimes remember seeing things they didn't see," as he put it?

Ruth himself didn't help out matters. Or perhaps he just loved adding fuel to the fire. Like a lot of athletes then and in years to come, Babe loved playing with sportswriters' heads, telling them anything—lies, the truth, half-truths, invented whoppers just to get rid of them and their pestering questions. Ruth was famous for it, as was Mickey Mantle in his time. Books upon books on the lies famous ballplayers tell could be written, along with lies of famous ballplayers often told by writers under deadline pressures to fill holes in their articles. So it's not surprising to read old stories unearthed about Babe telling a writer inquiring about the called shot, "Hell no it isn't a fact. Only a damned fool would do a thing like that... Nah, keed, you know damned well I wasn't pointin' anywhere. If I'd have done that, Root would have stuck the ball right in my ear. And besides that, I never knew anybody who could tell you ahead of time where he was going to hit a baseball. When I get to be that kind of fool, they'll put me in the booby hatch."

Myth? Romantic fiction? Years later, Yankees broadcaster Mel Allen said that if Mickey Mantle hadn't lived, he would have had to have been invented. In a sense, like most heroes, Ruth was a construction; he was not real. He was all that America wanted itself to be, and he was also all that America feared it could never be. In the 1920s, as sport itself took on the role in our culture that religion had often played in the past, Babe Ruth as the contemporary cultural hero contributed to American society's necessary business of reproducing itself and its values.

Years later the fictional literary character Terence Mann perhaps stated it more succinctly in the Hollywood film *Field of Dreams*, when he says to protagonist Ray Kinsella, "The one constant through all the years, Ray, has been baseball. America has rolled by like an army of steamrollers. It's been erased like a blackboard, rebuilt, and erased again. But baseball has marked the time. This field, this game, is a part of our past, Ray. It reminds us of all that once was good and it could be again."

16   The Feud

"They didn't get along. Lou thought Ruth was a big-mouth and Ruth thought Gehrig was cheap. They were both right."

—Tony Lazzeri

J.D. SALINGER ONCE WROTE THAT MOTHERS ARE ALL SLIGHTLY insane. The reclusive author of *The Catcher in the Rye*, a veritable bible for four generations of disaffected youth, sometimes had a penchant for exaggeration, but he might not have been off the mark where it comes to Christina Gehrig. Overbearing and insanely protective of her son, Christina could be much the same about anyone to whom she took a fancy. She thought she knew best and was not above voicing her opinion where it wasn't sought nor even needed. But sadly, you can't change someone who doesn't see problem with their actions.

By the time Lou had become an integral part of the phenomenon known as Gehrig and the Babe, Christina thought she was a central cog of that Yankees family that extended beyond her own. She went to spring training. She regularly hosted Babe and other Yankees players at her home. She went to every Yankees home game, and often followed Lou on the road as well. She knew all the players' wives and children, sitting alongside them in the box seats behind the Yankees dugout in an area reserved for team families. They called her Mom Gehrig, after all.

Despite that, she had never been close to Claire Hodgson in the years preceding the death of Helen Ruth. The issue of Babe's marriage was never spoken of publicly among the Yankees wives, especially at the stadium. Hodgson also made sure not to overstep among the wives, guarding her privacy as well as that of her daughter, Julia. But Helen's death and Babe and Claire's marriage in April 1929 changed the dynamic for the new Ruth family.

In June, Dorothy joined her father, Claire, and Julia in their Upper West Side apartment. Considering they were almost complete strangers, the two girls at first bonded surprisingly well. Julia, who turned 13 that summer, welcomed assuming the big sister role with Dorothy, who turned eight a month earlier. Julia had taken after her mother as a young fashion plate who was spoiled by Babe with new clothes. Ruth had not had the same kind of relationship with Dorothy, whose wardrobe consisted mostly of the uniforms required at her school and the casual play clothes that she wore when she visited her mother. Babe had bought her dresses for her occasional visits to New York, when he sometimes took her with him to visit the Gehrigs. Dorothy, though, was a rambunctious youngster who found the fancy dresses restrictive when running around the Gehrigs' backyard, climbing trees and getting dirty. So, once reunited in New York with her favorite worn-out play clothes, Dorothy felt in her element. Ruth didn't object. Claire, just getting to know her new stepdaughter, felt there was all the time in the world to acclimate Dorothy to the style and fashion sense of a child who now had a new comfort and security she had never before known.

The memoirs of Babe, Claire, and Julia, all indicate that Claire was a good mother to both girls. Julia, of course, was her own child. She took Dorothy under her wing with all the love that she could give to a youngster to whom Babe was devoted and cared for as if she were his own flesh and blood (which, of course, she was). But the girls were not the same age, or even close. Julia was a teenager in the late-1920s and almost a grown woman by 1933, when Babe's playing career was nearing its end. Dorothy was barely 12. Young women of those ages have different interests, wear different clothes and styles, and are treated differently by their parents. The children themselves, especially the younger, might not understand or like it. They may even become jealous of their older sister. And the people on the outside looking in—especially if they have not raised children of different ages themselves—may have no clue about the realities of life in a home with sibling rivalries.

Perhaps that offers an insight into Christina Gehrig, who had raised an only child. She also had never been to the Ruth home and barely knew Claire and Julia. Christina saw only the outside trappings, and she had known only Dorothy, a moody, insecure girl who had been living her childhood in a boarding school, as devoid of loving contact as St. Mary's had been for Ruth. Years later, one of Dorothy's daughters, Linda Ruth Tosetti, conceded that her mother, like Babe, could "be a real rebel. She'd get in trouble all the time."

Though Christina Gehrig saw Dorothy only occasionally, she became almost as obsessed with her as she had been with Lou. And when Christina began to take umbrage at the way Claire was raising the girls, it blindsided Claire and created a rift that no one saw coming. Apparently it all began innocently enough: with an overnight visit Dorothy took to the Gehrig's house. Claire Ruth was out of town, and young Dorothy decided to pack her own overnight suitcase, tossing in all her tattered clothes and leaving aside nice dresses that her parents had bought for her. At the Gehrig home, when she helped the child unpack, Christina couldn't help but notice—and to jump to conclusions. In her mind, it was just another example of Claire Ruth's neglect of her adopted daughter. Maybe had Mom Gehrig raised the issue privately and delicately, she might have gotten an explanation that would have put her mind at ease. Subtlety, though, was not one of Christina's virtues. She was opinionated and closed-minded. It's possible her own frustration with Lou's romantic involvement with Eleanor was playing on her emotions. Lou was pulling away from her, soon headed for marriage and wary about how his mother's meddling had ruined past relationships and could still potentially threaten this one.

Christina was unceasing in her manner. She meddled and needled, and she was unrelenting. She also rarely stopped talking about something once it was on her mind, and she had gotten it into her head, evidently, that Ruth and Claire mistreated young Dorothy. That needed expressing to anyone who would hear. And in fairness to Christina, she may have picked up on something that no one ever saw—no one, that is, except Dorothy. In a controversial memoir of her own many years later, Christina wrote of an unhappy childhood and accused Claire Ruth of mistreating her.

As Julia recalled in her own book, "Mrs. Gehrig said, 'Mrs. Ruth's daughter [me], she goes to the ballgames in silks and satins, and poor little Dorothy has nothing but rags to wear. When mother heard about that, she said, 'Tell Lou's mother to keep her mouth shut.' And that was that. Lou wouldn't stand for anyone speaking about his mother."

She later wrote, "You couldn't say a word to Lou about his mother. Well, I guess that's all right, I guess, for a son to defend his mother. But Daddy just wanted to let Lou know that his mother was sticking her nose in somebody else's business and it didn't belong there. And Lou was greatly offended by it, so that was the whole thing."

And that was the polite version. In truth, when she heard what Christina was going around saying about her, Claire Ruth rushed to Babe in tears and demanded that he tell Lou to muzzle his mom. Babe was equally enraged, and confronted Lou in the Yankee clubhouse, causing a fracas in which they had to be separated. "Your mother," Ruth told Gehrig when he confronted him, "should mind her own goddamned business." Some versions of the story maintained that Ruth dispatched someone to deliver the message to Gehrig—his agent Christy Walsh or teammate Sammy Byrd or Ben Chapman.

Years later, Babe told Hollywood pal Johnny Grant that it was he alone who confronted Gehrig. "Babe said that maybe he should have cooled down before talking to Lou, but he didn't," Grant said, recalling his conversations with Ruth. "He was just too upset and felt betrayed by Lou's mother. 'Where did she get off saying that about how Claire looked after and dressed the girls?' Babe said. 'Claire loved Dot like she was her own. I don't think Dot couldn't have had a more loving mother, and she loved Claire.'"

It took four decades after Babe's death for Dorothy to take issue with the pretty view of her young life that her father, stepmother, and stepsister remembered. In *My Dad, the Babe,* her autobiography published in 1988, Dorothy wrote, "As the months went by, my position in my new mother's heart became clear: I was excess baggage. Raising me was a burdensome job, like a stack of unexpected paperwork dropped in her lap." Dorothy said her stepmother withheld affection and treated her cruelly. She recalled feeling slighted by her bedroom, converted from maid's quarters and facing a courtyard, while Julia's bedroom was next to her mother's. The publication of Dorothy's memoir led to her estrangement from Julia, and the two stepsisters never spoke again. "If mother had been alive, Dorothy would never have written the book," Julia said in an interview, "because mother would have blasted her from here to kingdom come." Claire Ruth had died in 1976.

From Dorothy's perspective, consider that she never had a mother in her life. Helen, her adoptive mother, had the child forced on her by Babe through adoption. Even had Dorothy been Ruth's flesh and blood—and especially if she were indeed Babe's illegitimate child—it would have been emotionally difficult on Helen's part to raise a child who was the product of her husband's womanizing. Juanita Jennings, assuming she were the birth mother, was around Dorothy for years only as a friend of Claire and Babe, never as her mother. Jennings did not admit to being Dorothy's biological mother until she was near death in 1980. Dorothy died nine years later.

"What bothered my mother the most was that her birthright seemed stolen from her," Babe's granddaughter Linda Ruth Tosetti said in 2006 interview. "She was told all of her life that she was adopted—and there is absolutely nothing wrong with being adopted, if you are, [but] she was not. My mother only blamed my grandfather a little for [the misunderstanding]. She reasoned that he belonged to everyone [in the world]."

But could there have possibly been more that led to the feud between the two Yankees legends to cause a rift that would be so deep and last for years? Some have found it hard to believe that an old woman's ill-thought comments about how someone dressed their daughters could lead to such an estrangement. Tomboy attire for a child versus high style? Seriously? Or was inevitability at play? They had been the two most dissimilar men to form a mutual admiration society, after all. Ruth: outrageously undisciplined in every aspect of his personal life; Gehrig: put off by flamboyance and empty boasting. Ruth: rebellious of all authority; Gehrig: the consummate team player.

Had they grown closer during those Yankees years of the mid- and late-1920s as they played, traveled, barnstormed, and hung out together? Or had they grown apart over time, as Gehrig came into his own and exceeded Ruth's performance on the baseball field? In those earlier days, the common refrain in stories was that Gehrig seemed content to live in Babe's gargantuan shadow. But as the years passed, Lou had increasingly sought his independence—especially after marrying Eleanor, who insisted that her husband seek out his own commercial endorsements. After a while, when Lou's hitting statistics closely matched Babe's, it became difficult for Gehrig not to be aware that the Yankees were paying him less than a third of Ruth's $80,000 annual salary. As Frank Ardolino, an English professor who has written extensively about the history and culture of baseball, astutely observed in an article for the Society for

American Baseball Research, "The friction between Ruth and Gehrig in their baseball careers developed primarily from their different personalities, their divergent public images, and from the influence of other people on their relationship. Given all of these factors, their feud seems inevitable and regrettable."

Both Babe and Lou were extremely proud in their own ways, and each was dependent on and devoted to the women at the heart over the alleged incident. Claire Ruth was credited for being a positive influence on Babe's life, for curbing his appetites of excess and getting him into shape in the mid-1920s. But she also had become so controlling of Babe that it was obvious to all who knew them. And Gehrig's attachment to his mother bordered on the psychologically unhealthy. Has there ever been a major sports figure who has hung on to his mother's apron strings the way Lou had?

Over the years there have been other theories thrown into the feud fire: Ruth's anger and disappointment with Gehrig's refusal to stand strong on holding out for more money from the Yankees in their negotiations. Babe speaking disparagingly of Gehrig's cherished consecutive-game streak, calling it little more than a boring statistic. "This Iron Horse stuff is just a lot of baloney," Ruth told one reporter. "I think he's making one of the worst mistakes a player can make. He ought to learn to sit on the bench and rest. They're not going to pay off on how many games he's played in a row." Then there was Ruth's resentment of Gehrig for his failure to support him in his bid for Yankees manager, both after Miller Huggins' death and again in 1935, after the team suffered disappointing back-to-back seasons.

Ruth's final effort to manage the Yankees in 1935 came after an off-season barnstorming tour of Japan. An incident happened onboard the *Empress of Japan* luxury liner, on which Eleanor Gehrig went missing for two hours. Gehrig had panicked, even fearing his wife had fallen overboard. Eleanor later wrote in her memoir about having run into Claire Ruth and gone to have a drink with her in her cabin. "I stepped into their little world: the resplendent Babe, sitting like a Buddha figure, cross-legged and surrounded by an empire of caviar and champagne," she recalled. "It was an extravagant picnic, especially since I'd never been able to get my fill of caviar, and suddenly I was looking up at mounds of it. So I was 'missing' for two hours.... The one place that Lou had never thought to check out was Babe Ruth's cabin."

However, by that point, Ruth and Gehrig—the two sluggers who formed the heart of the Yankees' omnipotent ball club for the decade spanning 1925 to 1934—had barely spoken to each other for a couple of years. Old film footage of the Yankees playing in 1934 and even part of 1933 even shows a curious sight: Babe, having homered and circling the bases, touching home plate while Gehrig stood nearby with his back turned, not bothering to give him a congratulatory handshake as he had in the past. Of course there were times they did shake hands at home plate in the traditional post–home run tradition, and they managed to be accommodating when photographers asked them to pose together. Lou, though, was forced to play-act his familiar grin in the presence of Ruth.

No one will ever know how the feud my have impacted the team in those seasons. In 1933, the Yankees finished with a record of 91–59, seven games behind the Washington Senators. In

1934, the Yankees had a record of 94–60, seven games behind the Detroit Tigers. That season, Gehrig became only the fourth player in American League history to win the Triple Crown, though he finished a distant fifth to Tigers player-manager Mickey Cochran for the Most Valuable Player Award.

Of course, it had been so difficult for baseball historians to pinpoint precisely when the relationship between Ruth and Gehrig turned frigid. Or had it? Did it go sour after the 1932 World Series championship with Babe's "called shot?" Or sometime in 1933, after Lou and Eleanor Gehrig were married? Leigh Montville's 2006 biography *The Big Bam: The Life and Times of Babe Ruth* offers perhaps another, deeper truth, (assuming, of course, it was true): "Before she had known Gehrig," Montville writes of Eleanor, "she had known the Babe. She met Gehrig, in fact, at one of those free-flowing sessions at the Babe's suite in Chicago. To have known the Babe at that time was, well, to have known the Babe. He didn't suffer many platonic relationships with women."

In fact, Montville and sportswriter Fred Lieb make the case that the feud may have had little to do with how Claire Ruth dressed little Dorothy and Christina Gehrig's complaints about it—and everything to do with Eleanor and whatever her relationship may have been with Babe Ruth. "I'm not knocking Eleanor, but very few women went into Ruth's room for sightseeing," Lieb said in an interview. "And I don't think Babe welcomed very many that he didn't want to get in bed with."

Was that in the back of Gehrig's mind after he had married Eleanor, some image of his wife in the arms of baseball's Don Juan, a carnal conquest he found morally repulsive? Was the real reason for the feud just another twist of one of the oldest jealousies between men over "their" women? And then, once the feud is on, it is further fueled by the incident of Gehrig finding his wife, half-drunk, in Babe's Japan-bound stateroom? Eleanor said the incident led to "a long siege of no-speaking" between she and Lou, and that Babe later came to their room trying to make peace. "Ruth burst in—jovial, arms both stretched out in a let's-be-pals gesture," she wrote. "But my unforgiving man turned his back, extending the silent treatment to the party of the second part, and the Babe retreated. They never did become reconciled, and I just dropped the subject forever."

Eleanor denied ever having had a romantic relationship with Ruth. Of course, an admission likely would have made her the most despised woman of the 1930s this side of Wallis Simpson, the American socialite who caused King Edward VIII to abdicate the throne of England. Someone who might have had some clue, Yankees catcher and Lou's best friend Bill Dickey, wasn't keen to talk about the subject, though what he said raised more questions. "It just is unpleasant to think about even now," he said in an interview. "When I went [to the Yankees] they were good friends and kidded each other a lot and they got along fine. Then something happened. I don't want to tell you about it."

It would be a feud that, according to some, would cost Babe his late-career dream of becoming a major league manager. Or was it? The Yankees had no interest in replacing Joe McCarthy with Babe, and most teams seemed to balk at the notion of putting Ruth in charge of their on-field management. Babe also was not good at the subtleties of business. He didn't recognize some of the opportunities beyond the obvious involved in the postseason 1934 barnstorming tour of Japan that Connie

Mack was promoting and managing. Mack, who was going to turn 72 that December, had been managing the Philadelphia Athletics—of which he was also treasurer and part owner— since 1901. His teams had displaced the Yankees from 1929 to 1931 as rulers of the American League and World Series champions in 1929 and 1930.

However, on-again, off-again money problems had beset the Athletics in the past and came back around in 1932. Mack had dreams of rebuilding his team once again and hoped he could take a break from the pressures of managing on the field to devote himself to the business side of operations. How would the aging Babe Ruth fit into his program as a player-manager, Mack wondered. Some of Babe's antics didn't bother him as much as it did other people. As a manager, Mack never imposed curfews or bed checks, and his managerial style was not tyrannical but easygoing. Mack had observed Babe closely in the years following the death of his wife and his remarriage, and he thought he had seen a change in his behavior—important, because he looked for players with quiet and disciplined personal lives. Unfortunately, for Babe, the trip aboard the *Empress of Japan* was like being trapped in a small town, where gossip quickly made the rounds, which apparently is what happened with the incident involving the Ruths and the Gehrigs. The onboard feuding, according to reports at that time, quickly divided the shipload of baseball travelers into two chilly camps.

For his part, Connie Mack blamed Claire Ruth. Her influence over Babe was just too strong, he told Joe Williams, longtime sports editor of the *New York World Telegram*. "I couldn't have made Babe manager," he said. "His wife would have been running the club in a month."

17   Post-Ruth

"I have played with the greatest batter of all time: none other than Babe Ruth. My home runs are fouls in comparison with the Babe's drives."

—Lou Gehrig

HAD HE DONE NOTHING MORE THAN WAITED OUT THE YANKEES in 1935, Babe Ruth possibly could have stayed in pinstripes in New York for as long as he wanted. He would have had to take a massive pay cut—all the way down to $20,000 for the season. Babe, admittedly, was over the hill. At 40, he was overweight, he had difficulty running, and he was a detriment to the team in the outfield. On almost any other team, Babe might have played first base. But with the Yankees, they had established first baseman Lou Gehrig, who was now in his prime. Still, he *was* Babe Ruth, the Sultan of Swat. He could still hit, and, more important, he was still the biggest draw in all of baseball. Fans couldn't fathom the idea of the New York Yankees without Babe Ruth, no matter his physical conditioning or skills.

The problem facing the Yankees over what to do with the Bambino was with the team's front office, general manager Ed Barrow and owner Jacob Ruppert. They weren't about to make

him manager—no way—and Ruth outright rejected their offer
that he spend 1935 managing the Yankees' top minor league
team in Newark. The Yankees had a potential public rela-
tions nightmare on their hands: the prospect of Ruth as an occasional player riding the bench could invite second-guessing
about Joe McCarthy should the Yankees not play well. This
Joe McCarthy, after all, was not yet the manager who would
become a legend with the success of Joe DiMaggio. Then there
was Lou Gehrig and the ongoing Ruth-Gehrig feud, the ele-
phant in the clubhouse. Lou and Babe no longer spoke, and the
rumors of whatever had happened aboard the *Empress of Japan*
were unceasing.

So Ruth could stalemate for as long as he wanted. What were
the Yankees going to do, cut the Babe? Not if the Yankees front
office could avoid it, and Barrow and Ruppert went to work
behind the scenes to see if they could make their Babe Ruth
headache someone else's. The Yankees found a solution by col-
luding with the worst organization in Major League Baseball,
the Boston Braves, who offered Ruth a meaningless multi-tiered
deal and the titles of assistant manager and vice president while
leading him to believe he would soon become the manager of
the team. They also offered the lures of stock options and ownership, meaningless because they brought with them no stock
or ownership. The Braves were counting on Babe still being
a box-office draw in Boston, and they were asked to give up
nothing to the Yankees in return. Had they pressed their case,
the Braves might have even gotten the Yankees to throw in
some cash, if they could have kept it secret. That's how badly
the Yankees wanted Babe out of New York.

The two biggest influences on Babe's thinking, Claire Ruth and Christy Walsh, who had talked him out of managing in Newark for the Yankees, now urged him to take the offer from the Braves. They were all duped. Ruth signed a contract making $25,000 for the season based on "gross receipts above the average of the previous five years," all legalese misleading Babe to think he was getting something he wasn't. But everyone, from the *New York Times* to major league team owners, praised the deal.

Babe Ruth's start with the Boston Braves was something out of a fairy tale. He crushed a home run off New York Giants' ace Carl Hubbell before an Opening Day crowd of 20,000 fans, including the governors of five of the six New England states. In the previous year's All-Star Game, Hubbell had taken a big step toward immortality by striking out Ruth, Gehrig, and Jimmie Foxx in order and then mowing down Al Simmons and Joe Cronin to start the next inning. Unfortunately, Ruth's time with the Braves quickly turned into an unmitigated disaster. He soon learned that the Boston Braves had lied to him about almost everything. There was no profit-sharing and part-ownership deal, and the Braves had no plan of making him the field manager either. Instead, the team's owner tried desperately to get Ruth to invest his own money in the team. And they certainly couldn't afford to have him on the payroll. On June 2, 1935, the Boston Braves, on the verge of financial collapse, pulled the plug on their Babe Ruth deal. They publicly "fired" Babe, even before he could quit. He was batting .181 through 28 games with six home runs and a dozen RBIs. The high point of Ruth's brief time with the Braves came on May 25, at Forbes Field in Pittsburgh, where he went 4-for-4, hitting three home runs and driving in six. His final home run was No. 714 of his career.

At the end of the 1935 season, Boston Braves owner Emil Fuchs went bankrupt. He gave up control of the Braves, and the National League took over the franchise. The Braves that year were a reflection of its front office. They were the worst in baseball history, finishing the season with a 38–115 record.

"Judge Fuchs is a double-crosser," Ruth said when he announced what effectively became his retirement. "His word is no good. He doesn't keep his promises. I don't want another damn thing from him, the dirty double-crosser." Babe never again played professional baseball.

In New York, Lou Gehrig no longer had Babe Ruth's long shadow looming over him, though his 1935 numbers seemed to suggest otherwise. Lou had a noticeable statistical drop-off from his 1934 MVP season, when he won the Triple Crown with a .363 batting average, 49 home runs, and 166 RBIs. In 1935, Lou's batting average slipped to .329 with 30 home runs and 120 runs batted in. In his defense, Gehrig was not fully to blame for the Yankees' second-place showing (three games behind Detroit)—their third straight runner-up finish. The team offense fell off so dramatically that American League pitchers chose to pitch around Lou, who walked a career-high 132 times that season. Gehrig was also the Yankees' new captain, filling the role last held by Everett Scott from 1922 to 1925. Ruth had been captain for just a week in 1922 before being stripped of the title because of his off-the-field shenanigans. But Ruth the player had left some big shoes to fill, and some were willing to believe that Gehrig could fill them. It was notable perhaps that when Joe DiMaggio arrived at spring training in 1936, Dan Daniel of the *New York World Telegram* declared, "Here is the replacement for Babe Ruth."

Though only a rookie, DiMaggio had caught the attention of writers and the media in a way that Gehrig never did. In those first weeks of the 1936 season, newspaper accounts of Yankees victories often had DiMaggio's name in the headlines, even when Gehrig had been the real star of those games. If Gehrig was upset at being upstaged, he didn't let on. Lou himself had quickly joined the chorus cheering on the new rookie. "DiMaggio will develop into one of the greatest right-handed hitters of all time within the next three years," Gehrig predicted. "He has an amazing calmness, a thorough preparedness at the plate.... We are indeed fortunate to have so great a prospect."

Even for his teammates, however, it was impossible not to be aware that DiMaggio had taken the thunder that many had thought Gehrig had rightfully earned. "The man I felt sorry for was Lou," Lefty Gomez said of the situation. "Joe became the team's biggest star almost from the moment he hit the Yanks. It just seemed a terrible shame for Lou. He didn't seem to care, but maybe he did. Sure, the relationship between Joe and Lou seemed pretty good. They never had a cross word that I heard of. They got along, but how could you ever know how Lou really felt?"

Together, Gehrig and DiMaggio would develop a chemistry that never existed between Lou and Babe. It would help produce a new Yankees dynasty with a succession of championships surpassing Murderers' Row. The 1936 team had five players who each drove in 100 or more runs: Gehrig,

DiMaggio, Tony Lazzeri, Bill Dickey, and George Selkirk, the last of whom had succeeded Ruth in the outfield and taken his No. 3. This club set a new major league team record of 182 homers—24 more than the 1927 Yankees. These Yankees also scored a record 1,067 runs in 155 games. Catcher Bill Dickey set a record at his position by batting .362, and Lazzeri enjoyed the biggest day of any Yankee with three home runs—including two grand slams—with an all-time American League record 11 RBIs in a 25–2 rout of the Philadelphia Athletics in May. Of the eight regulars on that team, the lowest on-base percentage belonged to a rookie—Joe DiMaggio. But he had an otherwise phenomenal year, batting .323 with 29 homers and 125 RBIs. Gehrig led the league in slugging, runs, and walks on top of his 49 homers, 152 RBIs, and .354 batting average. His production led to him being voted league MVP by both *The Sporting News* and Baseball Writers. Even the pitching staff contributed to the offense. Red Ruffing crushed five home runs and Johnny Murphy batted .361.

As *Sports Illustrated* summed up in a retrospective decades later, "The pitching was deep and extremely effective, Dickey hit .362, and Gehrig won the Most Valuable Player Award, but the key man was Joe DiMaggio, in his rookie year. An outstanding fielder with a magnificent arm, a powerful batter and a great base runner, DiMaggio established the tone of the McCarthy-era Yankees: a quiet but brilliant all-round efficiency."

In the '36 World Series, the Yankees beat the Giants in six games, DiMaggio batting .346 with three doubles while Gehrig and Selkirk each slugged two home runs. The Yankees won World Series titles again in 1937, 1938, and 1939, and then in 1941 and 1943. Gehrig, of course, would be forced into retirement because of illness in 1939, but his legacy would endure. An appreciative DiMaggio would never forget Gehrig's mentoring and remained an unabashed fan of Lou's power. "I had watched Lou Gehrig hit down in St. Petersburg, and I couldn't see how there ever could have been a more powerful batter, including Babe Ruth, whom I had never seen," DiMaggio recalled. "And I couldn't understand how so great a hitter could be taken so matter-of-factly by the rest of the squad and by the sportswriters."

But he was. Perhaps on another team in another city, Lou Gehrig might have owned the town. New York, though, was America's city of lights, where Gehrig's low-wattage star shone too dimly for the masses. Babe Ruth, even in retirement, was still the prince of the city, at least in spirit. He had set the bar high.

"Strangers in town used to go to Yankee Stadium to see Ruth," Jack Miley of the *New York Daily News* wrote just a couple of weeks before the start of the 1937 season. "He was one of the city sights, like the Empire State tower and the Statue of Liberty. Today they go to see the Yankees, not Gehrig. Young Joe DiMaggio, a first-year rookie, has more color than Gehrig.... When it comes to that personal magnetism, you've either got it or you don't. Roosevelt has it. Hoover hasn't. Dempsey has it, but not Tunney. DiMaggio, like Ruth, has. But not Gehrig. This is a shame, for Lou is a great athlete. He's probably worth more to the Yanks than DiMag, but it is Joe, through no efforts of his own, who captures the imagination of the fans."

The reason may have been more than simply charisma. Gehrig certainly had a share of that. He was a New York Yankee, a World Series champion, and Babe Ruth's partner in making

America fall deeply in love with baseball. How can you not be romantic about the game? But there was something about Lou Gehrig's approach to life that was incompatible with the psyche of New York where, like in America at large, failure is forgiven of the big swingers, in whom even foolishness is flamboyant, and where the world will always belong to those who swing from the heels. That was not Lou Gehrig. The essential Lou Gehrig was the customer that Dom Bruzzese, a delivery boy for Dillon's pharmacy in New Rochelle, met that spring, as relayed in Jonathan Eig's *Luckiest Man*. Bruzzese delivered a package to the Gehrig home, where Lou answered the door. The item had been paid for, but Gehrig did not have any change on him to tip the youngster.

"Eleanor," Lou called out to his wife, "do we have any change for the boy?" Gehrig disappeared into his apartment, returning moments later when he gave the teenager five pennies—a laughable tip, even by 1937 standards. "He was cheap," recalled Bruzzese. "As cheap as they come."

Lou Gehrig, even as the highest-paid Yankee after Ruth's departure, was still Christina's little boy, scrambling for pennies. Off the field, Gehrig tried to cash in as Babe had, but without his success. Lou was the first athlete to appear on a Wheaties cereal box. Then he became a laughingstock when he made a financial deal with General Foods to endorse its breakfast cereal Huskies. General Foods had a network radio program with a broad national audience on which Gehrig was booked to appear. Unfortunately, when host Robert Ripley asked him if he enjoyed any special breakfast food, Lou instinctively blurted out, "Wheaties!" He corrected it in future programs, but his Wheaties flub became a national news story.

Eleanor also pushed Lou to hire Babe's agent, Christy Walsh, whose brainchild was to get Gehrig an audition to succeed Johnny Weissmuller as Tarzan in the movies. Publicity photos were taken of Lou in nothing but leopard-print briefs that showed him in an embarrassing, unflattering form. He looked ripped, too ripped perhaps in his lower body with freakish legs: overly developed thighs and calves that were as aesthetically unattractive as they were strong. *Tarzan* author Edgar Rice Burroughs was so put off by the pictures that he fired off a telegram, telling Gehrig, I WANT TO CONGRATULATE YOU ON BEING A SWELL FIRST BASEMAN.

Meanwhile, the feud with Ruth went on, even if Babe was no longer playing. In early 1937, Ruth made some comments that struck at the heart of Lou's ongoing streak of consecutive games played that continued to grow. "The next two years will tell Gehrig's fate," Babe told an interviewer. "When his legs go, they'll go in a hurry. The average ball fan doesn't realize the effect a single charley horse can have on your legs. If Lou stays out there every day and never rests his legs, one bad charley horse may start him downhill."

Babe struck a nerve with Gehrig. He had reached the point where his reason for being in baseball was about his consecutive game streak, which he felt Ruth had never respected. He hadn't, and with good reason. Babe felt a break here or there, a rest even if a player didn't want it, was a source of reenergizing. In the long run, more baseball people would have agreed with Ruth, given that few managers or front-office executives in the ensuing decades have allowed many of their high-priced athletes to play every game of every season. For Gehrig, though, everything he did in the game connected to his streak, which he believed would lead to him ultimately holding almost every offensive record. His streak was at 1,808 consecutive games after the 1936 season, and he was making public statements about having 2,500 straight games in his sights. Lou was still seething just before the start of the 1937 season when he sat down for an interview with that era's dean of sportswriters, Dan Daniel, who asked him who the greatest ballplayer he had ever seen was. Perhaps it wasn't so much a trick question as one to elicit a headline, and Gehrig took the bait. "Honus Wagner," Lou said, talking about the Pittsburgh shortstop who won eight batting titles but who had played from 1897 to 1917. Dan Daniel's conclusion from his interview: "War between Lou Gehrig and Babe Ruth? Well, we should say!"

18   The Streak Ends

*"I have read and heard people say
I'm near the end of my career, but I know I'm not."*

—Lou Gehrig

IT TOOK A TRAGIC DEATH SENTENCE TO FINALLY GET NEW YORK, and America for that matter, to fall in love with Lou Gehrig. Until then, it seemed, he had gotten about as much respect as Sancho Panza compared to Don Quixote, always playing second banana to the greatest player in baseball, Babe Ruth, and then to new Yankee sensation Joe DiMaggio. Gehrig was the Iron Horse, of course, playing day after day, season after season, never taking a day off, punching in a time card like a faithful employee who gets a gold watch at his retirement party but little more. The Bambino, who owned baseball's greatest records—60 home runs in a single season and 714 in his career, poked fun at Lou's record of playing all those consecutive games, a thankless task when it came to the front office acknowledging it at contract time.

Lou Gehrig's streak of consecutive games played ended on May 2, 1939, when he voluntarily took himself out of the lineup. He had played in 2,130 straight games. He would never return to the lineup again. Within a fortnight, his shocking news would stun baseball and the world beyond. Gehrig had been stricken by an incurable degenerative neurological disease that was decimating his body. Gehrig was only weeks from turning 36. He would not see forty.

Three days earlier, in a game when Gehrig had singled for what would be his 2,721st and last hit, few had taken notice or seemed to care. All attention was on Joe DiMaggio, who had been seriously hurt in the previous inning. Running to catch up with a hard line drive hit by the Senators' Bobby Estalella, DiMaggio got the cleats on his right foot stuck in the mud, tearing muscles just above his right ankle. Surrounded by anxious teammates, coaches, and trainers, Joe writhed on the Yankee Stadium outfield grass for eight minutes. Eventually, he limped off the field.

"I heard something snap in my leg," DiMaggio was quoted in one newspaper, and in another, "I felt something crack." He would be out of the lineup for six weeks, and it was an immediate concern for the Yankees and their fans. Joe DiMaggio had succeeded Babe Ruth as the star and leader of the Yankees in a way that Lou Gehrig never had. In 1938, as the Yankees won their third straight World Series, DiMaggio batted .324 with 32 home runs and 140 RBIs. After his return in 1939, in his fourth season, he would go on to hit a career-best .381. Gehrig, on the other hand, put up what amounted to subpar numbers in 1938: .295 with 29 home runs and 114 RBIs.

They were subpar, unless you consider that Gehrig in 1938 was likely in the early stages of amyotrophic lateral sclerosis, also known now as Lou Gehrig's disease—a fierce neurodegenerative disease that robs one of muscle control, swallowing, breathing, and, ultimately, life. Gehrig had just signed a contract for a career-high $39,000 for the season, and he again expected a great deal out of himself. "Irrespective of any other players on our club, I am the man to whom the team looks as a pacesetter every year," he said in one interview. "I am told I am the hitter who must lead the Yankees to the pennant. That suits me fine. I wanted to go on that way for many years to come." But Lou had an unusually difficult spring training, developing blisters and bruises on his hands for the first time in his career and having trouble hitting with power.

His problems continued when the season began, though the newspapers focused the Yankees' slow start not on Lou's problems but on Joe DiMaggio's holdout. He had refused to join the team unless he was given a contract for $40,000; Colonel Ruppert and the Yankees offered $25,000. Joe McCarthy went so far as to make the ridiculous statement that "the Yankees can get along without DiMaggio." Joe, just 23, eventually caved. When DiMaggio finally joined the team, Gehrig was dropped from the cleanup spot in the batting order to fifth and then sixth. "Let Lou hit his way back to the cleanup spot," McCarthy told reporters. Lou stayed silent and brooded. He was mocked by fans in Philadelphia and Washington when the Yankees played there. Even fans in New York began heckling him when he failed to drive in base runners and taunting him about his Hollywood ties, as he had a starring role in a new western. "Hi-ho, Silver!" they yelled at him when he came to bat, even though that was the Lone Ranger's famous line in the popular radio show and had nothing to do with Gehrig's film, *Rawhide*.

During the 1938 season, Gehrig's streak reached 2,000 games, even as he experienced the first neurological symptoms of his disease. Lou had no idea, of course, only that he was not performing on the baseball field as he had in the past. He went hitless in seven of his first eight games, and didn't hit his first home run until May 3. He was struggling, but obsessed with the fact that his precious consecutive-games streak was approaching the milestone number of 2,000. When he achieved it on May 31, he found that it was an accomplishment that did not get the attention he thought it would. Chances are he might have received considerably more fanfare and stadium celebration had he reached another milestone that seemed within reach at the start of the season: his 500th home run. He had entered the season with 464 career home runs, needing only 36 to join Ruth as the only two players to slug 500 or more homers. But his 29 home runs would be a major disappointment for Lou in 1938. As for reaching 2,000 consecutive games played, he was to find that it merited no in-game recognition, nor did the Yankees or anyone else present him with any certificate or award, not even a gold watch recognizing what he had done. No one seemed to care as much as he did for a record that, like perfect attendance in school, didn't have much to show for it. Even Eleanor Gehrig appeared to diminish its importance to Lou when she had suggested that he end the streak on his own terms at 1,999 consecutive games, a number she said would be more easily remembered than any random number after 2,000. Gehrig, however, was intent on playing. If anything, he found himself on the defensive in answering questions about an achievement in which many others could see little merit. "I can't see why anyone should attack my record," Gehrig said, controlling his exasperation. "I have never belittled anyone else's. I intend to play every day and shall continue to give my best to my employers and the fans. What about the guy who pays $1.10 to see the game? What if I sit on the bench and say I'm resting?"

And what if Lou played only one inning and called it a game played for the purposes of keeping his streak intact? He had propped up his streak that way most notably in 1934 in Detroit, the same place Gehrig's streak would eventually end. That day in 1934, suffering from lumbago, a form of rheumatism, Lou had begged Joe McCarthy to help him keep his streak going. "I don't think I can go nine today," Gehrig told his manager, wincing. "But I'd like to keep the streak alive, Joe, because I'm sure I can play tomorrow. Would you do me a favor? Let me lead off. I'll take my first bat, then I'll get out for the day." Gehrig batted once as the leadoff batter—he singled—and then came out of the game for a pinch runner. "Instead of enhancing his reputation for durability, he sullied it," insisted Bud Shaver of the *Detroit Times*. "He also impugned his reputation for sensibility. If a man is too ill to play, the sensible thing to do is refrain from playing. His physical handicaps are apt to be disastrous for his teammates. Records preserved in the manner in which Gehrig preserved his at Navin Field prove nothing except the absurdity of most records."

As Lou in 1938 tried to draw more attention for recognition of his accomplishment, some fans had begun calling him on that. They were writing letters to newspapers complaining that Gehrig had achieved his record by exploiting a loophole in baseball's rules that allowed players to appear for one inning but get credit for having played the game. Those fans had a point. Starting pitchers, for example, had to be in the game in their position for a full five innings to get credit for being the winning pitcher of a game. In achieving his streak, Gehrig played every inning of every game in only one season, 1931. In addition to his lumbago game in Detroit, Lou was substituted for on nearly 70 other occasions. Then there was the time Yankees general manager Ed Barrow called off a home game on account of rain, even though there was no rain falling and scarcely a cloud in the sky. At the time Gehrig was again nursing an attack of lumbago. But the extra day of rest allowed Lou's back the time to heal so that he could resume his streak the next afternoon. To his credit, Gehrig did play throughout his streak with an assortment of injuries and illnesses, including torn muscles, colds, concussions, headaches, stiff backs, and broken fingers.

What he had begun to suffer in 1938 was just another health issue that now began to raise questions. One of the ways some newspapers had recognized Gehrig's 2,000[th] consecutive game was by publishing photos of Lou in 1925, when he began the streak, and Lou in 1938. The photos were astonishing, showing not only the passage of time—of course, as 13 years had passed—but also in presenting Gehrig as increasingly gaunt and worn. Lou seethed and insisted that he still had a lot of baseball to play "because I know my legs are not going back on me." Yet all the signs were there that Gehrig's skills weren't just eroding, they were disappearing practically overnight. This wasn't just a ballplayer aging.

Even so, no one in authority with the Yankees thought about having Lou—one of the team's most valuable commodities—undergo a full physical examination. Later, Joe McCarthy maintained in a 1945 interview that he suspected in mid-1938 that something might be wrong with his star first baseman and slugger. "We were playing a midseason series with Washington," the Yankees manager said. "For some time I had noticed Gehrig wasn't getting his body into the swing, wasn't taking his full cut. I called this to his attention, and his answer startled me somewhat." What was Lou's response? "You know, Joe, I think it's best for me to make sure I get a piece of the ball. If I get enough little hits, I can lead the league in hitting."

To his credit, Lou performed slightly better in the second half of the season—but it was far below his usual standard. The previous season still seemed too recent to accept such a dramatic decline, and it was difficult to put aside that in 1937 Gehrig had compiled a .351 batting average and a .643 slugging percentage, exceeding his career norms. For a brief period, it looked as if Lou had found the key to unlocking what had chained him. It was also promising that he seemed to be making a recovery in August, which is always the most grueling and hottest month of any baseball season, especially in the middle of a pennant race. On August 12, 1938, Lou enjoyed something he hadn't had all season: a four-hit game, including a double and home run, reminiscent of the younger Gehrig. On August 20, he accomplished a feat that was greater than his consecutive-game streak. He belted a bases-loaded homer, the 23rd grand slam of his career. It was a record worthy of the Babe, and it was Gehrig's, and it would outlast Ruth's 60-homer single season record as well as his career home run mark. (It stood until September 20, 2013, when another Yankee, Alex Rodriguez, broke Lou's record and ultimately ended his career with 25 grand slams, the most by any player in Major League Baseball history.) For Gehrig, that August in 1938 gave him reason to hope. He had tinkered with so much of what he was doing and had finally resorted to a batting stance he had used earlier in his career. "I dunno what did it," he told the Associated Press, "except going back to my old stance. I couldn't figure out how the other one was wrong, but it looks like it was. I won't monkey with it again."

But after hitting his 26th home run of the season on August 26, Gehrig slipped back into a slump, even as the Yankees ran away with the pennant. He hit only three more homers the rest of the season, falling seven shy of the exclusive 500 Home Run Club. He would never reach it. In the 1938 World Series, in which the Yankees swept the Chicago Cubs, he had four hits in 14 at-bats, all singles. "I tired midseason," Gehrig said, talking about how he didn't feel like himself of past years. "I don't know why, but I just couldn't get going again."

It would be no different in 1939. In fact, by most accounts, Lou's spring training that year was so bad that he would have been released had he been anyone else. "He didn't have a shred of his former power," Joe DiMaggio recalled in his autobiography. In batting practice, DiMaggio watched from outside a safety cage at home plate as Gehrig missed easy pitch after easy pitch—19 in a row altogether. How bad Lou Gehrig looked, both as a hitter and in person, was the talk of spring training among players, staff, and writers. Those sports reporters covering the team couldn't ignore the story, but at the same time what they wrote for print were journalistic soft tosses like the ones Gehrig was no longer able to crush. Their stories attributed Lou's problems to "leg stiffness," "calf pains," and "Father Time." But Gehrig's problems were serious enough that Joe McCarthy and Ed Barrow were weighing options in case Lou was finished as a ballplayer.

So it was no surprise to anyone closely following the Yankees when Gehrig began the season in an abysmal slump. At the end of April, when he got his final hit, he was batting a meager .167 on just four hits in 24 at-bats with five walks and one RBI—and he had already committed two errors. His defensive play had made him a liability. He had begun missing ground balls that were hit straight at him, and he barely had the strength to make a throw to second or third base. He also had become so slow covering first base that fellow infielders had to wait for him before making a throw to throw out a runner. He was even noticeably clumsy off the field. One day he fell down while getting dressed in the clubhouse. No one on the team dared say anything about the incident. When he went hitless in a game on April 24, Arthur Daley of the *New York Times* seemed to signal the universal concern that Gehrig's ineffectiveness "has reached an alarming state of anemia."

Lou must have wondered if part of the problem was with his bats. The next day he ordered three new 33-ounce Louisville Slugger bats from Hillerich & Bradsby, a weight lighter than the 36¼-ounce bats he had used for years and the 35¼-ounce bats he used in 1938. But it was obvious the issue had more to do than just the wood. That same day he drove in his only run of the season, banging out two hits against the Philadelphia Athletics, including what should have been a double, had he been the Gehrig of old. He rounded first base but got caught, unable to complete the double and too far to return to first safely. Lou didn't even bother trying to get into a rundown. The *Times* charitably gave him the benefit of the doubt, reporting that Lou was tagged out in a "reckless attempt" to stretch a single into a double. Then came the game when DiMaggio went down in the outfield, with Gehrig's last hit an inning later. The next day, Lou failed to get a hit in four at-bats with runners on base each time. "Captain Lou Gehrig isn't hitting and may be demoted from his present slot," the *New York Mirror* reported the next day. The *New York Sun* went even further as the Yankees headed to Detroit, suggesting that Gehrig's "benching seems imminent."

Gehrig certainly had to be aware that he wasn't helping the team, and that there was grumbling in the clubhouse that his presence in the starting lineup and at first base was a detriment. So on May 2, before the start of the series with the Tigers, Lou took manager Joe McCarthy off the hook and benched himself. McCarthy, who had been very patient and still believed in him, said, "All right, Lou, take a rest, but I want you to know that that's your position and whenever you want it back, all you have to do is walk out there and take it."

Gehrig had been Pipped, as it were, by himself. Coincidentally, Wally Pipp, who had retired in 1929 and lived in Grand Rapids, Michigan, just happened to be at the game in Detroit when Lou benched himself. "Lou looks ill to me," he told reporters who interviewed him that day. "Back when he joined the Yankees he seemed bigger and broader."

"Maybe a rest will do me some good," Gehrig told writers reporting the sports story of the year when he took himself out of the lineup. "Maybe it won't. Who knows? Who can tell? I'm just hoping."

Of course, he would never return. Gehrig's record of consecutive games played would last for 56 years until Baltimore Orioles shortstop Cal Ripken Jr. surpassed it on September 6, 1995. Ripken extended his own mark to 2,632 consecutive games.

19   "The Luckiest Man"

*"I have read and heard people say
I'm near the end of my career, but I know I'm not."*

—Lou Gehrig

WHEN YOU LISTEN TO THE SCRATCHY RECORDING OF LOU GEHRIG'S "luckiest man" speech, it's difficult not to be touched, even to get a lump in your throat. He is Thomas More speaking bravely at his sentencing, Thomas Becket about to be martyred at the cathedral, St. Ignatius facing the lions at the Colosseum. And there, at baseball's own cathedral, is Gehrig, the Iron Horse—dealt a bad hand, dying from a horrible disease and making a heartfelt, poignant speech, sharing "his feelings to an enraptured audience that left tears rolling down the cheeks of all but a few," as the National Baseball Hall of Fame tells it.

It is July 4, 1939, and Gehrig bids farewell to the home crowd in a stirring on-field ceremony at Yankee Stadium: "Fans, for the past two weeks you have been reading about a bad break I got. Yet today I consider myself the luckiest man on the face of the earth." Heaven and earth are moved. How can you not be a romantic about baseball, a national pastime in which the legends and the myths so often tug at your heartstrings?

231

Gary Cooper received an Oscar nomination for portraying Gehrig in the 1942 film *The Pride of the Yankees.* The pinnacle of his performance, of course, was the speech. *The luckiest man on the face of the earth* echoes still. But could it have been that Lou Gehrig in real life was an even better actor than Gary Cooper on film? What was it Napoleon supposedly once said about history: that history is the myths men choose to believe? Exactly. We look at those moments in retrospect with what we know many years later, and imbue them with a meaning that may not accurately represent what was happening at the time.

In 1939, after Lou Gehrig had been diagnosed with the deadly disease that would bear his name in the future, the last thing he wanted the public to know about him was that he had only two years to live. He wanted to hide that he was dying for as long as he could. The diagnosis and the statements released by Gehrig, his doctors, and the Yankees to the public originally said nothing about him being gravely ill, or that there was no cure for amyotrophic lateral sclerosis. In fact, the statements were intentionally misleading, and Lou's world-renowned doctors from the Mayo Clinic in Rochester, Minnesota, carried the deception further by proclaiming him to be suffering from "a form of chronic poliomyelitis," a type of infantile paralysis. When he issued an announcement to the media, Yankees general manager Ed Barrow included a letter from the primary Mayo Clinic neurologist, but neither the letter nor the Yankees' statement suggested that Gehrig's disease was fatal. "Gentlemen, we have bad news," Barrow said. "Gehrig has infantile paralysis. The technical word for his illness is chronic poliomyelitis. Gehrig has been given a chart of exercises and a list of doctors by the Mayo Clinic... The report recommends that Lou abandon any hope of continuing as an active player." Lou Gehrig would have to retire, the Mayo Clinic effectively said in its letter, though, "he could, however, continue in some executive capacity."

It was, in essence, a deliberate ruse. Gehrig had been given the true and dire diagnosis by doctors at the Mayo Clinic, where he spent a week in June 1939 undergoing elaborate neurological tests by the leading authorities on amyotrophic lateral sclerosis, or ALS. Lou knew the score. Some accounts, including his wife's, have suggested that Eleanor Gehrig had orchestrated the trip to the clinic in addition to keeping the extent of his illness—that he was dying—from Lou. In truth, Eleanor hadn't made the trip to Rochester; she remained behind in New Rochelle. Gehrig himself told Eleanor of the diagnosis in a letter that is now in the archives of the National Baseball Hall of Fame: "The bad news is 'lateral sclerosis,' in our language infantile paralysis," the letter begins. "There isn't any cure, the best they can hope is to check it at the point it is now and there is a 50-50 chance for that."

Even to Eleanor, Lou was outlining a best-case scenario, intimating that perhaps 15 years down the road he would likely need the use of a cane to walk. That was also what Gehrig wanted to believe. Why wouldn't he? But what he wanted most of all was to have a life if not on the baseball field, then in the front office. He told doctors he was hoping to finish the season with the Yankees in some capacity. He hoped to collect his salary for the season. He had taken a $4,000 pay cut from 1938 and would earn $35,000 for the season, assuming the Yankees kept him in another position and were willing to pay him a baseball star's salary.

It was money, pure and simple—isn't it always about the money? It was money, his big contract, that was the motivation for giving the misleading diagnosis to the Yankees, media, and public. According to biographer Jonathan Eig, "He told one writer, in fact, that he couldn't afford to quit the game because poor investments, heavy taxes, and family problems had cut into his bank account." Gehrig's financial problems must have indeed been severe. He wasn't supporting just himself and his wife, after all. After marrying Eleanor, Lou had continued supporting his mother and father, for whom he had bought a house in New Rochelle in 1927. He couldn't buy his wife a house, but he was keeping momma in one. And it was already a drain on his finances apparently even before he got sick. On May 9, 1937, according to Westchester County court records, the Gehrigs missed a semiannual payment of $255, which set off a clause in the mortgage that allowed the children of previous owner Alexander List, as executors of their father's will, to call in the balance of about $8,800. Apparently neither Gehrig's parents nor Lou himself were able to pay the balance, leading to loss of the house in foreclosure on September 11, 1937, according to a deed in the Westchester County clerk's office.

So Gehrig appeared to be facing a serious financial crisis at the same time as a personal health catastrophe that threatened to make money problems even worse. Understandably, the last thing that Lou was looking forward to was an appreciation day in his honor, especially one that might be construed not as a retirement farewell but a living memorial to a walking dead man. The less said or written about Lou and his health, the less likely it was that his true diagnosis would become public, and jeopardize his future earnings either with the Yankees or in business.

He was firm about this. To this day, his medical records remain permanently sealed despite repeated requests by medical researchers, lawmakers, and journalists to have them opened.

At the time, the truth about Gehrig's diagnosis was known only to Lou, Eleanor, and a few close friends, among them writer Fred Lieb and his wife. Other writers, the Yankees players, and fans were in the dark, having only the public statement to rely upon. The reports about Gehrig's health were similarly absent of the seriousness of Lou's condition, let alone the fact he would almost certainly die soon from the rare disease. "Nobody knew what the heck that disease was," said teammate Tommy Henrich.

When Gehrig returned to New York in late June, his teammates began thinking of honoring Lou with a clubhouse presentation of a fishing rod and a trophy. But then the writers who covered the Yankees began pressing for a public ceremony, an appreciation day honoring Lou. Those writers campaigned for honoring Gehrig by giving him gifts to thank him for his years with the Yankees, as well as retiring his uniform No. 4, which they had not done yet for any player, not even Ruth. But they didn't foresee this as a somber event enveloped with sadness and tragedy due to his impending death because they had no idea that he was dying from the illness that was forcing his retirement. Some writers even suggested this appreciation day take place at the upcoming All-Star Game, which was scheduled at Yankee Stadium on July 11. Ed Barrow, though, didn't want to lose the thunder to the All-Star Game, not to mention the gate and concession receipts which would then be shared with the leagues and other teams. So with the Fourth of July approaching, Barrow agreed to a Lou Gehrig Appreciation Day ceremony to take place between games of that day's double-header with the Washington Senators. Yankee Stadium would already be adorned with red, white, and blue bunting in celebration of the country's Independence Day holiday, fitting for an occasion honoring Lou. Barrow even invited the great 1927 Yankees team for a reunion so that Gehrig might be surrounded by teammates from his first World Series championship.

The question on the minds of some Yankees and writers was whether the most important figure on the 1927 team, Babe Ruth, would be in attendance. There was no secret about the feud between Babe and Lou. They hadn't spoken in five years. There was also the matter of Ruth being denied a chance to manage the Yankees. Was Ruth harboring bad feelings about that slight—both at Ed Barrow, who hadn't wanted him, and Gehrig, who hadn't supported Ruth in his bid? The decision, unsurprisingly, wasn't made by Ruth alone. Claire Ruth's influence over Babe had grown even greater during his retirement. She still strongly disliked Christina Gehrig and for that matter she didn't think much of Lou for allowing his mother to speak about people, especially her and their girls, as she had. She also hadn't forgiven the Yankees for slighting her man—both for refusing to give him a chance to manage and for hatching the cruel deal that sent him to obscurity and embarrassment with the Boston Braves. Ruth later told Johnny Grant and others that Claire had insisted he not attend... but that he changed his mind the morning of the event.

A capacity crowd of 61,808 fans packed Yankee Stadium to see Gehrig honored by dignitaries and presented with gifts that included a silver service set from the Yankees front office; a fruit bowl and two candlesticks from the New York Giants;

a silver pitcher from the Harry M. Stevens company (the stadium's concessionaires); two silver platters from Harry M. Stevens employees; a fishing rod and tackle from the Yankee Stadium employees and ushers; a silver, three-handled loving cup from the Yankees office staff; and a ring from the jewelry firm Dieges & Clust. But perhaps the gift that may have touched Gehrig most was what had set in motion the idea of an this day, compliments of his 1939 Yankees teammates: a 21½-inch-tall silver trophy with wood base featuring an eagle perched atop a baseball supported by six bats. On one side of the trophy were the names of all his current teammates; on the other side a poem written by *New York Times* sports columnist John Kieran:

To LOU GEHRIG
We've been to the wars together;
We took our foes as they came;
And always you were the leader,
And ever you played the game.
Idol of cheering millions,
Records are yours by sheaves;
Iron of frame they hailed you,
Decked you with laurel leaves.
But higher than that we hold you,
We who have known you best;
Knowing the way you came through
Every human test.
Let this be a silent token
Of lasting friendship's gleam
And all that we've left unspoken;
YOUR PALS OF THE YANKEE TEAM.

Ed Barrow, as the Yankees general manager, took control of the field rituals, working with manager Joe McCarthy and columnist Sid Mercer, who served as master of ceremonies. What would give the event a stirring theatrical atmosphere was the public address system, which had been installed at Yankee Stadium in 1936 and whose echo from the outfield speakers repeated everything everyone said with a dramatic delay. Among the dignitaries on hand was Mayor Fiorello LaGuardia, who soon after offered Lou a job at the New York City Parole Commission. La Guardia called Gehrig "the greatest prototype of good sportsmanship and citizenship," and Postmaster General James Farley told Lou that "for generations to come, boys who play baseball will point with pride to your record."

The emotional tide continued building as Joe McCarthy described Lou as "the finest example of a ballplayer, sportsman, and citizen that baseball has ever known." Then he tearfully turned to Gehrig. "Lou, what else can I say," he said, "except that it was a sad day in the life of everybody who knew you when you came into my hotel room that day in Detroit and told me you were quitting as a ballplayer because you felt yourself a hindrance to the team. My God, man, you were never that."

At last came the Babe, looking resplendent in a white suit, two-toned shoes, and tan from all the golf he had been playing. He had been standing with Waite Hoyt, Tony Lazzeri, Joe Dugan, Herb Pennock, and members of the 1927 Yankees while players from the current Yankees team and the Senators lined up along the first- and third-base paths. Even at a ceremony for someone else, it was still tough to top Ruth. He hadn't said a word, and the packed crowd was suddenly abuzz, as if he had just come to the plate for another at-bat and the lightning that could accompany it. "In 1927, Lou was with us, and I say that was the best ballclub the Yankees ever had," Ruth said into the microphone of the public-address system. "Anyway, that's my opinion, and while Lazzeri here pointed out to me that there are only 13 or 14 of us here, my answer is shucks, we only need nine to beat 'em." Babe then made a joke about letting Lou free to now go out and catch all the fish he could, and moved back.

Everyone waited for Lou, who looked frozen, staring at nothing in particular. Eleanor Gehrig later said that Lou had written down some things he wanted to say, but then decided against making a speech. Somewhat awkwardly, Sid Mercer told the crowd, "Mr. Gehrig has asked not to speak, thank you for coming—" He hadn't finished when the crowd started to chant, "We want Lou! We want Lou!" A moment passed before Joe McCarthy came up to Lou and whispered, "Lou, you've gotta do this," giving him a little nudge in the back. Gehrig had no choice. What followed, of course, made history.

"Fans, for the past two weeks you have been reading about a bad break I got," he began, his voice cracking. He hesitated, lowered his head, and took a deep breath. "Yet today, I consider myself the luckiest man on the face of the earth."

The words caromed off the speakers in an echo—"*luckiest man... luckiest man... on the face of the earth... on the face of the earth*"—and he continued without looking up or changing the expression on his face.

I have been in ballparks for seventeen years and have never received anything but kindness and encouragement from you fans. Look at these grand men. Which of you wouldn't consider it the high-light of his career just to associate with them for even one day?

Sure I'm lucky. Who wouldn't consider it an honor to have known Jacob Ruppert? Also, the builder of baseball's greatest empire, Ed Barrow? To have spent six years with that wonderful little fellow, Miller Huggins? Then to have spent the next nine years with that outstanding leader, that smart student of psychology, the best manager in baseball today, Joe McCarthy? Sure I'm lucky.

When the New York Giants, a team you would give your right arm to beat, and vice versa, sends you a gift—that's something. When everybody down to the groundskeepers and those boys in white coats re-member you with trophies—that's something.

When you have a wonderful mother-in-law who takes sides with you in squabbles with her own daughter—that's something.

When you have a father and a mother who work all their lives so you can have an education and build your body—it's a blessing.

When you have a wife who has been a tower of strength and shown more courage than you dreamed existed—that's the finest I know.

So I close in saying that I might have been given a bad break, but I've got an awful lot to live for.

Was it "baseball's Gettysburg Address," as some called it? It was certainly one of the most emotional moments in the game's history, despite the fact that fans did not know the truth about his failing health. Lou was not one for feeling oppressed, sad-assed, and sorry for himself, nor did he want anyone's pity. For a game whose commentators so often love to pontificate about "character" emanating from the greats of the past or among its present heroes, Gehrig's "Luckiest Man" speech makes one wonder if we truly recognize that trait or if the word has simply become as overused as every other superlative.

As Richard Vidmer of the *New York Herald Tribune* wrote the next day:

> Throughout Lou Gehrig's career there was always the feeling he lacked that mythical something called color. Perhaps he did. And yet now that his playing days are over, he has more color than almost any athlete in the game. Somehow I felt that at the stadium yesterday they were honoring not a great baseball player but a truly great sportsman who could take his triumphs with sincere modesty and could face tragedy with a smile. His records will attest to future generations that Lou Gehrig was one of the greatest baseball players who ever lived, but only those who have been fortunate enough to have known him during his most glorious years will realize that he has stood for something finer than merely a great baseball player—he stood for everything that makes sports important in the American scene.

Wiping tears away from his face with a handkerchief, Lou was visibly shaken as he stepped away from the microphone, any sound drowned out for a moment as the crowd stood and applauded for nearly two minutes. A red-eyed Babe Ruth came over and hugged Lou, wrapping an arm around his neck as he broke five years of silence by whispering through his own tears, "C'mon, kid... C'mon, kid, buck up now. We're all with you." It was enough to make them both smile. "Lou spoke as I never thought I'd hear a man speak in a ballpark," Babe later recalled. "When he said, 'I consider myself the luckiest man in the world' [sic], I couldn't stand it any longer. I went over to him and put my arm around him, and though I tried to smile and cheer him up, I could not keep from crying."

It was the moment the photographers had been waiting for, and the picture of Gehrig and the Babe in a seemingly loving embrace became one of the best-known images of baseball's greatest slugging combo. Behind them, the Seventh Regiment Band, which had entertained, played the romantic ballad "I Love You Truly," which Bing Crosby had made famous again in 1934, and the crowd began chanting, "We love you, Lou!"

"It was left for the greatest showman of baseball history, Babe Ruth, to come forward with a much-needed tension-breaker," wrote Dan M. Daniel, reporting for the *New York Telegram.* "Before the biggest crowd of the baseball year, Ruth and Gehrig, who had quarreled before the Bambino left the Yankees, became reconciled. With his face wreathed in the old Ruthian smile, the Babe posted with his right arm around Lou's neck.

"The old king and the crown prince had become reconciled at last."

Epilogue

A WEEK AFTER THE LOU GEHRIG APPRECIATION DAY, BABE RUTH went up to Cooperstown, New York, where he was inducted among Ty Cobb, Honus Wagner, and Christy Mathewson in the first class of the Baseball Hall of Fame.

Gehrig finished out the season in uniform with the Yankees, though never seeing any action. At the end of the season, he accepted a job with the City of New York, taking on the quiet life of a bureaucrat. Meanwhile, he maintained regular correspondence with his doctors at the Mayo Clinic, who were monitoring his health and response to a course of treatment. His true condition remained hidden and possibly would have stayed that way if the Yankees had continued winning as they had in recent years. But when several Yankees reported injuries and physical aches related to muscle problems, Jimmy Powers of the *Daily News* published a story questioning whether Gehrig might have infected his teammates with the "polio germ" that supposedly had ravaged his body. Furious, Gehrig sued and opened a can of worms that exposed his secret.

If Gehrig had been diagnosed with poliomyelitis or infantile paralysis, which is communicable and with no vaccine at the time, then there was a basis for the polio germ fear. This diagnosis is what Gehrig, the Yankees, and the Mayo Clinic had maintained in their statements. The lawsuit, however, put an end to that charade when a lawyer for the *Daily News* went to the Mayo Clinic where he spoke to doctors there. Only then did the public begin learning that Gehrig had the deadly ALS and that the disease is not a form of polio. No one—not Gehrig, the Yankees, or the Mayo Clinic—offered an immediate explanation of why his true diagnosis had been hidden. The lawsuit placed the issue in the courts with more convoluted legalese that continued to cloud the understanding of what exactly Lou Gehrig was suffering from.

Would Gehrig have prevailed in court? By the end of 1939, he was already a shell of the wasted-away man people had seen at Lou Gehrig Appreciation Day. Or would the findings in a court case have only further exposed the fact that Gehrig had lied and misled everyone except his family and close friends? Lou Gehrig hadn't simply retired. He had a disease for which there was no cure, and he was dying before his fans' eyes. The *Daily News* paid $17,500 to settle the lawsuit. Ultimately, while Lou Gehrig Appreciation Day had not been a memorial to a dying man, that was exactly what it would be remembered as being.

As the symptoms of ALS further destroyed his body, a wheelchair-bound and then bed-ridden Gehrig continued entertaining friends and writers at his home. Babe Ruth was among those who visited. The rift between the two former teammates, though, never healed. On April 14, 1941, Lou finally took a leave of absence from the city job that he had come to love.

On the morning of Monday, June 2, 1941, Gehrig slipped into a coma. He died at 10 minutes past 10:00 that night, with Eleanor and his parents around his bed. He was 37.

Babe and Claire Ruth arrived around 1:00 in the morning after getting word that Gehrig had died. They offered Eleanor and Lou's parents their condolences then quietly left. "[Eleanor] became very angry when Ruth and his wife came in very intoxicated," wrote songwriter Fred Fisher, a good friend of the Gehrigs, in a letter to one of Lou's doctors at the Mayo Clinic. "He certainly wasn't wanted by the Gehrigs, as there was friction between them for years."

New Yorkers paid their respects at a public viewing at the Church of the Divine Paternity at Central Park West and 76th Street. When he showed up, Babe Ruth wept in front of Lou Gehrig's open casket. The next day, Lou's body was cremated at the Fresh Pond Crematory in Queens.

Flags were flown at half-staff throughout New York City and at every major league ballpark. At the Hall of Fame in Cooperstown, New York, Lou's plaque was draped in black. The previous winter, the five-year waiting period for induction had been waived for Gehrig, and he had been enshrined while he was still living.

Gehrig's will left his estate—valued at about $160,000, including a stock portfolio of roughly $50,000 and $14,000 in bonds—to Eleanor. It gave his parents an allowance of $205 a month. They contested the will and wound up settling out of court, the terms never disclosed. Henry died in 1946 at the age of 79. Christina died in 1954 at the age of 72. Eleanor, who never remarried, died on March 6, 1984, her 80th birthday.

Babe Ruth died of throat cancer on August 16, 1948. He was 53. "The Babe died a beautiful death," Father Thomas Kaufman of St. Catherine of Siena Parish told reporters outside the hospital. "He said his prayers and lapsed into a sleep. He died in his sleep." Thousands of New Yorkers, including children who idolized him, had stood vigil outside his hospital in Babe's final days.

Ruth's open casket was placed on display in the rotunda of Yankee Stadium. More than 77,000 people filed past to pay tribute. At his funeral Mass at St. Patrick's Cathedral in Manhattan, a crowd estimated at 75,000 waited outside. Ruth was buried on a hillside at the Gate of Heaven Cemetery in Valhalla, New York.

Just two months earlier, on June 13, 1948, wearing his No. 3 pinstriped uniform, Babe Ruth appeared at Yankee Stadium one last time to have his number retired. "I am proud I hit the first home run here," Babe said that day, his raspy voice barely above a whisper. "God knows who will hit the last one. It is great to see the men from 25 years ago back here today and it makes me feel proud to be with them."

Acknowledgments

MY LATE FRIEND AND AGENT MIKE HAMILBURG LOVED TO SAY THAT every book has its own godfather. In the case of *Gehrig and the Babe,* there were two. My longtime writer pal Dave Thomas used to spend too much time for his own good on the basketball courts and at Los Angeles Lakers games. Like a lot of Lakers fans, he lamented the feud between stars Kobe Bryant and Shaquille O'Neal that broke apart their dynasty, possibly while they still had a few more NBA championships in their future. Knowing I was a die-hard Yankees and baseball fan, Dave turned to me one day and said, "Kobe and Shaq are the modern day Ruth and Gehrig. Their feud ruined their Yankees teams, and who knows how many more pennants and World Series championships they could have won?"

I was raised a Yankees fan, with huge color posters of Joe DiMaggio and Mickey Mantle on my bedroom walls. I met Mantle on my first newspaper job shortly after his retirement, and we played golf together in Dallas in the early 1970s. In the late 1970s, while a Nieman Fellow at Harvard, I hosted Robert Creamer, author of what many consider the definitive biography of Babe Ruth, *Babe: The Legend Comes to Life*, at a dinner and wine and cheese gathering. He stayed in Cambridge an extra two days while we took in a Boston Red Sox game together and spoke extensively about Ruth, Gehrig, the Yankees of yesterday and today, and Mantle too, of course. In the mid-1980s, when I joined *Sports Illustrated*, I was hired to replace Robert Creamer, though replacing Creamer would be like trying to replace Babe Ruth. Then, of course, there was my work on my two previous baseball biographies, *Mickey Mantle: America's Prodigal Son* and *DiMag & Mick: Sibling Rivals, Yankee Blood Brothers.*

So, undertaking *Gehrig & the Babe,* I thought I knew almost all there was to know about Ruth and Gehrig, but, wow, was I wrong. I knew they had been great players, so you assume those had been great teams with hardware by the caseload. Perhaps that's how we always think about the great ones in any sport. And, if we haven't lived in their time or anywhere close to their era, we just think their greatness equaled World Series titles, for to the truly great ones, championships are the mark of greatness. Mantle used to say that the only time he cried after losing was after the seventh game of the 1960 World Series that the Yankees lost to the Pittsburgh Pirates. The Yankees won three blowout games and scored more than twice as many runs as the Pirates, but Pittsburgh won the championship on Bill Mazeroski's ninth-inning walkoff home run. "All our home run power and greatness," Mantle said, recalling that series with a bitter scowl. "Some greatness, huh?"

Those legendary Ruth-Gehrig teams from 1925 to 1934—known as Murderers' Row, and especially the 1927 Yankees, recognized as the greatest of all baseball teams? Well, for all their Bambino and Iron Horse bluster, they won only three World Series titles: in 1927, 1928, and 1932. In six of those other years—1925, 1929, 1930, 1931, 1933, and 1934—the Ruth-Gehrig teams didn't even win the American League pennant. In contrast, consider that Joe DiMaggio's Yankees of the 1930s, 1940s, and early 1950s won 10 World Series championships, and Mickey Mantle's teams of the 1950s and early 1960s won seven. Heck, the Reggie Jackson–led Yankees of the 1970s won only one fewer title than Gehrig and the Babe.

So I began looking into why those of us who grow up with baseball are raised with these stories of the greatness of Babe Ruth and Lou Gehrig. Yes, individually they were incredible, saving and reinventing the game while putting up records and statistics that lasted half a century and more, many of them broken only by bionic-like men created by science. But their incredible individual accomplishments, while dynastic statistics, failed to translate into a dynasty of championships.

This book's other godfather is Johnny Grant, the long-time Hollywood promoter who befriended Babe Ruth in Tinseltown while he was in Los Angeles filming *The Pride of the Yankees*. Johnny had a knack for engaging people in marathon personal conversations, which is how he got to know the Bambino so intimately. Over time, Johnny became known as the "Mayor of Hollywood," an honorary title given to him for his years of service to the Hollywood Chamber of Commerce. About the time that Dave Thomas suggested the Ruth-Gehrig friendship and feud as a subject of a book, Johnny Grant approached me to assist him in helping organize and write a retrospective of his life in Hollywood. Johnny's career included helping save the famous HOLLYWOOD sign and having hosted hundreds of Walk of Fame inductions, being photographed alongside a succession of stars as their names were immortalized on the sidewalks of Hollywood Boulevard. During our work on this project, I learned of his friendship with Ruth, and he was most gracious and unselfish in sharing his recollections. Johnny and I spent countless hours talking about Babe at the Roosevelt Hotel, which was Grant's home and hangout and where Ruth lived during his visits to Hollywood.

"There are two people I've known that I could spend a lifetime talking to," Johnny used to say. "One was Babe Ruth. The other was Marilyn Monroe."

Well, of course!

Gehrig and the Babe would not have been possible without the assistance of many individuals. First, acknowledgment must go to my literary agent and friend, Leticia Gomez, without whose professional skills, constant encouragement, and unstinting moral support, this book would never have been completed.

James Bacon, my former deskmate at the *Los Angeles Herald Examiner*, was an inspiring mentor. His friendship and countless stories about Hollywood stars and their stories and anecdotes about Babe Ruth in New York and Los Angeles—not to mention his whiskey and his introduction to numerous contacts, among them Reno Barsocchini, Joe DiMaggio's lifelong friend, who offered additional insight into the relationship of DiMaggio and Gehrig—are invaluable.

Pete Rose was magnanimous in sharing his thoughts about both Ruth and Gehrig, how they hit the way they did, and in helping me understand the unique culture and dynamics of the major league clubhouse. Pete has been a friend since the 1990s.

His youngest son, Tyler, and my oldest son, Trey, grew up together playing Little League, travel teams in their teens, and playing baseball and basketball at Glendale College.

Blackie Sherrod, the late sports columnist of the *Dallas Morning News* and a role model from my early days in journalism, was helpful in his final years in giving me his assessment of Ruth and Gehrig as pop culture figures in post–World War I America and the Depression era.

Longtime baseball scouts George Genovese and Phil Pote were extremely kind in their recollections of Ruth and Gehrig, especially of their barnstorming throughout the country.

I am deeply appreciative of the acceptance and assistance from my publisher, Triumph Books, and my editor there, Jesse Jordan.

Special thanks also to these individuals for their support or assistance in tangible and intangible ways: Hank Aaron, Marty Appel, Bobby Asnas, Jim Bacon, Sallie Baker, Jim Bellows, Keven Bellows, Yogi Berra, Hollis Biddle, Barry Bonds, Jim Bouton, Jimmy Breslin, Tony Brooklier, Jerry Brown, Jim Brown, Jeff and Cindy Brynan, Jim Bunning, Ken Burns, George W. Bush, Roger Butler, Al Campanis, Dave Campbell, Rick Cerrone, Laura Chester, Barbara Cigarroa, Paul Cohen, John B. Connally, Alfredo Corchado, Bob Costas, Kevin Costner, Warren Cowan, Robert Creamer, Billy Crystal, Francis Dale, Tina Daunt, Teo Davis, Cody Decker, Frank Deford, Joe DiMaggio, James Duarte, Mel Durslag, Jonathan Eig, Carl Erskine, Roy Firestone, Robert Fitzgerald, Whitey Ford, Don Forst, Dudley Freeman, Glenn Frey, Carlos Fuentes, Randy Galloway, Peter Gammons, Gabriel Garcia Marquez, Mikal Gilmore, Rudolph Giuliani, Carole Player Golden, Peter Golenbock, Johnny Grant, Kathy Griffin, Carlos Guerra,

Mary Frances Gurton, Chris Gwynn, David Halberstam, Mike Hamilburg, Thomas Harris, Lew Harris, Jickey Harwell, Don Henley, Mickey Herskowitz, Joe Holley, Ken Holley, Ed Hunter, Matty Ianniello, Alex Jacinto, Derek Jeter, Chipper Jones, David Justice, Ron Kaye, Preston Kirk, Doug Krikorian, Sandy Koufax, Tony Kubek, Deborah Larcom, Ring Lardner Jr., Don Larsen, Lisa LaSalle, Tommy Lasorda, Tim Layana, Timothy Leary, Jane Leavy, Jill Lieber, Carole Lieberman, Mike Lupica, Ralph Lynn, Bob Mallon, John Mankiewicz, Mickey Mantle, Willie Mays, Barbara McBride-Smith, Julie McCullough, Mark McGwire, David McHam, Frank Messer, Lidia Montemayor, Jim Montgomery, Leigh Montville, Louis F. Moret, Mark Mulvoy, Marcus Musante, Stan Musial, Joe Namath, Jack Nelson, Don Newcombe, Jose Oliveros, Peter O'Malley, Edward James Olmos, Bill Orozco, Robert Patrick, Octavio Paz, Thomas Pettigrew, Dorothy Ruth Pirone, Harry Provence, John Robert Pharr, George Pla, Robert Redford, Jimmie Reese, Pee Wee Reese, Rick Reilly, Bobby Richardson, Wanda Rickerby, David Riesman, Phil Rizzuto, Tim Robbins, Phil Alden Robinson, Gregory Rodriguez, Jim Rome, Carol Rose, Susan Sarandon, Dick Schaap, Dutch Schroeder, Vin Scully, Modesta Garcia Segovia, Diane K. Shah, Gail Sheehy, Charlie Sheen, Ron Shelton, Bob Sheppard, Blackie Sherrod, Buck Showalter, T.J. Simers, Paul Simon, Marty Singer, Bill Skowron, April Smith, George Solotaire, Stephanie Sowa, Lee Strasberg, Susan Strasberg, Ben Stein, George Steinbrenner, Julia Ruth Stevens, Gay Talese, Don Tanner, J. Randy Taraborrelli, Joe Torre, John Tuthill, Peter Ueberroth, George Vecsey, Judy Wammack Rice, Sander Vanocur, Robert Vickrey, Don

Wanlass, Ted Williams, Tom Wolfe, Gene Woodling, Steve Wulf, and Don Zimmer.

My appreciation to the entire staff of the National Baseball Hall of Fame Museum Library in Cooperstown, New York, for their cooperation on so many levels. Thanks also to the library staffs of *Time* and *Sports Illustrated, The Sporting News,* the Associated Press, the *Los Angeles Times,* the *New York Times,* the *New York Post,* the *New York Daily News, Newsday,* the *Washington Post,* the *Brooklyn Daily Eagle,* the *Boston Globe,* the *Dallas Morning News,* the *Houston Chronicle,* the *Detroit Free Press,* the *Kansas City Star,* the *Oklahoman,* and the *Tulsa World;* ESPN Archives, MLB.com, the New York Yankees, Susan Naulty of the Richard Nixon Presidential Library in Yorba Linda, the National Archives and Records Administration, the reference departments at the New York Public Library, the City of Baltimore Public Library, the Beverly Hills Public Library, the Santa Monica Public Library, the Dallas Public Library, and the Library of Congress.

I want to thank, too, Christina Kahrl, my editor on my Mickey Mantle biography at Brassey's Inc., for her sensitive editing and commentary on drafts of the manuscript. Christina isn't just a great editor but one of the most knowledgeable baseball writers in America. Although she wasn't involved in editing *Gehrig & the Babe,* her early input on the book, especially on the contributions of Miller Huggins and Joe McCarthy, was invaluable in developing this dual biography.

As always, I am especially indebted to my late parents: my mother, Maria Emma, for always encouraging my interest in heroes in general and Mickey Mantle in particular; my father, Antonio Sr., for sparking my love of baseball as a youth and spending countless hours over the years talking baseball and forever debating the merits of Ruth and Gehrig, as well as DiMaggio and Mantle.

Special gratitude goes out to my muse, Jeter, the prince of all Labrador retrievers.

As with my other books, *Gehrig and the Babe* might never have been written without the inspiration and sacrifice of my wife and our sons, Ryan and Trey, and daughter-in-law, Frances. My wife, Renee, the fairest of them all, has been the person who has kept after me about this book, as she has with all of them—willing to sacrifice vacations, movie nights, and more for whatever research and work the project required. Her devotion and love—and the love of my sons—are my reason for being.

—Tony Castro
Los Angeles, 2017

Appendix 1: Babe Ruth's Farewell Speech

APRIL 27, 1947, YANKEE STADIUM, BABE RUTH DAY

Thank you very much, ladies and gentlemen. You know how bad my voice sounds? Well, it feels just as bad.

You know this baseball game of ours comes up from the youth. That means the boys. And after you're a boy and grow up to know how to play ball, then you come to the boys you see representing themselves today in your national pastime—the only real game, I think, in the world: baseball.

As a rule, some people think if you give them a football or a baseball or something like that—naturally they're athletes right away. But you can't do that in baseball. You've gotta start from way down [at] the bottom, when you're six or seven years of age. You can't wait until you're 15 or 16. You gotta let it grow up with you. And if you're successful, and you try hard enough, you're bound to come out on top—just like these boys have come to the top now.

There's been so many lovely things said about me, and I'm glad that I've had the opportunity to thank everybody. Thank you.

Appendix 2: Lou Gehrig's Farewell Speech

JULY 4, 1939, YANKEE STADIUM, LOU GEHRIG APPRECIATION DAY

Fans, for the past two weeks you have been reading about a bad break I got. Yet today, I consider myself the luckiest man on the face of the earth.

I have been in ballparks for 17 years and have never received anything but kindness and encouragement from you fans. Look at these grand men. Which of you wouldn't consider it the highlight of his career just to associate with them for even one day?

Sure I'm lucky. Who wouldn't consider it an honor to have known Jacob Ruppert? Also, the builder of baseball's greatest empire, Ed Barrow? To have spent six years with that wonderful little fellow, Miller Huggins? Then to have spent the next nine years with that outstanding leader, that smart student of psychology, the best manager in baseball today, Joe McCarthy?

Sure I'm lucky. When the New York Giants, a team you would give your right arm to beat, and vice versa, sends you a gift—that's something. When everybody down to the groundskeepers and those boys in white coats remember you with trophies—that's something.

When you have a wonderful mother-in-law who takes sides with you in squabbles with her own daughter—that's something. When you have a father and a mother who work all their lives so you can have an education and build your body—it's a blessing. When you have a wife who has been a tower of strength and shown more courage than you dreamed existed— that's the finest I know.

So I close in saying that I might have been given a bad break, but I've got an awful lot to live for.

Appendix 3: Letters Of Note

LETTER FROM LOU GEHRIG TO ELEANOR

This letter, now preserved at the Baseball Hall of Fame library, was handwritten by Lou Gehrig to his wife on stationery from the Book-Cadillac Hotel in Detroit, where the New York Yankees stayed when Gehrig's consecutive-games streak ended at 2,130 on Tuesday, May 2, 1939. The letter, which appears to have been written the next day, is undated and the ending is missing.

> My sweetheart—and please God grant that we may be ever such—for what the hell else matters—That thing yesterday I believe and hope was the turning point in my life for the future as far as taking life too seriously is concerned—It was inevitable, although I dreaded the day, and my thoughts were with you constantly—How would this affect you and I—That was the big question and the most important thought underlying everything. I broke just before the game because of thoughts of you—not because I didn't know you are the bravest kind of partner, but because

my inferiority grabbed me and made me wonder and
ponder if I could possibly prove myself worthy of
you—As for me, the road may come to a dead end
here, but why should it?—Seems like our backs are
to the wall now, but there usually comes a way out—
where, and what, I know not, but who can tell that
it might not lead right out to greater things?—Time
will tell—

    As for our suggestion of farewell tour and farewell
day [manager] Joe [McCarthy] had a different but
sensible idea—He said there wasn't anybody more
deserving of the remaining salary—and he wasn't
afraid of [Yankees president] Ed [Barrow], but with
this new setup [Gehrig had been named non-playing
captain] that questions might arise, and if we planned
a farewell day to record, newspapermen would in-
terpret it as the absolute finish and that might cause
quite a squabble among all the new directors, whereas
if we said just a temporary rest and lay off—to come
back in warmer weather, there could hardly be any
doubt—I couldn't tell you this over the phone because [roommate] Bill [Dickey] was—

With this, the letter ends abruptly. The Gehrig family did
not provide the rest of the letter when handing over a number
of belongings after the death of Eleanor Gehrig in 1984.

Appendix 4: Career Statistics

BABE RUTH'S PITCHING STATISTICS

Year	Age	Tm	Lg	W	L	W-L%	ERA	G	GS	GF	CG	SHO	SV	IP	H
1914	19	BOS	AL	2	1	.667	3.91	4	3	0	1	0	0	23	21
1915	20	BOS	AL	18	8	.692	2.44	32	28	3	16	1	0	217.2	166
1916	21	BOS	AL	23	12	.657	1.75	44	40	3	23	9	1	323.2	230
1917	22	BOS	AL	24	13	.649	2.01	41	38	3	35	6	2	326.1	244
1918	23	BOS	AL	13	7	.650	2.22	20	19	0	18	1	0	166.1	125
1919	24	BOS	AL	9	5	.643	2.97	17	15	2	12	0	1	133.1	148
1920	25	NYY	AL	1	0	1.000	4.50	1	1	0	0	0	0	4	3
1921	26	NYY	AL	2	0	1.000	9.00	2	1	1	0	0	0	9	14
1930	35	NYY	AL	1	0	1.000	3.00	1	1	0	1	0	0	9	11
1933	38	NYY	AL	1	0	1.000	5.00	1	1	0	1	0	0	9	12
10 Yrs				94	46	.671	2.28	163	147	12	107	17	4	1221.1	974

BABE RUTH'S HITTING STATISTICS

Year	Age	Tm	Lg	G	PA	AB	R	H	2B	3B	HR	RBI	SB	CS	BB
1914	19	BOS	AL	5	10	10	1	2	1	0	0	0	0	0	0
1915	20	BOS	AL	42	103	92	16	29	10	1	4	20	0	0	9
1916	21	BOS	AL	67	152	136	18	37	5	3	3	16	0	0	10
1917	22	BOS	AL	52	142	123	14	40	6	3	2	14	0	0	12
1918	23	BOS	AL	95	382	317	50	95	26	11	11	61	6	0	58
1919	24	BOS	AL	130	543	432	103	139	34	12	29	113	7	0	101
1920	25	NYY	AL	142	616	458	158	172	36	9	54	135	14	14	150
1921	26	NYY	AL	152	693	540	177	204	44	16	59	168	17	13	145
1922	27	NYY	AL	110	496	406	94	128	24	8	35	96	2	5	84
1923	28	NYY	AL	152	697	522	151	205	45	13	41	130	17	21	170
1924	29	NYY	AL	153	681	529	143	200	39	7	46	124	9	13	142
1925	30	NYY	AL	98	426	359	61	104	12	2	25	67	2	4	59
1926	31	NYY	AL	152	652	495	139	184	30	5	47	153	11	9	144
1927	32	NYY	AL	151	691	540	158	192	29	8	60	165	7	6	137
1928	33	NYY	AL	154	684	536	163	173	29	8	54	146	4	5	137
1929	34	NYY	AL	135	587	499	121	172	26	6	46	154	5	3	72
1930	35	NYY	AL	145	676	518	150	186	28	9	49	153	10	10	136
1931	36	NYY	AL	145	663	534	149	199	31	3	46	162	5	4	128
1932	37	NYY	AL	133	589	457	120	156	13	5	41	137	2	2	130
1933	38	NYY	AL	137	576	459	97	138	21	3	34	104	4	5	114
1934	39	NYY	AL	125	472	365	78	105	17	4	22	84	1	3	104
1935	40	BSN	NL	28	92	72	13	13	0	0	6	12	0	0	20
22 Yrs				2503	10623	8399	2174	2873	506	136	714	2214	123	117	2062

HR	BB	IBB	SO	HBP	BK	WP	BF	ERA+	FIP	WHIP	H9	HR9	BB9	SO9
1	7		3	0	0	0	96	70	3.65	1.217	8.2	.4	2.7	1.2
3	85		112	6	1	9	874	114	2.81	1.153	6.9	.1	3.5	4.6
0	118		170	8	1	3	1272	158	2.43	1.075	6.4	0	3.3	4.7
2	108		128	11	0	5	1277	128	2.65	1.079	6.7	.1	3	3.5
1	49		40	2	1	3	660	122	2.75	1.046	6.8	.1	2.7	2.2
2	58		30	2	1	5	570	102	3.58	1.545	10	.1	3.9	2
0	2		0	0	0	0	17	94	4.25	1.250	6.8	0	4.5	0
1	9		2	0	0	0	49	49	7.10	2.556	14	1	9	2
0	2		3	0	0	0	39	150	3.50	1.444	11	0	2	3
0	3		0	0	0	0	42	81	3.80	1.667	12	0	3	0
10	441		488	29	4	25	4896	122	2.81	1.159	7.2	.1	3.2	3.6

OBP	SLG	OPS	OPS+	TB
.200	.300	.500	50	3
.376	.576	.952	188	53
.322	.419	.741	121	57
.385	.472	.857	162	58
.411	.555	.966	192	176
.456	.657	1.114	217	284
.532	.847	1.379	255	388
.512	.846	1.359	238	457
.434	.672	1.106	182	273
.545	.764	1.309	239	399
.513	.739	1.252	220	391
.393	.543	.936	137	195
.516	.737	1.253	225	365
.486	.772	1.258	225	417
.463	.709	1.172	206	380
.430	.697	1.128	193	348
.493	.732	1.225	211	379
.495	.700	1.195	218	374
.489	.661	1.150	201	302
.442	.582	1.023	176	267
.448	.537	.985	160	196
.359	.431	.789	119	31
.474	.690	1.164	206	5793

LOU GEHRIG'S HITTING STATISTICS

Year	Age	Tm	Lg	G	PA	AB	R	H	2B	3B	HR	RBI	SB	CS	BB
1923	20	NYY	AL	13	29	26	6	11	4	1	1	8	0	0	2
1924	21	NYY	AL	10	13	12	2	6	1	0	0	5	0	0	1
1925	22	NYY	AL	126	497	437	73	129	23	10	20	68	6	3	46
1926	23	NYY	AL	155	696	572	135	179	47	20	16	109	6	5	105
1927	24	NYY	AL	155	717	584	149	218	52	18	47	173	10	8	109
1928	25	NYY	AL	154	677	562	139	210	47	13	27	147	4	11	95
1929	26	NYY	AL	154	694	553	127	166	32	10	35	125	4	3	122
1930	27	NYY	AL	154	703	581	143	220	42	17	41	173	12	14	101
1931	28	NYY	AL	155	738	619	163	211	31	15	46	185	17	12	117
1932	29	NYY	AL	156	708	596	138	208	42	9	34	151	4	11	108
1933	30	NYY	AL	152	687	593	138	198	41	12	32	140	9	13	92
1934	31	NYY	AL	154	690	579	128	210	40	6	49	166	9	5	109
1935	32	NYY	AL	149	673	535	125	176	26	10	30	120	8	7	132
1936	33	NYY	AL	155	719	579	167	205	37	7	49	152	3	4	130
1937	34	NYY	AL	157	700	569	138	200	37	9	37	158	4	3	127
1938	35	NYY	AL	157	689	576	115	170	32	6	29	114	6	1	107
1939	36	NYY	AL	8	33	28	2	4	0	0	0	1	0	0	5
	17 Yrs			2164	9663	8001	1888	2721	534	163	493	1995	102	100	1508

OBP	SLG	OPS	OPS+	TB
.464	.769	1.234	218	20
.538	.583	1.122	189	7
.365	.531	.896	127	232
.420	.549	.969	152	314
.474	.765	1.240	220	*447*
.467	.648	1.115	193	364
.431	.584	1.015	165	323
.473	.721	1.194	203	**419**
.446	.662	1.108	194	*410*
.451	.621	1.072	181	370
.424	.605	1.030	177	359
.465	*.706*	*1.172*	*206*	*409*
.466	.583	1.049	176	312
.478	*.696*	*1.174*	*190*	403
.473	.643	*1.116*	**176**	366
.410	.523	.932	132	301
.273	.143	.416	10	4
.447	**.632**	**1.080**	**179**	**5060**

Bibliography

Barrow, Edward Grant with James M. Kahn. *My Fifty Years in Baseball.* New York: Coward-McCann, 1951.

Braund, W.G. *Babe Ruth and the 1927 Yankees Have the Best Summer.* New York: Out of the Park, 2016.

Christopher, Matt. *Babe Ruth.* New York: Little, Brown and Company, 2005.

Cobb, Ty with Al Stump. *My Life in Baseball, the True Record.* Garden City, NY: Doubleday and Company, 1961.

Carney, Gene. *Burying the Black Sox: How Baseball's Cover-up of the 1919 World Series Fix Almost Succeeded.* Washington, DC: Potomac Books, 2006.

Castro, Tony. *DiMag & Mick: Sibling Rivals, Yankee Blood Brothers.* Guilford, CT: Lyons Press, 2016.

———. *Mickey Mantle: America's Prodigal Son.* Washington, DC: Brassey's Inc., 2002.

Cook, William A. *The 1919 World Series: What Really Happened?* Jefferson, NC: McFarland & Co., 2001.

———. *Waite Hoyt: A Biography of the Yankees' Schoolboy Wonder.* Jefferson (NC): McFarland & Co., 2004.

Cottrell, Robert C. *Blackball, the Black Sox, and the Babe: Baseball's Crucial 1920 Season.* Jefferson (NC): McFarland & Co. 2001.

Cramer, Richard Ben. *Joe DiMaggio: The Hero's Life.* New York: Touchstone Books, 2000.

Creamer, Robert W. *Babe: The Legend Comes to Life.* New York: Simon and Schuster, 1974.

————. Babe: *The Legend Comes to Life.* New York: Fireside Books, 1992.

Deford, Frank. *The Old Ball Game: How John McGraw, Christy Mathewson, and the New York Giants Invented Modern Baseball.* New York: Atlantic Monthly Books, 2005.

Eig, Jonathan. *Luckiest Man: The Life and Death of Lou Gehrig.* New York: Simon & Schuster, 2005.

Eisenberg, John. *The Streak: Lou Gehrig, Cal Ripken Jr., and Baseball's Most Historic Record.* Boston: Houghton Mifflin Harcourt, 2017.

Fleitz, David. *Shoeless: The Life and Times of Joe Jackson.* Jefferson, NC: McFarland & Co., 2001.

Frommer, Harvey. *Five O'Clock Lightning: Babe Ruth, Lou Gehrig and the Greatest Baseball Team in History, the 1927 New York Yankees.* New York: Wiley, 2007.

Gallico, Paul. *Lou Gehrig: Pride of the Yankees.* New York: Grosset & Dunlap. 1942.

Gehrig, Eleanor, and Joseph Durso. *My Luke and I.* New York: Thomas Y. Crowell Co., 1976.

Gilbert, Brother C.F.X. *Young Babe Ruth: His Early Life and Baseball Career, from the Memoirs of a Xaverian Brother.* Jefferson, NC: McFarland & Co., 1999.

Graham, Frank. *Lou Gehrig: A Quiet Hero.* New York: G.P. Putnam's Sons, 1942.

Hoyt, Waite. *Babe Ruth As I Knew Him.* New York: Dell Publishing, 1948.

Hubler, Richard. *Lou Gehrig: The Iron Horse of Baseball.* Boston: Houghton Mifflin, 1941.

Kashatus, William C. *Lou Gehrig.* Westport, CT: Greenwood Press, 2004.

Katcher, Leo. *The Big Bankroll: The Life and Times of Arnold Rothstein.* New

Rochelle, NY: Arlington House, 1959.

Kelley, James. *Baseball.* New York: DK Publishing, 2005.

Levitt, Daniel R. *Ed Barrow: The Bulldog Who Built the Yankees' First Dynasty.* Lincoln, NE: Bison Books, 2010.

Leavy, Jane. *The Big Fella.* New York: Harper, 2018.

Lieb, Fred. *Baseball As I Have Known It.* New York: Grosset & Dunlap, 1977.

Meany, Tom. *Babe Ruth: The Big Moments of the Big Fellow.* New York: Bantam Books, 1947.

Montville, Leigh. *The Big Bam: The Life and Times of Babe Ruth.* New York: The Doubleday Broadway Publishing Group, 2006.

Pirone, Dorothy Ruth. *My Dad, the Babe: Growing Up with an American Hero.* Boston: Quinlan Press, 1988.

Reisler, Jim. *Babe Ruth Slept Here: The Baseball Landmarks of New York City.* South Bend, IN: Diamond Communications, 1999.

Rice, Grantland. *The Tumult and the Shouting.* New York: A.S. Barnes, 1954.

Robinson, Ray. *Iron Horse: Lou Gehrig in His Time.* New York: W.W. Norton. 1990.

Ruth, Mrs. Babe with Bill Slocum. *The Babe and I.* Englewood Cliffs, NJ: Prentice Hall, 1959.

Ruth, George Herman with Bob Considine. *The Babe Ruth Story.* New York: E.P. Dutton, 1948.

Sandomir, Richard. *The Pride of the Yankees: Lou Gehrig, Gary Cooper, and the Making of a Classic.* New York: Hachette Books, 2017.

Sarnoff, Gary A. *The First Yankees Dynasty: Babe Ruth, Miller Huggins, and the Bronx Bombers of the 1920s*. New York: McFarland, 2014.

Seymour, Harold. *Baseball: The Golden Age*. New York: Oxford University Press, 1971.

Sherman, Ed. *Babe Ruth's Called Shot: The Myth and Mystery of Baseball's Greatest Home Run*. Guilford, CT: Lyons Press, 2015.

Smelser, Marshall. *The Life That Ruth Built: A Biography*. New York, Quadrangle, 1975.

Sobol, Ken. *Babe Ruth and the American Dream*. New York: Ballantine, 1974.

Steinberg, Steve and Lyle Spatz. *The Colonel and Hug: The Partnership That Transformed the New York Yankees*. Lincoln, NE: University of Nebraska Press, 2015.

Steinberg, Steve. *Urban Shocker: Silent Hero of Baseball's Golden Age*. Lincoln, NE: University of Nebraska Press, 2017.

Stevens, Julia Ruth with George Beim. *Babe Ruth: A Daughter's Portrait*. Dallas: Taylor, 1998.

Stevens, Julia Ruth and Bill Gilbert. *Babe Ruth: Remembering the Bambino in Stories, Photos, and Memorabilia*. New York: Stewart, Tabori and Chang, 2008.

———. *Major League Dad: A Daughter's Cherished Memories*. Chicago: Triumph Books, 2001.

Stewart, Mark, and Mike Kennedy. *Long Ball: The Legend and Lore of the Home Run*. Minneapolis: Millbrook Press, 2006.

Stout, Glenn. *The Selling of the Babe: The Deal That Changed Baseball and Created a Legend*. New York: Thomas Dunne Books, 2016.

Stump, Al. *Cobb: A Biography*. Chapel Hill, NC: Algonquin Books, 1994.

Thomas, Keltie. *How Baseball Works*. Toronto: Maple Tree Press, 2004.

Wagenheim, Kal. *Babe Ruth: His Life and Legend.* Chicago: Olmstead Press, 2001.

Verral, Charles S. *Babe Ruth, Sultan of Swat.* Champaign, IL: Garrard Publishing Company, 1976.

Votano, Paul. *Tony Lazzeri: A Baseball Biography.* Jefferson, NC: McFarland & Co., 2005.

About The Author

TONY CASTRO, WHOM THE *NEW YORK TIMES* HAS CALLED THE definitive biographer of Mickey Mantle for his best-selling *Mickey Mantle: America's Prodigal Son* (Brasseys, 2002), is the author of several books, including the 2016 releases *DiMag & Mick: Sibling Rivals, Yankee Blood Brothers*, and *Looking for Hemingway: Spain, The Bullfights & A Final Rite of Passage.*

He is also the author of the landmark civil rights history *Chicano Power: The Emergence of Mexican America* (E.P. Dutton, 1974), which *Publishers Weekly* hailed as "brilliant... a valuable contribution to the understanding of our time." *Chicano Power* was re-issued in 2014 in a special 40th anniversary edition.

Castro is a former Nieman Fellow at Harvard University, where he did graduate work on American Studies and comparative literature—studying under Homeric scholar and translator Robert Fitzgerald and Mexican Nobel laureate Octavio Paz. He lives in Los Angeles with his wife, Renee LaSalle, and Jeter, their black Labrador retriever. Their two grown sons, Trey and Ryan, also reside in Southern California.